A CENTURY OF HUMILIATION

A CENTURY OF HUMILIATION

The Domination and Exploitation of China
1839–1949

ANDREW P. HYDE

AMBERLEY

For Kaià, Ermias, Wynter, Tayjah, Cloe and Deandre

First published 2024

Amberley Publishing
The Hill, Stroud
Gloucestershire, GL5 4EP

www.amberley-books.com

Copyright © Andrew P. Hyde, 2024

The right of Andrew P. Hyde to be identified as the Author of this work has been asserted in accordance with the Copyright, Designs and Patents Act 1988.

All rights reserved. No part of this book may be reprinted or reproduced or utilised in any form or by any electronic, mechanical or other means, now known or hereafter invented, including photocopying and recording, or in any information storage or retrieval system, without the permission in writing from the Publishers.

British Library Cataloguing in Publication Data.
A catalogue record for this book is available from the British Library.

ISBN 978 1 3981 1598 9 (hardback)
ISBN 978 1 3981 1599 6 (ebook)

1 2 3 4 5 6 7 8 9 10

Typesetting by SJmagic DESIGN SERVICES, India.
Printed in the UK.

Contents

Introduction	7
1 I Rule All under the Heavens	13
2 Our Celestial Empire Possesses All Things in Prolific Abundance	28
3 The Vile Dirt of Foreign Countries	57
4 Freedom of Trade for All the World Alike	87
5 A Piece of Stupidity Which Will Be Remembered for All Time	111
6 They Would Never Try to Fight Us	127
7 A Place of Dingy Dilapidation	140
8 The Very Scum of the Population	169
9 China Belongs to the Chinese	197
10 We Do Not Want to Become Like the Koreans	208
11 A Mutually Beneficial Relationship	224
Notes	261
Bibliography and Sources	274
Index	282

Introduction

The transformation of Red China since 1949 has been meteoric, standing today second only to the United States as a global superpower. Having become the largest trading partner for many countries in the Asia Pacific Region, Latin America and Africa, its wealth is distributed internationally in the form of trade, foreign aid and investment. In addition to cars, computer technology, electronics, office machine parts and clothing, it is a major exporter of coal, aluminium, iron ore and copper, and a huge market for chemicals and fuels. Being a major borrower on international capital markets it attracts inward investment from countries including the UK, France, Germany and the Netherlands. In exchange, its scientists develop much of the information technology – artificial intelligence, fifth generation telecommunications, nanotechnology and robotics – which help to drive the economies of many Western states. Beijing is also assuming an increasing role on issues such as the environment, health and poverty and has become an active participant in UN peacekeeping missions, disaster relief and anti-piracy operations. These are all positive indicators of a country playing a full and constructive role in the world, but sceptics watch these developments with growing concern. They believe many of these activities to be a veil behind which more sinister motives are at play, and by any metric there would appear to be a case to answer.

Many projects undertaken in Africa and elsewhere under the auspices of the so-called Belt and Road Initiative leave recipient governments hugely indebted to Chinese banks and financial institutions. They are then left exposed to political coercion or risk the consequences of defaulting. As well as borrowing huge sums, it also holds much foreign debt, placing it in a potentially powerful position should it wish to exploit its creditor status. Investments in foreign mines and factories are viewed as part of a wider scheme to control rare natural resources. The computer software it produces is suspected of containing potential trojan horses and other malware in preparation for launching cyber-attacks when the time is ripe. The Covid pandemic has been cited as a further example of Beijing exploiting its strengths to act independently of the same international bodies it strives to dominate. There are also suspicions that influence in key government institutions is being sought through nefarious bodies cloaked behind a veneer of legitimacy.

Whilst paying lip service to the UN Charter on Human Rights, Covid regulations are exploited to restrict them within its own borders. Political opponents are silenced and Christians, Uyghurs and other minorities face harassment through regulations designed to enforce religious conformity. In the process many face losing their cultural identities completely, suffering imprisonment and ethnic cleansing. In the former British colony of Hong Kong, various undertakings made with the United Kingdom to protect democratic institutions and its way of life are coming under pressure from a relentlessly irredentist regime, determined to absorb the territory back into the mainland.

The same compulsion has seen persistent claims to the territorial waters and islands of the South China Sea, the militarising of reefs and the building of man-made islands. The frontier with India is in constant flux and its legitimacy repeatedly challenged. Similarly, maritime and physical borders shared with North and South Korea, Nepal, Laos and Myanmar are questioned. Growing antagonism towards Taiwan has been fuelled by the mantra of national reunification and seen threats to its territorial integrity escalate. In response, Australia, the UK and the United States have signed the AUKUS Treaty, whilst other states including Japan, South Korea, the Philippines and Indonesia seek the security of commitments enshrined in the Manila Pact. In practice they are limited to protests, sanctions or the exercise of freedom of navigation, but even these gestures are met with studied indifference, the use of the UN veto or veiled threats of retaliation. Such conduct serves to vindicate those who assert that Xi Jinping and the rest of the Chinese Communist Party are relentlessly pursuing a Machiavellian strategy, one with the ultimate aim of achieving global hegemony.

Nonetheless, even if such assertions do have traction, there are many who sympathise with the notion that the West's chickens are finally coming home to roost. They see parallels with the European powers of the eighteenth and nineteenth centuries who unashamedly vied for natural resources, markets and political influence around the world. They rarely felt inhibited in the methods they employed, using bribery, coercion or gunboat diplomacy to achieve their aims. Significantly, a key battleground in the struggle for dominance was China itself, and if we examine the complex dynamics that once shaped its own involvement in this great struggle, we may better understand what governs the mindset of its political class today.

Until Westerners arrived in any appreciable numbers in the sixteenth century China had been a remote, isolated empire, save for contacts via the Silk Road and the sea. An ancient civilisation, it had innovated numerous technological advances long before they reached Europe, and long after the Portuguese arrived in the early 1500s it remained the equal of the West in many fields. Furthermore, Court mandarins judged all beyond its borders to be mere vassals, and any visitors no more than tribute bearers. Consequently, successive emperors maintained an iron grip on these 'foreign devils', with whom they supped with a long spoon, and trade was subject to strict rules. Limited concessions were reluctantly made over time, but they fell far short of what ambitious and profit-hungry merchants were aspiring to secure. Appeals, particularly by Britain, to liberalise the arrangements were repeatedly rebuffed, and any nation reckless enough to attempt to force change was crushed by a militarised state powerful enough to assert its will. However, over time hubris and ignorance made the ruling classes complacent and incapable of adapting to the realities of a changing world. Hidebound by tradition and protocol, and doggedly refusing to accept that the West had anything to offer in exchange for its silks, tea and porcelain, they failed to read the room.

By the end of the eighteenth century and into the nineteenth, their power was diminishing as that of their future nemesis was growing. Although the chimera was maintained for a few more years, war in 1839 finally exposed the empire's shortcomings, and its power and prestige was shattered almost overnight. Britain led the way by seizing Hong Kong, opening several so-called treaty ports and gaining access to increased trade. Fresh crises were then exploited or contrived in order to erode Beijing's authority to the point where it became almost irrelevant to the fate of the empire.

This toxic relationship, known reductively as the Century of Humiliation, was compounded by other foreign governments who joined in imposing unequal treaties, demanding extraterritorial rights and expropriating territory. To the north, Russia first insinuated itself by planting colonists and establishing illegal settlements, and then forced the cession of huge tracts of land. To the east, Japan fulfilled long-cherished ambitions to annex Formosa, Korea and the Ryukyu Islands. To the south, France detached former tributary states from the control of the metropole whilst Germany participated in securing privileges of its own. Other smaller powers secured various advantages too, leaving little of the empire completely free of any foreign presence. In the meantime, the United States eschewed overt aggression and preferred to pursue its objectives vicariously, promoting an open-door policy.

This self-evident impotence in the face of persistent foreign encroachment stimulated rebellions which weakened the central government further. In the face of such turmoil, tens of thousands sought to escape abroad to work as labourers in South America and the Caribbean. Many more helped to build railways in North America, or risked their lives in the mines of South Africa. Wherever they went they experienced further humiliation in the form of racism and exploitation.

Erratic and half-hearted attempts to reverse this decline through modernisation and reform were scuppered by reactionary conservatives and culminated in the anti-foreign so-called Boxer Rebellion of 1900. This was easily crushed and instead of liberating the country subjected it to further humbling punishments. It also produced revolution, establishing a republic that held out the prospect of salvation, but failed to fulfil its promise. The First World War came and went, but the Wilsonian vision of a utopian new world order was not applied here. Having aided the Allies in the conflict, there

Introduction

were demands for an end to its vassal status and the revocation of the privileges it had dispensed. Instead, it was subjected to the same horse trading that had distributed German and Turkish colonies among the victorious Entente Powers. From this duplicity Japan emerged as the main beneficiary, using its privileged position to extend its influence in, and finally to annex, the province of Manchuria. In the meantime the machinations of the Allies had contributed to the emergence in the 1920s of extreme Nationalist and Communist ideologies, which were then embroiled in a bitter civil war.

Following full-scale invasion in 1937, the Japanese pursued a cruel and relentless campaign to eradicate all opposition; indiscriminately bombing, shooting and raping civilians, and deploying biological weapons against innocent men, women and children. Barbarous and pointless human experiments were also carried out in the name of scientific research. Defeat of Japan in 1945 brought an end to that particular nightmare, but there was little respite as the civil war between Red and Nationalist China continued. It ended with Communist victory in 1949, and only then could the Century of Humiliation be said to have finally come to an end. Apart from Portuguese Macao and British Hong Kong, the treaty ports and concessions had been reclaimed and all the extraterritorial privileges enjoyed by foreigners annulled. Furthermore, the territory occupied by Japan, apart from Taiwan, had been repatriated and Korea liberated. For the first time since 1839, Beijing was beholden to no other power and was master in its own, albeit now devastated, house.

Nonetheless, the mental and physical scars could not be easily eradicated, and it would have been surprising had its sufferings not informed Beijing's subsequent view of the world. Such a negative mindset was not helped by being ostracised by the US and facing international hostility. Consequently, conflicts such as those in Korea and Vietnam became surrogate wars against American-led ideologies and the support given to anti-colonial movements in European colonies were inspired by a desire to humiliate its one-time bullies. The hostility shown towards Taiwan, and other claims to what Beijing believes to be its territory indicate a determination to eliminate every reminder of its former agonies, and having an economy second only now to the United States, these aspirations would appear to have an almost unstoppable momentum. This account is therefore a journey, at the end of which we may better appreciate what the future holds for a world where the tables have been turned and which is dominated by China rather than the West.

This has been a project upon which I had embarked under similar onerous Covid restrictions to those which governed my previous book, *The Sun Must Set*. With libraries, museums and other repositories off-limits, research material had to be accessed in large part by painstakingly trawling through the internet. Fortunately, vast wellsprings of knowledge and information exist here if searched for with sufficient determination and this allowed me to judiciously consult a wealth of original documents and primary data. Although there is nothing as satisfying for the scholar as interacting with original documents, papers and published material, without these alternatives Covid would almost certainly have made my endeavour impossible to pursue.

One aspect of my research that I did not anticipate was the hornet's nest that Chinese naming conventions might stir up. Thomas Wade and Herbert Giles's interpretations of both traditional and simplified characters have long since been eclipsed by Hangu-Pinyin, but in some cases the new spellings can present issues. For example, although that of Mao tse-tung poses no problem, having long since evolved into Mao Zedong, Sun Yat-sen is now frequently written as Sun Chung-San, but I have nevertheless opted to retain the former iteration. Similarly, although Confucius has been translated into Kong Fuzi I decided to retain the old form in the interests of clarity. Fortunately, Peking has been referred to as Beijing for many years, Canton Guangzhou, Tientsin Tianjin, and Shanghai as Shenzhen, and I foresee no issues for the reader as these names evolve through the course of the story. Likewise, the historic island of Formosa changed to Taiwan after the Second World War. British writers and travellers did add to the confusion by spelling place names either phonetically or simply from their own best guess, and some of these have been cited, even though their contemporary beginnings elude me. I hope therefore that my need to compromise in some cases will not confuse the reader, or be to the detriment of this history.

Andrew Hyde

1

I Rule All under the Heavens

As a culture, China has been ahead of the curve almost from its inception. The earliest known subspecies of homo erectus is Peking Man, who lived in the north around 400,000 years ago, approximately 350,000 years before the first humans set foot in Europe. During his tenure he is credited with mastering skills such as making fire, utilising crude stone implements and possibly hunting and making clothes. About 10,000 years later his descendants were living within the orbit of the Yangtze and Yellow Rivers, evolving into small communities of hunter gatherers, foraging for food and living off the land. As they slowly adapted themselves to the caprices of nature and civic life they put down roots, merging into more ordered societies to farm and keep domestic animals. Expansion gradually heralded more structured lives under the dynastic rule of kings. The first of these was probably the Xia around 2070 BCE, roughly coinciding with the peak of the Bronze Age Minoans in Europe. The Xia kings presided over feudal lords who acted as viceroys, below whom lesser nobles and inferior classes of commoners served. The dynasty oversaw the tradition of ancestor worship, polytheism and the principle of primogeniture. They constructed massive canal systems to manage the flooding of the two great rivers, developed brick ovens, plaster, potters' wheels, bronze casting and created the earliest astronomical calendar.

They were eventually overthrown by the Shang, also referred to as the Yin, around 1600 BCE, coinciding roughly with Europe's Mycenaean civilisation. It is the first for which archaeological evidence has been found, and from this it has been deduced that writing and mathematics first began with the Shang. Astronomy and art also thrived, along with the development of chariots and bronze weapons. The period is particularly renowned for king Wu Ding and his legendary warrior Queen Fu Dao, whom he married around 1,200 BCE. The discovery of her tomb in 1976 revealed much about the dynasty, as it contained a wealth of artifacts including hundreds of bronze objects. The dynasty eventually succumbed to outside pressures, and the Zhou overran the Shang in 1050 BCE, dominating the landscape until around 256 BCE, a period corresponding roughly with Ancient Greece. The period saw further sponsorship of writing and literature and the introduction of innovations such as the multiplication table. Under Zhou rule, irrigation techniques were enhanced through the use of hydraulics and the building of dams, which improved crop production. The 'nine squares' system of land ownership was also instituted and farmers would later be growing rice, soyabeans and other crops using sophisticated land management techniques. They found that by planting in rows in a grid pattern and spacing the seeds well apart, higher production was achievable, permitting the soil to be hoed, allowing it to aerate and improve moisture retention. Ploughshares were another brainchild of this period, made using bronze and iron, and by the third century BCE improvements in casting meant that much bigger implements could be produced, ploughing deeper and breaking up the soil more effectively.

Military leader, strategist and philosopher Sun Tzu is credited with writing the military manual *The Art of War*, one of the earliest treatises on strategy and tactics. The fourth century BCE witnessed many military developments, including the invention of the crossbow. In its heyday it was one of the most sophisticated and effective weapons on the battlefield, and would see service for the next 2,000 years. Cavalry also began to play a significant role in combat and by the third century BCE stirrups would free the rider's hands so that he could use weapons more effectively in the saddle and guide the horse with his feet. The Zhou also oversaw peaceful discoveries such as the *Ci-Shi*, or lodestone. Its magnetic properties led to the development of the compass or 'south pointing needle'. Initially they were employed by travellers on land, but their advantages were eventually appreciated by mariners. Back on terra firma, farriers had developed a harness with a breast strap, known as the trace harness, for domesticated horses and oxen. It allowed heavier loads to be hauled by the creature, and by the first century BCE would be further refined by the addition of a padded collar. They are also credited with being among the earliest civilisations to appreciate the qualities of and potential for natural gas. Later still, they would search for deposits of the fuel, and use bamboo to pipe it for use in cooking and other applications.

Yet for all these achievements, as the Zhou polity footprint expanded it failed to adapt to the demands of its sheer size. Beyond the reach of the centre, governors evolved into semi-autonomous warlords, with separate systems of taxation, currency and defence. Eventually, they detached themselves from the metropole entirely, looking to carve out fiefdoms of their own. As they competed for succession, Zhou dominance waned and fractured into Western and Eastern spheres. These, too, eventually succumbed during the Warring States Period, 247-221 BCE. However, from this chaos emerged the Ch'in or Qin dynasty, bequeathing the name by which the country is known today. Its founder, Emperor Shi Huang, seized control of and absorbed the warring states one by one, vanquished the warlords, and began a process of reintegration. He started the Great Wall, constructed a network of interconnecting roads and created thirty-six military and civil districts. He also reformed the government and further standardised weights, measures, currency, writing and the law. The welfare of his people was also catered for with the building of the Lingqu Canal and the Dujiangyan irrigation systems, which brought more land under cultivation.

The empire's inevitable decline coincided with the rise of the Han, who would govern from 206 BCE to 220CE, roughly parallel to the Roman Empire. They would see Buddhism introduced, having been brought to China by nomads, and a uniquely Chinese Mahayana form evolved over time. Emperor Wu di, however, had more of a predilection for immortality than religion, and sponsored experiments to find the secret of eternal life. His loyal alchemist Wei Boyang sought to provide such a miracle, trialling various substances including sulphur and saltpetre in pursuit of the elusive elixir. Although he failed to satisfy his master's wishes, some of the compounds with which he experimented later proved essential ingredients for gunpowder.

Meanwhile, engineers had been producing more pragmatic gadgets such as the rudder, replacing the cumbersome and less efficient oars which had up until then to be suspended from the side of the ship. The Dragon Spine Water Lift was also developed, overcoming the need to collect water in buckets and carry it to where it was needed. Instead, sprockets moved a chain with paddles over a trough. Water was pumped as the paddles pushed the water up the trough and it was deposited in the required location.

The first practical paper was developed in 105 CE by Cai Lun, using hemp, mulberry bark, bamboo, silk rags or rice straw. He pounded the material continuously until it finally disintegrated, then added liquid to create a mushy pulp, which was spread evenly over a fabric screen or mould. Allowed to drain through the screen until it dried, it produced a reasonably serviceable sheet. It was a particularly timely invention, because during this era poetry and literature would see something of a renaissance after it suffered neglect under the Qin. Another significant technological stride made in this period was the bronze earthquake detector. Invented by astronomer Zhang Heng around 132 CE, it consisted of a domed jar six feet across, upon the exterior of which eight dragon heads were spaced, and within the jaw of each rested a ball. Below lay a model of a toad with its mouth open, and when seismic activity occurred a rod inside the jar pushed the ball out of one of the jaws and into the mouth of the toad, making a loud noise. The dragon whose ball was displaced indicated the direction of the earthquake.

The later Han dynasty was characterised by a succession of natural disasters, earthquakes, famines and floods which it proved ill-equipped to address. These problems were compounded by an increasingly discontented people, weighed down by the burden of taxation, and the state faced exterior forces seeking to encroach upon its territory. This culminated in serious revolts threatening its integrity in the 180s CE, which, combined with factional in-fighting, finally led to its disintegration by around 220 CE. The power vacuum that emerged was soon seized upon by Tartar and Tibetan raiders who engaged in numerous invasions and produced the Three Kingdoms period, which survived until 265 CE. This was followed by the Jin dynasty from 265 to 420 CE, before a complete split led to the Northern and Southern dynasties. These states co-existed from 420 until 581 CE, when nobleman Yang Jian, or Wendi, founded the Sui Dynasty. By allying himself with warlords in the north and building a complex network of interconnecting waterways he began another process of reunification. The 1,100-mile Grand Canal, originally started in the fifth century BCE between Beijing and Hangzhou, was also much improved and extended. He popularised his rule by cutting taxes, redistributing land and building granaries. In this period the formal examinations for civil servants were reintroduced, and the law and education reformed.

Once more, however, poor governance replaced good, as power was increasingly concentrated in the hands of a privileged elite. Rulers became more remote and corrupt, neglecting the people and inciting social unrest. By 618 CE China again experienced civil war, from which emerged the Tang to restore some stability, surviving until 907 CE. Under its watch the empire expanded to encompass northern Vietnam and Korea, the territory later known as East Turkestan and as far as the Caspian and Aral Seas. Turkic tribes also came within its orbit, and limited incursions were mounted against Tibet. One of its greatest cultural contributions was the sponsorship and encouragement of poetry, and a large academy was founded which would store some 49,000 works by 2,000 artists. In the field of medicine, a diagnosis for diabetes was developed, with effective cures found through the use of vitamins. In 725 CE, a Buddhist monk, Yi Xing, invented the first mechanical clock, made of bronze and iron and powered by a waterwheel. Advances were also being made in printing, and around 868 CE a method was devised by which text written in ink on a piece of paper was pressed on top of a block of wood. All the wood surrounding the word or character was then chipped away, leaving its mirror image on the block. This was brushed with ink and pressed on a fresh sheet of paper to produce legible script. Another innovation was the paddle boat, initially used commercially as tugs and passenger transport, and later employed as warships with purpose-built versions protecting the crews from enemy attack.

The earlier, unstable ingredients for gunpowder which had been developed by Wei Buoyang were now reputedly finding new uses. Instead of endowing eternal life, medical applications were discovered like as an insect repellent and a cream for treating cuts and wounds. Its volatile nature when mixed in the right ratios was not overlooked for long. When ignited it made a loud noise, and various experiments led to the development of weapons such as 'flying fire'. This was a rather crude affair consisting of a tube packed with powder and attached to an arrow, but when ignited and launched in the direction of the enemy it caused quite a stir. More serious applications followed, among them a rudimentary cannon called the fire lance, poison gas, hand grenades and mines. Consequently, by 1076 CE its potential as a force multiplier had become obvious, and it had to be kept a closely guarded secret. The sale of saltpetre to foreigners was outlawed in the hope of depriving potential enemies of the formula, but it proved an impossible secret to keep indefinitely. Once the genie was out of the bottle, tales of its amazing properties eventually travelled through India and the Middle East to Europe, where by the late 1200s CE the existence of this wonder weapon was finally known. Nonetheless, it was not until 1346, nearly 140 years after first being developed in China, that practical cannons were deployed in Europe.

Alongside Buddhism, the Tangs also began to embrace Confucianism as the official state ideology. Its founding father Confucius, born in 551 BCE in what would later become Shandong Province championed a credo which he believed should guide all those who governed. He taught values such as worth (Xian), nobleness (Shang), Righteousness (Yi), Honesty and Trustworthiness (Xin). He also believed that loyalty to the state (Chung), Ritual, Propriety and Etiquette (Li) and love within the family (Hsiao) must be the essential tenets of all practitioners. These demanding and prescriptive benchmarks would eventually become an article of faith, and although they were honed and adapted over the centuries, would remain the fundamentals of Imperial government almost until the very end. Such a rigid mantra would also prove a serious impediment to reform, thwarting those who later in its history attempted to adapt the empire to the challenges of a changing world.

Meanwhile, more practical disciplines were also being pursued, and around 1048 CE fellow visionary Bi Sheng developed moveable type, some 400 years before the German inventor Johannes Gutenberg introduced the process to Europe. After much trial and error, he found that individual characters could be carefully carved onto small cubes of slightly wet clay and then baked in a kiln. Once they had dried, they could be arranged on a frame to create pages of text, smeared with ink and pressed onto a sheet of paper. Unlike woodblock, the individual characters could be re-used many times over, but due to the complexity of the Chinese language it required many different characters, and made the process extremely time consuming and laborious. In any case, in 907 CE a coup brought the Tang to an end and ushered in the short-lived Liang, which in turn heralded the upheaval of the so-called Five Dynasties and Ten Kingdoms, which followed one another in quick succession until 960 CE.

These were supplanted by the Song, the dynasty widely credited with having presided over the country's golden era. Its cultural, engineering and social advancements, as well as its administrative reforms transformed the empire from a motley collection of bickering fiefdoms into a strong, well governed state. The role of the civil service was expanded and the influence of the military in the executive replaced by men who, having passed a stringent neo-Confucian examination offered a more professional and civic form of governance. Measures were taken to unify the tax system and rebuild its road and canal communications, and earlier innovations such as the magnetic compass, moveable type, gunpowder and military ordnance were improved upon; the arts, literature and painting, science and education all experienced a renaissance. Land ownership was encouraged and agricultural improvements increased the production of rice, millet and wheat, contributing to an increase in the population from 50,000,000 to 118,000,000. This in turn saw massive urbanisation, in the process broadening the consumer base for the empire's products. The introduction of paper currency made commercial transactions more efficient, stimulating trade and contributing to the growth of the empire's internal market. Foundries produced millions of tons of iron and steel for weapons and tools, and the finest ceramics were created. These products were in such demand that trade with Japan, Korea, Southeast Asia, east Africa and the Persian Gulf flourished, making China the richest country in the world for perhaps the next 500 years. Yet even as it prospered, from 1211 CE the Mongols under Genghiz Khan, and later his grandson Kublai Khan would strike and wreck it asunder.

Finally, after forty-four gruelling years of conflict the Song were driven south, heralding the establishment of the Mongol or Yuan dynasty around 1271. This led to expansion north and west, its furthest extent reaching as far as Europe and west Asia. However, being of nomadic stock, accomplished in conquest rather than statecraft, Khan was wise enough not to dispense with the governmental structures he inherited, instead refining them to his own ends. He did nonetheless create a strict racial hierarchy based upon the Four Class System, which placed the Mongols firmly at the apex and the ethnic Han and southern Song remnants at the bottom. Power was entrenched further by the creation of eleven departments, which consolidated his conquests and unified the various ethnic groups which had come under his sway. By the time of his death in 1294 aged seventy-nine, his guiding hand had established the geographical compass of modern China. Behind these secure borders the condition of the agrarian economy, which had been seriously damaged by constant fighting could be addressed, and various infrastructure projects were undertaken. The most significant of these were the construction of two new canals which greatly enlarged the areas which could be brought under cultivation.

Although he also encouraged the arts and literature, he could not get the urge to widen his conquests out of his system, resulting in invasions of Tibet, Burma, Borneo and Korea, one abortive attack on Java and two against Japan in 1274 and 1281 CE. His grasp of economics was also somewhat flawed and although he continued to sponsor the use of paper money, the temptation to overprint the currency created an inflationary spiral which ultimately caused the impoverishment of many of his subjects. The thirty years which followed his death saw little respite in the suffering of the people, a situation exacerbated by a succession of rulers mired in venality and corruption. Their luxurious lifestyles and those of their Courts and the ruling class juxtaposed with a resentful peasantry, forced to neglect their land to labour on expensive infrastructure projects. This left them ill prepared when a series of natural disasters caused more misery, and a number of fruitless wars sapped the wealth of the country further. Finally, a succession of rebellions left the dynasty irrevocably weakened, and in 1368, a peasant army under

I Rule All under the Heavens

Zhu Yuanzhang delivered the coup de gras. The Mongols were swept back up north and replaced by the Ming dynasty.

Under its watch most of the Great Wall was strengthened to ward off further Mongol incursions, and in 1406 Emperor Yongle embarked upon the construction of the Forbidden City in Beijing. It took fourteen years to complete and was built in strict accordance with *feng shui*, or 'the way of wind and water'. This convention dictated how buildings, objects and space had to be arranged to ensure harmony and balance, and to this end the palace had been constructed on a north-south axis. Moreover, all doors, steps and access ramps had to be uneven in number, the complex consisting of 999 buildings and 9,999 rooms. Every item of furniture, from the throne to his dining table had to be arranged in accordance with its strict principles. When finished, he and his entire governmental apparatus moved there from Nanjing, and it would remain the seat of imperial government until 1912. In addition to changes in government and administration, great strides were made in other areas of life. There were further improvements in the practice of medicine, and the dynasty saw a renaissance in vernacular literature, with millions of books published, including the largest encyclopaedia ever compiled.

Like the Song and the Yuan it demonstrated an interest in what lay beyond its immediate confines, and engaged in various campaigns including that against Yunnan to the south between 1380 and 1388. Emperor Yongle also sent naval commander Cheng Zu on ambitious maritime expeditions between 1405 and 1433 to extend trade and secure more vassals from which to secure tribute. In seven voyages made by a total of 2,000 ships he travelled to the Philippines, the Malayan Peninsula, the Malacca Strait, Calicut on the west coast of India, the Persian Gulf and the east coast of Africa. His voyages also led to the discovery in Persia of the blue paint which would be employed in crafting some of the most exquisite porcelain ever created.

Nonetheless, the dynasty's fortunes began to wane following a dire shortage of silver in the 1630s, the economic consequences of which were particularly severe for poor farmers. They sold their produce for copper but had to pay their taxes in silver, and thus found themselves facing complete ruin. Their predicament was compounded by a succession of droughts, floods and earthquakes, the effects of which the government proved ill-equipped to ameliorate. The cumulative effects were more rebellions among the peasantry and growing dissent within its army, where discipline was suffering and increasing numbers deserting. As these tribulations unfolded, they coincided with the growing strength of hostile neighbours to the north, the most powerful of whom watched and bided its time.

These were the Tungusic Manchus, descendants of the Jurchen horsemen of north-eastern China, proficient with bow and arrow and the sword. From 1582 their chieftain Nurhaci began forging alliances with neighbouring clans, which he formed into 'Banners' and in 1616 brought them all together under his Jin dynasty. In 1618 he produced the 'Seven Grievances', which denounced Ming rule as despotic and corrupt, and concluded that the only way the people could prosper would be by its complete removal. He followed with a succession of incursions into Ming territory, capturing key cities and recruiting Mongol and Han deserters in the process. These became crucial elements in preparing his army to crush the Ming, and although his death in 1626 put paid to his ambitions, the mantle immediately fell to his son Hong Taiji. He further strengthened his position by infiltrating into Mongolia, Korea and the Amur region of Manchuria. In 1636, the name of his people was changed to Manchu, the dynasty renamed Da Qing or Great Pure, and upon his death in 1643 he was succeeded by his six-year-old son Shunzhi. Because of his age his paternal uncle Dorgon was appointed regent and the honour of delivering the coup de grace fell to him.

Despite implementing a number of reforms, the prestige of the seventeenth Ming Emperor Chongzhen was in terminal decline. He had been further undermined by infighting, corruption and natural disasters, including a devastating earthquake which killed thousands across a number of provinces. The dynasty also faced growing opposition to the heavy taxation needed to fight incursions and internal rebellions, the most dangerous of which by 1644 was being led by Zi Zicheng. When his forces occupied Beijing and Chongzhen called a council, he realised that he had been deserted by his ministers and hanged himself in disgrace. The government then called upon Dorgon for assistance, but having crushed the rebellion he now held the balance of power. Free to impose his will, he installed the infant Shunzhi on the throne, ordered the execution of all counter claimants and proceeded to eradicate whatever Ming opposition remained.

By 1650, the north had been largely overcome, and in 1659 Shunzhi dispersed the last Ming forces from the south, forcing many to seek sanctuary on the island of Formosa. Furthermore, the dynasty would see further expansion into Korea, Tibet, East Turkestan, Mongolia, Kazakhstan, Kyrgyzstan, Tajikistan, Kashmir and later still into the dynasty of Burma. The relative speed with which these conquests were achieved was in large part due to the fact that the Qings, like the Mongols before them, had retained the essentials of the administration bequeathed to them by their predecessors. Although they chose for the most part to segregate themselves from the Han, living in separate areas in the cities and forbidding intermarriage, the majority of Chinese officials had been kept in post, albeit under the authority of senior Manchus. They were thus able to facilitate an almost seamless transition from Ming to Qing rule, running the government much the same as they had always done.

This complex apparatus was the product of centuries of adaptation and refinement, so that by the time of the Manchu invasion it ran like a finely tuned timepiece. At its apex sat the emperor, hermetically sealed in one of the opulent courts housed in the Forbidden City, exercising his power over the so-called Celestial Empire through *Tianming*, or the 'Mandate of Heaven', a system first adopted during the Zhou period. Under his aegis, power was exercised at the pleasure of the gods and followed the Confucian principle that emperors must reign benevolently in the interests of the people, or *Ren,* the benchmark by which all incumbents were measured. He was therefore expected to act paternally, demonstrating wisdom, fortitude, omniscience, and infallibility. He also needed to be judge, jury and final arbiter over a vast array of matters both spiritual and temporal. Yet although he lived a life of unlimited power, privilege and luxury it was not his own, every hour of every day dictated by the unremitting demands of government and the daily grind of official duties.

Furthermore, all his decisions and actions meant he had to be constantly on his guard for any sign that he may have incurred the displeasure of the gods and breached his Mandate. Such transgressions might be augured by disasters such as flood, famine, or earthquake, rebellion or invasion. Court astronomers, astrologers and meteorologists observed the stars, consulted cloud charts or looked for ominous changes in weather patterns. If the predictions were unfavourable he was then expected to take steps to prevent or ameliorate the effects through food relief or flood prevention. He might also be faced with economic problems, and failure to take the necessary steps could again be interpreted as his having abandoned his responsibilities and forfeited his right to rule. This had been the fate of Chongzhen when he was faced with rebellion and invasion.

Each incumbent therefore bore a heavy weight of responsibility, and naturally not every ruler could hope to possess all the necessary skills and acumen that his role demanded. One commentator would later observe that many knew 'nothing of the world outside … nothing of any science or any useful thing whatsoever',[1] and therefore ruled badly and made poor decisions. Checks were held in reserve so that if the worse came to the worse, those judged to be ill-equipped for the role could be side-lined or passed over, or regents appointed if the emperor came to the throne too young to rule. Under these circumstances, experienced and savvy officials or relatives could rule on their behalf and leave their own stamp on the fortunes of the empire. Another check on potential misrule or despotism was provided for by a firewall of counsellors and ministers who served in various capacities to guide and advise the monarch.

This function had assumed many guises over the generations, but all served essentially the same purpose. The earliest had existed before the conquest, and was named the Deliberative Council of Princes and Ministers, which was then staffed almost exclusively by Manchus until superseded by the Grand Secretariat. This in turn became the Grand Council in the 1730s and was responsible for various governmental functions. In conformity with the decision to retain Han officials, each had two presidents, one Manchu and one Chinese, and four vice-presidents, two Manchu and two Chinese. The theory behind this was that whilst the Manchu member would serve the interests of the dynasty, its Chinese participant would have at heart the well-being of the Han majority. This system of 'equipoise' may have provided balance and fairness, but it also had its drawbacks. China expert Putnam Weale later observed that because neither wished to be held accountable for failure or decisions that may incur the wrath of the emperor, 'the well-known propensities of each are so hedged round that all danger of inconvenient action is removed'.[2] As we shall see, this accommodation was destined to dog the administration of the empire in the future, with disastrous consequences.

Another important body was the Provincial Censorate, the emperor's diligent eyes and ears responsible to the Court of Censors in Beijing. It, too, consisted of one Manchu and one Han president who managed its senior and junior vice-presidents, twenty censors and forty-four inspecting censors. These men held the whip hand, exercising sweeping powers to audit, criticise and censure any official regardless of seniority, and their visits were awaited with anxiety. Not surprisingly they were also widely loathed as 'obnoxious ... a species of degenerate Star Chamber'.[3] Nonetheless, they could not be openly challenged, and their conclusions and recommendations carried the weight of the emperor's own person. These were contained in the memorials formally submitted to the relevant board or department, or directly to the sovereign. Once he had evaluated their findings he could issue his own 'Imperial Edicts', which had the force of law and were then dispensed throughout his realm.

These documents flowed to-and-fro between one or other of the provinces in the empire, an area of around 400,000 square miles, taking just twelve days to cover a distance of 1,200 miles. Each province was divided into prefectures and sub-prefectures, and within these were six or seven *Xian*, counties or districts, of which there were approximately 1,300. Each province was run by a governor and its military commander, who digested the contents of the edict and distributed it to their prefects and sub-prefects. The emperor's writ then landed on the desk of the magistrate, the lowest ranking official, but who had perhaps the most direct contact with the people. Consequently he was the human face of *Ren*, earning him the epithet 'Mother and Father Official', whose task it was to implement the orders.

Nonetheless, these weighty documents were only as effective as the emperor who authored them. If the governors or the magistrates did not like the contents of the edict, or felt that it contained orders with which they disagreed, they might ignore them and fail to pass them on. To commit such a breach however, depended upon whether they feared the repercussions of such defiance. As one commentator noted, 'it was much like the rule of the Pope in Europe. If the ruler happened to be a strong one he was able to make his will respected; but generally speaking, each "duke" was independent.'[4]

This authority relied in great part upon his official's adherence to and exercise of the Confucian principles with which they which had been imbued, such as procedure, protocol, convention and above all loyalty and obedience. To demonstrate these qualities, they had to prepare for and pass the notoriously difficult civil service examination. It was not a test of practical subjects such as science, mathematics, or engineering but of Confucian musings. His Four Books and Five Classic works had to be thoroughly digested, some of which were texts 400,000 characters long. Because they had to be learnt by rote this task was considered so difficult that no one was expected to pass until he was around thirty years of age. The challenge and the pressure to pass was so great that cheating was not unknown, nor was the greasing of palms to try to ensure success. It was worth the risk of expulsion or even execution to acquire the tremendous prestige, power and influence which accompanied membership of this elite group. For the unscrupulous, it also gave access to the huge venal opportunities that became available, the exploitation of which over time would contribute to the eventual decline and demise of the empire. The Court was also the workplace of equally powerful eunuchs, who by coercion, poverty or punishment had undergone not a strenuous exam, but an excruciating physical test to gain access to this exclusive club. They had to accept castration as part of their admission to imperial service, and although they were originally employed as harem guards, over time they managed to insinuate themselves into government and acquire positions of increasing influence. By the time the Manchus arrived there were 40,000 or so, occupying various positions throughout the Forbidden City. Their new masters did not share their predecessors' predilection for eunuchs, however, and immediately proceeded to curtail their numbers, eventually whittling them down to around 3,000, although they were never completely eradicated and remained a feature of government almost to the end of the dynasty.

The guiding principle for service in this arcane and rigid system was strict observance of the unwritten code of *Mianzi*, an almost abstract concept which rested upon the obsession with 'saving face' at all costs. It was a notion that governed the lives of everyone from viceroys down to the humblest court functionary. Its practitioners needed to be well-versed in the arts of dissembling, anodyne language, semantics and sophistry, whilst maintaining a façade of self-control, dignity and propriety. It was perhaps no better exemplified than by the cumbersome apparatus of 'equipoise', within which saving face was valued above all. Arguably, the epitome of both Confucian teaching and *Mianzi* was the observance of court etiquette. This included the 'kou tou' the obligatory 'three kneelings and nine kowtows' which was required prior to being granted an audience. This act of obeisance consisted of crawling on the floor on one's stomach when entering the Imperial presence, then pausing to bump the head on the floor at intervals until coming before the emperor himself. This was followed by kneeling from a standing position three times and again performing the kowtow, all whilst knocking your head on the ground. When the audience was concluded the entire exercise had to be repeated in reverse.

Foreign visitors were also expected to adhere to the inflexible procedures demanded of this Ruritanian court, because the so-called 'Sino-Barbarian Order' or *Hua-Yi Zhixu* made no distinction between China proper and the world beyond. Although classified as tribute states, 'Yi' to their 'Hua', Ming Emperor Yongle explained that nonetheless, 'I rule all under the heavens, pacifying and governing Chinese and Barbarians alike, looking upon them with equal humanness and without separation between the two'.[5] Yet although the Chinese interpretation of Yi was closer in phraseology to 'southern people' or simply 'the other', the vagaries of translation meant that when it was rendered into foreign tongues 'barbarian' was the version which stuck. Nonetheless, if outsiders hoped to penetrate this mysterious inner sanctum of the Celestial Empire, then they would have to resign themselves to the indignities both the kowtow and the designation Yi carried with them.

2

Our Celestial Empire Possesses All Things in Prolific Abundance

Contact with this opaque circle would be a lengthy incremental process, and there has been considerable scholarly debate as to when this began. Some claim it was with Alexander the Great around 328 BCE, and if this is accepted as a working hypothesis, the next contact would not have been until perhaps 130 BCE. This corresponds with the Han period, when the Silk Road was established allowing traders to extend their orbit further west and south into Uzbekistan, India, Mesopotamia, Antioch and the Levant. This eventually facilitated the earliest recorded contacts with the extremities of the Roman Empire, estimated at sometime between 27 BCE and 14 CE. When a maritime route was opened, direct contacts are thought to have started about 166 CE and between 226 and 643 CE diplomatic relations were established.

What stimulated this increased interaction was the demand for China's unique manufactures, one of which was attributed to Queen Leizu, fabled wife of Yellow Emperor Huang-Ti. Legend tells that sitting in her garden one day, she observed certain types of moth feeding on mulberry leaves. Closer inspection revealed that their eggs produced a jelly-like substance which developed into fibrous cocoons. After eight or nine days they could be gently teased apart to reveal silk filaments approximately 900 metres long and 0.025mm in diameter. If five to eight of these were spun together they made one thread, and in the hands of skilled artisans thousands of strands produced fine silk fabrics of amazing opulence and beauty. These eventually found their way westwards along the Silk Road to Rome, where their name for silk – ceres – became synonymous with the people who created it. At one stage, so much gold and silver was being exchanged in return that the exchequer was nearly exhausted, prompting the Senate to seek to prohibit further imports. Nonetheless, the highly profitable traffic continued, finding its way as far north as Scandinavia via the Russian rivers. This growing interest also made it critical to keep the method of production a closely guarded secret.

In 552 CE, the empire became an early victim of intellectual property theft, when the Byzantine Emperor Justinian I found himself at war with the Persians. As a result his precious silk supply dried up and in desperation he despatched two monks to China to uncover the technique, steal some eggs and return with the contraband concealed in their pilgrim staves. It was then only a matter of time before the process became common knowledge, spreading first to Greece and Syria, and reaching Spain around 711 CE. By the twelfth century, Sicily and Naples were in on the act, followed by Italy in the sixteenth and France in the seventeenth centuries.

Alongside silk, porcelain had also become a highly desirable commodity. The Yuan had mastered the process, combining a mixture of a white clay called kaolin with powdered 'China Stone', a rock containing feldspar. When fired at very high temperatures it turns into something translucent, harder and stronger than ordinary pottery, and when potential buyers discovered it, another vibrant market opened up. Later still, another product destined to become a popular staple in the West would find its way on to the market. This was tea, although it would not come to the notice of Europeans until the middle of the sixteenth century, when it was popularised by the Portuguese.

In the meantime, among those tempted to venture east in search of these wonders were Venetian merchants Niccolo Polo and his brother Maffeo. They set off in 1260, and eventually returned around 1270 with a note from Kublai Khan inviting the Pope to send missionaries and teachers to his Court. In 1271 they embarked upon a second trip, accompanied by Niccolo's fifteen-year-old son Marco, who later recorded what he encountered and experienced in a volume published in 1300. By all accounts (or at least his) the young Marco was an engaging and charismatic enough character who became a confidant and companion of Kublai Khan, entrusted with diplomatic missions to Burma, Sri Lanka and Vietnam. So useful did his services become that he, his father and uncle were only allowed to make their way back home around 1294.

After the Ottomans closed the Silk Road in 1453, trade with India, which began around the second century BCE, continued along the so-called Maritime Silk Road via the narrow Malacca Strait, on the west coast of the Malay Peninsula opposite Sumatra. Already a strategic crossroads, it became of even greater significance once Europeans began venturing east by sea. In the vanguard of these explorations was Portuguese explorer Vasco da Gama. He had been sponsored by his king, Manuel I, to seek a sea route to India via the Cape of Good Hope, and set off from Lisbon in July 1497. It proved a tempestuous journey, with storms and strong currents resisting him at every turn, and it took until late November just to round the Cape. After stopping off in today's South Africa, Mozambique and Kenya, he crossed the Indian Ocean and landed at Calicut on the west coast of India on 20 May 1498. Here, locals told of the strange men they had met previously, and who 'wore [their] hair long and had no beards except around the mouths'.[1] These may well have been the crewmen of Cheng Zu's fleet that made landfall about sixty years before. Their appetites were further whetted by stories of the 'big and beautiful vases of porcelain ... musk, amber and quicksilver'[2] brought from a place the Indians called 'Malochina', the 'land of the Chins'.[3]

A few years later, more was learned of Malacca, which by now had become 'the terminal of the voyages of the traders from China', who sailed there in 'very fine four masted junks ... with cargoes of sugar, great store of fine raw silk, porcelain, damasks, brocade and satins'.[4] From the recently occupied Indian enclave of Goa, its governor Alphonse de Albuquerque was among those enthralled by these reports, and he wrote to the king that it was evidently 'a very great place'.[5] Keen to establish an official presence there, in September 1509 Admiral Diogo Lopes de Sequiera set off from Goa to make overtures to its Sultan, Mahmud Shah. However, he was uncooperative and the negotiations made little progress. After a dispute turned to violence some of the Portuguese were killed, the rest thrown into gaol, and Lopes de Sequiera barely escaped with his life. When, in August 1511, news of the incident reached Albuquerque, he immediately organised an expedition, determined to avenge this slight on his country. After Mahmud defied an ultimatum to hand the prisoners over, Albuquerque captured the town and the sultan fled to the Malay peninsula, making this the first Ming tributary to fall to foreigners.

Portugal was now another step closer to the elusive land of the Chins, and Albuquerque wasted no time in despatching missions in search of the mainland. One of these was led by adventurer Jorge Alvares and Malaccan-based Captain Rui de Brito Patalim, who in early 1513 set off with a fleet of six small junks. Driven by trade winds and lashed by the southwest monsoon, they reached the South China Sea around May and proceeded northeast. Eventually, they came to the mouth of the Choo-Keang or Pearl River Estuary, and ventured deeper inside. By now they badly needed to make landfall to rest and find provisions, and Alvares plumped for a small island later referred to as Tamao. This was either modern day Lantau or Hong Kong island, but whichever it was they were the first Europeans to set foot on Chinese soil since the Polos. Alvares' glory would be cut short. He perished there of undisclosed causes seven years later, reputedly buried beneath the *padrao* or stone pillar planted to claim the territory for their king. Since neither have been recovered to allow the landing site to be definitively identified, we can assume it was Lantau.

After a hiatus of three years, Malacca's governor George Albuquerque commissioned Rafael Perestrello to follow in Alvares' footsteps. He retraced the sea route north through the East China Sea before venturing into the delta, passing Lintin Island and proceeding into a narrow strait called the Bocca Tigris, or Bogue. Through this waterway he passed tiny Pazhou, Whampoa Island, before the thriving port of Guangzhou finally hove into view. They soon discovered that they had long before been preceded by Arabs, Persians, Indians and Syrians, and the river thronged with both their vessels and those of the Chinese. All kinds of craft, from small sampans to large junks were busy ferrying goods to and from the hectic wharves to larger merchant vessels destined for ports along the coast. The town itself, built strictly in accordance with the principles of *feng shui*, was a network of interconnecting avenues dissecting its various quarters; to the north the government district and below that the gated residential, market and commercial areas. Beyond its walls, and segregated from the native population was an area set aside for its 10,000-strong foreign community.

As they observed the frenetic activity around them, the Portuguese knew that they had reached their goal, an El Dorado the equal of the gold mine their Spanish competitors had found in the New World. However, although the locals were friendly enough, at least at first, there was one large fly in the ointment. Guangzhou, like all the other ports up and down the coast, was subject to the intermittent bans imposed on foreign trade by the emperors. These periodic embargoes came and went at the whim of the ruler, usually when he suspected that contact with the barbarians was making his subjects too familiar with foreign ways. Fortunately, such edicts could be circumvented if the price was right, so they approached the local governor Wang bo, who, in return for help suppressing Wokou pirates, turned a blind eye to their activities. Lantau Island became their de facto base, and from there merchants travelled surreptitiously to the silk fairs held in January and June every year in Guangzhou. They would stay for a few weeks, buy goods, and then return with their purchases to Malacca and Goa. But King Manuel wanted to formalise the arrangement, and in 1521 sent Fernao Pires de Andrade to Beijing to negotiate a treaty and install an ambassador.

Meanwhile, increasingly frustrated by the restrictions under which they were operating, his brother Simao de Andrade threw a spanner in the works. With the embassy trying to woo the emperor, he decided to take the law into his own hands. He built a fort on Lantau without asking permission and then unceremoniously ejected all its other foreign residents. His reckless behaviour naturally riled the governor, who sent one of his officials to take Simao down a peg or two. He refused to back down and an almighty row broke out. The locals were already maddened by rumours that their children were being kidnapped to eat or to sell as slaves in Malacca, and this was the last straw. The authorities promptly imposed a blockade and when this proved ineffective, ejected the Portuguese by force. Furthermore, when news reached the Forbidden City, Fernao and his mission were thrown out of Beijing. They were now completely persona non grata and a formal edict followed in 1524 confirming their pariah status. It threatened anyone trading or conducting business with them with severe punishments, and to hammer the point home ordered the destruction of every ocean going two-masted ship in the region. Henceforth, the only activity allowed along the coast was to be fishing.

Although the ban remained in force until the 1560s, it, too, proved easier to circumvent than to enforce. The coast was porous, officials amenable to persuasion and Chinese merchants anxious to trade. Palm greasing gave the Portuguese use of Shang Chuan Island off the Guangdong coast in 1549, but they had really set their hearts on the small island of Macao, lying close to the mainland at the mouth of the estuary. Its location, natural harbour and clement climate made it a very attractive prospect, and naval officer Leonel de Sousa approached Governor Wang bo hoping to secure its use. The tiny spot was of little use to him, and if the foreigners were so keen then he may as well cash in on it. Nonetheless he proved a tough negotiator, only agreeing to hand it over after some hard bargaining. He authorised traders to operate on the island in return for a fee of 500 taels of silver per annum, the levying of 20 per cent taxes on half the cargo traded, and on condition they did not try to erect any fortifications. These terms were considered quite acceptable, and the subsequent Luso-Chinese Agreement of 1554 made Portugal the recipient of the first treaty port on Chinese territory. This arrangement proved so successful that by 1557 Shang Chuan could be abandoned altogether, and its operations transferred to Macao. These developments had not gone unremarked by equally ambitious rivals, prompting constant competition and turf wars that would become the hallmark of the next few decades.

Among the first to try to challenge their monopoly were the Dutch, who had rebelled against King Philip II's Spain following its union with Portugal in 1580. This prompted the imposition of a blockade, preventing their ships from using the port of Lisbon and cutting them off from trade with the East. So a group of intrepid Dutch merchants formed the 'Far Distant Lands Company' intending to establish their own trading links. Its mission was twofold, to eliminate Portugal and Spain as competitors, and to establish trade relations with Beijing. Four ships set off in fulfilment of this remit in 1595, but the early signs were not propitious, as the journey took fifteen months just to reach the island of Java, over 2,000 miles short of their objective. The expedition's backers only barely made any return on their investment, and when another expedition in 1601 did manage to reach China, the Portuguese used their influence to have the crews hanged as pirates.

In 1602, the recently declared Dutch Republic decided to amalgamate the existing companies into one huge concern, which they called the *Vereernigde Oost-Indische Compagnie* (VOC), or Dutch East India Company. When the first expedition reached China in 1603, an attempt was made to wrest Macao from the Portuguese, but they not only failed, the Chinese stubbornly refused to entertain their demands for a similar arrangement. In frustration they turned instead to piracy, intercepting and seizing Portuguese trading vessels so that they could carry off their valuable cargoes as booty. It proved to be a successful strategy, as their ships proceeded to sail the waters off China in search of victims for the next twenty years. One particularly profitable raid in 1627 resulted in four heavily laden vessels being boarded off Malacca. They were transporting large stocks of porcelain and ginger to Goa, and these were seized and the captured ships put to good use, attacking other unsuspecting merchantmen.

A favoured base for these operations were the Penghu Islands, which the Portuguese had named the Pescadores or 'Fishermen's Islands', conveniently sited between the island of Formosa and the mainland. Numerous small inlets provided excellent concealment in which to repair and revictual their ships, and so long as the Dutchmen confined their activities to attacking other Europeans the mandarins were prepared to tolerate the arrangement. However, when in 1622 the pirates started raiding Amoy and Macao and forced locals to work for them building a fort on Penghu, the Chinese decided it was time to teach them a sharp lesson. In 1624 an expedition of 4,000 troops was despatched which cleared the islands of the pirates and forced them to seek shelter elsewhere. They made for Formosa.

Our Celestial Empire Possesses All Things in Prolific Abundance

Known to the Chinese as Tai Liu-Khiu and the natives as Pak-an, it lay beyond Chinese jurisdiction and contained most of the amenities the pirates needed to continue their activities. They established themselves at Taoyuan, a sandy peninsula on the south-west of the island, where about fifteen hundred Chinese traders and farmers and the indigenous population also lived. It was therefore, according to historian Reverend W. M. Campbell, deemed judicious to build a fort 'for defence not so much against some great enemy as against the islanders and ... Chinese farmers'.[6] It was called Fort Zeelandia after the ship which had taken them to the island, 'square, neatly built of baked brick, with surrounding walls six feet thick at the strongest parts',[7] considered adequate for fending off any unwanted attention from hostile locals. It also served a more pragmatic purpose, as they appeared 'to have made their selection of a spot where they could more easily land and ship their wares',[8] which they planned to procure by interrupting Spanish trade between the Philippines and Japan.

They also discovered that the island contained many natural resources, which offered further scope for profit. Particularly, there were huge herds of deer which were hunted by both the Chinese and the aboriginals, and as early as 1625 Governor-General Pieter de Carpentier was able to report to the VOC Board that up to 200,000 a year were being taken. Their venison found a ready market in China, and the skins were sold to Japan where they were used in the manufacture of body armour.[9]

Spain's own presence had been growing in the region since they seized Manila in 1571, and they had also been trading in the Amoy area of Fukien. In 1575 they made overtures to the authorities to make their business official, but when these were turned down they resorted to smuggling along the Guangdong and Fujian coasts. Finding the Dutch a growing problem, Manila's Governor, Fernando da Silva despatched an expedition to the island from where he intended to police the seas and keep it clear of pirates. In 1626, they occupied the northern end of the island and built Fort Salvador on Hoping Island in the Bay of Keelung. In 1629, a second base was established at Tamsui, named Fort San Domingo. Although the forts lost much of their significance after the Japanese closed their country to foreigners in 1630, their Chinese interests still needed protecting. In 1637, incensed by the taxes levied on them by the Spanish, the natives attacked Fort San Domingo and razed it. Unperturbed, the structure was rebuilt in stone, twenty feet high, just in time to face a more serious challenge from the Dutch, who by the close of the 1630s had decided that with the Spanish thwarting their piratical activities, the time had come for a showdown.

On 26 August 1641, Dutch governor Paulus Traudenus gave advance warning of his intentions and issued a rather polite ultimatum to his Spanish counterpart, Gonsalo Portilio, calling upon him to surrender: 'Avail yourself of the opportunity of avoiding bloodshed.'[10] Portilio however, was disinclined to accommodate his request, replying equally courteously but no less firmly that 'I and my men are resolved to defend ourselves ... we are Christian Spaniards, and God is our protector... God preserve you.'[11] When the ultimatum expired, Traudenus ordered his men to attack the Spanish positions, but they proved a tougher nut to crack than he anticipated and he was forced to abandon his efforts. In the meantime though, the Governor of Manila had sent word to Portilio that he needed most of his men for a campaign against natives in the Philippines. So in August 1642, with the garrison leaving, the Dutch resumed the attack and this time the stronghold was captured after just six days. Although the fighting was bitter and little quarter was given, the victors proved magnanimous enough. They conveyed the survivors to Java where its governor is said to have treated them as his honoured guests, showering them with ' all kinds of consideration and respect',[12] before they were eventually returned to Manila.

Thereafter, the Dutch enjoyed a thirty-year monopoly on the island, and by the 1650s Formosa had become one of the VOC's most lucrative product sources. Income from trade, piracy, a residency tax on the Chinese, levies on butter and alcohol, and licence income from Chinese fishermen all contributed to the Company coffers. After the potential for rice and sugarcane cultivation was appreciated, it undertook a campaign to encourage Chinese migrants to the island to work on the land. This proved so successful that there would eventually be 25,000, supplemented by Ming loyalists exiled there by the Qings. But they were resentful at their treatment as second class citizens, especially with regards to the onerous taxes they were having to pay, restrictions on where they could live, and the exploitation of their labour on the plantations. In 1652 they had had enough and broke out in a rebellion which was crushed by the Dutch, but left behind a festering sense of resentment. Tensions were further exacerbated by a series of natural disasters, first in 1651 when drought prompted a famine, and from 1654 onwards when the island was shattered by locust plagues, epidemic diseases, storms and earthquakes. These travails were compounded in 1657 by an outbreak of smallpox, leaving the population weak, hungry and seething.

This discontent came at an injudicious time, for on the mainland Ming loyalist Zheng Chenggong, known to them as Koxinga, had been resisting the Manchu conquest, raising insurrections, and hoping to restore the old dynasty. He had become such a thorn in the side of the new regime that in 1659 emperor Kangxi ordered the 'Great Clearance' in an effort to cut Chenggong off from sources of supply. He evacuated all the coastal areas of Fujian Province south to Guangdong, which deprived Chenggong of his powerbase, and in the process cut its ports off from foreign trade. He now badly needed a new bolthole from which to operate and continue the fight, so like the Dutch before him decided that Formosa, still nominally beyond Qing jurisdiction, offered the perfect solution.

The Dutch did not want this troublesome rebel in their backyard, so they started to strengthen their defences in anticipation of any planned landing, including calling for reinforcements from Java. Unfortunately, relations with the local Chinese population had become so acrimonious by this time that they were also expecting him, and they organised a fifth column which engaged in various forms of sabotage in preparation for his arrival. But as time passed and there was no sign of the anticipated invasion, the garrison began to relax and was lulled into a false sense of security. The men from Java were returned and it appeared that that the crisis was over. All the time however, Chenggong had been preparing, and when he appeared with 25,000 troops in April 1661, the defenders found themselves completely wrongfooted.

A protracted and bloody nine-month siege of Keelung followed, which gradually wore them down so that by the time further reinforcements did arrive, they were too late. Some 1,600 of the defenders had perished, and the survivors were tired, hungry and had little fight left in them. Finally, the governor Frederick Coyett resigned himself to the inevitable and on 1 February 1662 agreed to abandon the island and leave it to Chenggong and his army. He then established his own rule, boosting the population with campaign veterans, their dependents and other refugees from the fighting on the mainland. He did not outlive his victory for very long though, dying from malaria in June 1662 at the age of thirty-seven, leaving his son Zheng Jin to continue the war against the Qings. He fought on for another twenty years until he died in 1681, and two years later the Qings mounted an expedition to take possession of the western and northern coastal tracts. So it would remain, half settled and half wild, until it became the backdrop for further bitter conflict two centuries later.

With the Portuguese largely contained, and the Dutch and Spanish consigned respectively to the East Indies and the Philippines, threats had also been materialising from the north. For some years the Russians had been establishing small ad hoc settlements in Manchuria and along the Amur River, where livings were made hunting, fishing, or extorting furs from local villagers. The border in this region was extremely fluid and ill-defined, so in 1618-19 envoys sought to open negotiations with Beijing to formalise their activities in the area. Instead, they fell at the first hurdle when they encountered the complex Court etiquette and refused to perform the kowtow. Furthermore, having travelled 5,000 miles via the challenging Mongol Desert and Kalgan River, circumventing physical hazards and avoiding bandits, they had none of the customary gifts or tribute to offer their hosts. Singularly unimpressed by this lack of good manners, their faux pas was duly noted. They returned empty-handed, except for a curt letter which rather tetchily informed the Czar that the Chinese were not interested in negotiation, only in receiving tribute and the political submission it signified.[13] It would be over thirty years before the Russians risked another official approach, and in 1654 Czar Alexis entrusted diplomat Feodor Iskowitz Backhoff with a similar mission. Although he had availed himself of an introductory letter and the requisite tribute, he was also under strict instructions not to kowtow or act in any way that might concede that the Czar was subordinate to a Chinese emperor. This second snub to Chinese sensibilities was met with a similar rebuke, and the ill-fated mission was left marking time in lodgings. Faced with the prospect of a long and frustrating wait, he gave up and returned home.

Russia's commercial ambitions were nonetheless drawing it deeper into Manchuria and along the Amur River. In 1651 the small settlement of Albazin was founded, followed in 1654 by Nerchinsk and a number of other forts and trading posts. Beijing had not been entirely ignorant of this activity, monitoring it and waiting to see how far the Russians were hoping to push their luck. They had also begun a colonising programme of their own, and were starting to settle Han peasants in the area. In 1658, determined to assert their sovereignty, a large force of Bannermen encountered a much smaller party of Russians who were forced to flee for their lives. Thereafter, frequent confrontations sparked clashes and skirmishes which were making life for the interlopers difficult. In 1675, Nicolai Spathari, a writer and experienced traveller and diplomat, took a set of proposals to Beijing which it was hoped would facilitate a free trade agreement, giving the subjects of each country the right to trade inside the borders of the other. This third approach was also rebuffed, and again the Russians resorted to stealth.

In 1681, the governor of Nerchinsk, now an important transport hub serving Transbaikalia and the Amur, instructed Ignatius Milovanof to undertake a survey of the Dzeya and Selimba rivers and identify potential sites for further settlement. A year later he presented his report, which prompted the first of about 10,000 colonists to migrate to the region, and by 1683 they had enlarged the trapping operations, constructed small towns and brought land under cultivation. Such large-scale activity again aroused the ire of the Chinese, who promptly reinforced the town of Aigun on the right bank of the Amur in anticipation of a showdown. In July 1683, a detachment of around a hundred Cossacks under Gregory Mylnikof was despatched to the Amgun River, where they were confronted by 15,000 Manchu cavalry. In an apparent gesture of goodwill their commander invited him to parley, but when Mylnikof accepted the offer he was promptly seized. At the sight of this treachery the rest of his men bolted, with the Manchu cavalry in hot pursuit. A number were captured and sent to Beijing, where they were paraded before the Court for the amusement of the emperor.

The Bannermen also increased their military presence in the region, burning down all the illegal settlements with the exception of Albazin, where around 500 Russians stubbornly held out. Late in 1684, with no sign of them leaving, the Chinese sent two of the hostages captured at the Amgun River to the town, demanding that they begin evacuation or face the consequences. But the commander rejected the ultimatum and began strengthening the fort's defences. In June the following year a force of around 18,000 Bannermen equipped with heavy cannon arrived and repeated the call for the defenders to evacuate. They were promised safe passage if they offered no further resistance, but the Russians held firm and the attackers proceeded to prepare siege lines. An unrelenting bombardment ensued, which wrought considerable damage with mounting casualties, but they managed to hold out. However, after ten days of unrelenting punishment the exhausted defenders were depleted in numbers and low on food and ammunition. With little choice than to throw in the towel or face being slaughtered, they opted to live to fight another day, and the survivors marched off to Nerchinsk.

Albazin was then demolished, and the Chinese returned to Aigun where a garrison of about 2,000 men was stationed to watch over the Russians. Later, following reports that the Chinese had withdrawn their forces, 600 Russians returned to Albazin and set about its reconstruction, prompting the furious Chinese to mount yet another expedition. This time the defenders were better prepared and managed to hold out for three months before they were down to 115 men, with ammunition and supplies running dangerously low.

In the meantime, the Czar decided to try diplomacy again, and in January 1686 an envoy made for Nerchinsk to broker a peace deal. But his journey was so dogged by mishaps and delays that the mission did not reach its destination before August. Then, whilst the fighting at Albazin raged in the background, negotiations dragged painfully on, with the Chinese doggedly refusing to make any concessions whatsoever. They made it clear that their adversary had pitifully few cards to play, isolated, far from sources of resupply and massively outnumbered. Finally, the Czars' plenipotentiary reluctantly agreed to the Treaty of Nerchinsk, which they signed on 6 September 1689. It was the first of its kind entered into with an Asiatic power, and the Russians had its terms virtually dictated to them; their helplessness was something the gloating Manchus were determined to underline. This was made crystal clear in the opening preamble, which stated pointedly that they had been forced to act 'to suppress the insolence of certain scoundrels who cross the frontier to hunt, plunder and kill, and who may give rise to much trouble and disturbance'.[14] The rest of the document was an equally salutary lesson in humility.

The key aim of the negotiations it stated, was to 'determine clearly and distinctly the boundaries between the Empires of China and Russia',[15] so that the scoundrel Russians could be kept on a tight leash in future. To that end the rivers and streams south of the Stanavoy mountains and entering the Amur were assigned to China, and those to the north went to Russia. Aigun was fixed as the boundary between the two countries, and all the Russian settlements situated on the south bank of the Amur had to move to the north. Russia had lost access to the sea of Okhotsk, its far eastern markets, and it was cut off from the Pacific Ocean. The Chinese also insisted that Fort Albazin had to be demolished once and for all. The Russians had achieved one albeit minor concession, however. Nerchinsk could remain for the time being as a trading post and limited commerce could be conducted by bearers of just ten Chinese-issued passports. Anyone attempting to do so without the necessary documentation was liable to arrest and execution. These clauses apart, the treaty was anything but clear and distinct, because no reliable survey was made to ensure both sides knew precisely what they had agreed to, with only vague geographical references which could be interpreted either way. Matters were not helped by the fact that the treaty had been translated into Latin, Manchu and Russian, each language with its own particular nuanced interpretation of what had been agreed. Nevertheless, and despite the Russians' undisguised disappointment at the outcome, the Chinese added their hope that the two empires could now 're-establish peace and good understanding for the future', so that their differences could pass into 'eternal oblivion',[16] an overly optimistic aspiration in view of what was to follow.

In 1692 Peter the Great decided to put this new era of detente to the test, and sent German merchant Eberhard Isbrand to Beijing as head of a 250-man mission. They took a gruelling eighteen months to make the journey, but at least found their hosts in an accommodating mood, agreeing that up to 200 merchants could now trade in the capital once every three years.[17] Whilst there, Isbrand also met a few of Gregory Mylnikof's captive Cossacks, some of whom were serving in the emperors' bodyguard. They had even been granted permission to build their own church,[18] but with the exception of these few waifs and strays, Manchu hospitality proved to be in short supply. This was made abundantly clear when in 1721 another envoy made the journey to Beijing hoping to build on the previous concessions. Believing that he had been granted the right to leave behind a permanent representative in the capital, he found that his erstwhile hosts had taken the man a virtual prisoner. Another tentative approach was made in 1741, when permission was sought to navigate the Amur in order to supply the penal settlement they had established on the Kamchatka Peninsula. Beijing again stood firm, and was adamant there would be no amendments to the 1689 Treaty or the 1692 concessions, a point driven home when a further emissary visited in 1806 and received little more than icy stares for his trouble.

Whilst the drama with Russia was being played out, French interest in the Celestial Empire was also being awakened. Early samples of porcelain had been acquired via the Dutch, prompting Jean-Baptiste Colbert, Louis XIV's Minister of State, to form the *Compagnie des Indes* or French East India Company in 1664. Traders returned laden with silk, porcelain, art, clothing and furniture, and Louis' curiosity was further aroused by a visit in 1684 by convert Shen Fuzong. This encounter stimulated cultural exchanges between himself and emperor Kangxi, on the one hand of western science, and on the other of Chinese art and design. It was largely through their blossoming personal relationship that commerce increased, and in 1698 merchant Jourdan de Grouce equipped the armed frigate *Amphitrate* for the long trip to China. It returned to Nantes in 1701 with 167 pieces of the finest porcelain, and he followed up this success with a second voyage a year later. Contact deepened further with the arrival of visitors such as Arcadio Huang, who toured the country in 1702 and then went on to the Holy See in Rome. He returned in 1704 to serve as Louis' interpreter whilst also working on the first Chinese-French dictionary. Cartographers began producing maps of the Celestial Empire, and in 1736 Jean Baptiste de Halde edited the *Description de Chine et de la Tartarie Chinoise*. Jesuit missionaries helped emperor Qianlong build European-style additions to the Old Summer Palace, an opulent complex of pavilions, lakes, rivers, bridges and gardens that had been started by his predecessor Kangxi. Painter Jean Denis Attirel then became his court artist, whilst Joseph-Marie Amiol took up the post of interpreter.

The earliest, largely abortive attempts by the English to make contact are believed to have been around 1553, when King Edward VI sent a mission in search of markets for the country's wool, but it only got as far as the Caspian Sea. A book published in 1577, entitled 'Certyne Reportes of the Province of China, learned though the Portugalles' and translated by Richard Willes, reignited interest and in 1579 Queen Elizabeth I sent a mission which included a personal letter to the emperor. In this she optimistically proposed the 'transporting out of things whereof we have plenty, and in bringing in such things as we stand in need of'.[19] However, his attempt to make contact was foiled by the Portuguese, as were two further attempts in 1581 and 1585. Following the publication of another work describing China in 1588, Sir Robert Dudley financed a mission under the captaincy of Benjamin Wood, but it foundered somewhere in the West Indies, never to be seen or heard of again. Undeterred, English traders already making their fortunes in far-flung parts urged their compatriots to resume their endeavours.

Once the East India Company (EIC) was founded in 1602, its Charter gave it a monopoly of trade in China, but this was only half the battle. It found this market a much harder nut to crack than India, in spite of repeated calls to make inroads. In 1627, English factors in Batavia wrote of 'the abundant trade it affordeth' but added cautiously that 'they admit no stranger into their country'.[20] Although it took another nine years to act on such urgings, the Company's Captain John Weddell would have been wise to heed the accompanying caveat.

He set out with four armed ships in April 1636, finally reaching Macao in June 1637. Here he was to secure from the Chinese the right to 'traffic freely with them, on the same footing as our European precursors',[21] but the Portuguese had different ideas. Again they sought to interfere with the English plans, and repeatedly sabotaged Weddell's efforts to open a dialogue with the authorities. So he sailed up the Pearl River intending to make landfall in Guangzhou, only to be confronted by forty war junks barring his way. Not to be denied, he opened fire on the coastal batteries guarding its approaches, demolishing and then occupying one fort and skirmishing with local troops. Thinking his show of strength had changed their minds, he sent two representatives ashore to negotiate, but they were duly arrested as pirates and thrown in prison, most likely at the instigation of the Portuguese. His humiliation was compounded by having to then ask them to arbitrate his men's release, after which he turned round and sailed away empty-handed. Finding themselves thwarted by this Sino-Portuguese combination, merchants had to look for alternative outlets. The EIC then tried to take advantage of the ejection of the Dutch from Formosa and set up a factory there in 1670, but that enterprise only survived a few years before the island was conquered by the Qings.

The suppression of the Ming rebels had, however, finally made it prudent to reopen the coastal areas to trade, and in 1684 Emperor Kangxi issued a formal edict legitimising foreign access to Chinese markets. Although this was a pivotal moment in Beijing's relationship with the outside world, there were still strings attached. Traders were restricted to the ports of Guangzhou, Amoy, Fuzhou, Ningbo and Shanghai and as we shall see, they were obliged to abide by a number of onerous conditions which dictated when and how they could conduct business. Nonetheless, the door was now at least ajar, if not yet completely open, and the English and French East India Companies were the first to take advantage of the new arrangements. The Austrians followed their lead around 1717, the Dutch in 1729, and the Danish made their first appearance around 1731. The Swedish followed in 1732 and Prussia in 1744, but the first Americans and Australians did not come onto the scene until 1784 and 1788 respectively.

Men like Captain James Flint and his associates were in the vanguard of exploiting the choice of ports to the full. They preferred Ningbo to Guangzhou, which being further north was not only closer to where tea and silk was produced, but could save them money on taxes and dues. Consequently, from 1755 to 1757 they undertook most of their business there, much to the annoyance of the Chinese merchants in Guangzhou. They soon realised how much money they were losing to this freedom to shop around, and lobbied Emperor Qianlong to restrict all commerce to Guangzhou instead. They added for good measure the perceived threat from the armed Western merchant ships which were now frequenting the area, and their arguments won the day. In 1757 the *Yi Kou tongshang*, or Single Port Commerce System, was introduced, switching all operations to Guangzhou. This radical measure certainly made life easier for the authorities, a fact visitor Charles Toogood Downing was quick to appreciate. He calculated that 'its distance from the capital is considered an advantage, as the emperor and his court are thus separated as far as possible from the foreigners, whom they both fear and dislike; the duties arising from the transit of the goods through the canals of the interior are thus increased; and the dreaded traitorous intercourse of the natives with the [foreigners] is in a great measure prevented'.[22]

Any traitorous intercourse was in any case largely avoided by a longstanding convention known as the Guangzhou, or Canton System. This confined foreign traders to the banks of the Pearl River in the southwest of the city, where a complex of buildings, the Thirteen Factories or *Shisan Hang*, was set aside for their use. Each business was known by the name of the nationality operating from it, and although they seemed to get along pretty well, they also kept themselves to themselves. Aeneas Anderson noted how they appeared to do business 'without the least communications with each other ... their general distinction is the flag, or standard of their respective countries'.[23] He was nonetheless impressed:

> The porcelain warehouses are said to exceed any similar repositories in the world for extent, grandeur, and stock in trade. The warehouses of the tea merchants ... are also filled with extensive ranges of chests.[24]

Moreover, the Canton System did not apply solely to the function of the Thirteen Factories. Before any business at all could be transacted, merchant ships heading for the port had to stop at Lintin Island to have their cargoes inspected and pay their dues. They were then allowed to make their way up the Pearl River where, twelve miles from the Factories, they weighed anchor at the 5.8-square-mile Whampoa Island. Here all cargoes were transferred upstream by the ships' crews in their own boats, and for the return trip local chop boats were used. Once the formalities were concluded, so-called 'supercargoes', the merchants who accompanied the vessels out from Europe, liaised with the factors or acted independently to buy and sell their respective commodities. Neither were allowed to do business directly, they had to use intermediaries belonging to merchant guilds known as cohongs. These were the port's authorised agents charged with ensuring all taxes and duties were paid and that merchants complied with the rules. They in turn were monitored by Ministry of Revenue officials, or Hubus. Inevitably referred to by the English as hoppos, they enjoyed direct access to the emperor and exercised virtually the power of life and death over everyone working in the port.

To smooth relations between foreigners and officialdom, more middle men, known as compradors, were recruited. Because direct communication with hongs and hubus was not allowed, they supplied interpreters who were fluent in Mandarin and Cantonese and proficient in classical Chinese text. Other services were also on offer, including collecting wages, organising transport to and from Macao and arranging for all the documentation, or 'chops' issued at Lintin Island. They could provision the factories and ships with everything they needed, from firewood, coal and charcoal to dairy products and meat, and offer security for the factories when they were unoccupied off-season. They could even arrange laundry, other forms of housekeeping and indeed more nefarious services.

On the river, so-called 'Flower Boats', illegal floating brothels, were operated by pimps to which like much else in Guangzhou, hubus turned a blind eye to for a piece of the action.

It was indeed unfortunate that foreigners were not supposed to learn any Chinese, because it might have helped them fill their leisure hours. Although commerce occupied much of the traders' time, there was little else to do, as Charles Toogood Downing observed:

> The mode of living of the residents of Canton is very monotonous, from the restricted limits of their quarters, and the very few pleasures they are able to enjoy... the chief recreation of the younger residents is that of rowing and sailing in the water... Later, in the spring season, when the greater part of the business has been transacted ... regattas and rowing matches are got up.[25]

He concluded that such tedium was due in large part to official policy, a critical element of which was the exclusion of women. He reasoned that 'besides their wish to render the residence of foreigners temporary and uncomfortable, they evidently have a very wrong opinion of the amiable qualities of the fair sex; and therefore consider perhaps that they have enough to do to keep the male barbarians in order, and would find it altogether impractical to manage the females'.[26]

Nonetheless, once the system had bedded in and officialdom appreciated that there was much to gain from liberalising the arrangement, concessions began to be granted. Originally, merchants were supposed to return to Whampoa Island at the close of the day's trading, but later they were allowed to rent rooms in the Factories instead. In 1759 another instruction, the 'Vigilance Towards Foreign Barbarians Regulations' had forbidden trade in winter, and merchants were supposed to leave Guangzhou between November and February, take their business to Macao or go home. When it was discovered that ships no longer had to rely on the monsoon winds to reach Guangzhou, and could instead round the Philippines and visit at any time, the ban on winter trading became an anachronism. Consequently, as the restrictions were lifted business began to flourish. In 1784, of thirty four ships using

Guangzhou, twenty-one were British, four French, four Dutch, four Danish and one American. Of 194,665 piculs of tea carried 91,000 was British, and of 1,089 piculs of raw silk, 800 was British.[27] The following year, twenty-eight out of forty-five ships, 119,000 of 232,030 piculs of tea and 623 of 2,305 piculs of raw silk were British, and of the eighty-six ships entering the harbour in 1789, sixty-one were British.[28] With their commercial activity eclipsing that of their rivals, wrote observer John Barrow, 'the trade of the Dutch, French, Americans, Danes and Swedes in China is likely in a few years to be almost annihilated'.[29]

But as the port boomed there remained one vexing drawback, the restrictive system of hong guildsmen and hubus, which offered almost unlimited scope for venality, corruption and the swindling of traders. This was in large part due to the fact that the position of hong had to be bought from the hubu for around 10,000 Spanish dollars, or 74,000 taels of silver, plus 3 per cent of their takings. Furthermore, their contracts expired after three years, so there was a strong incentive to squeeze as much as possible out of the traders before they had to relinquish their sinecures. Otherwise, as John Barrow noted, 'they could not be able to bear the expense of the numerous and magnificent presents which they are expected to make to the superior officers of government at Canton, who in their turn, find it expedient to divide these with the emperor and his ministers in the capital'.[30] On top of this burden, they had to recoup their initial outlay and emerge at the end showing a profit.

Consequently, traders were regularly presented with fees and charges above and beyond those they were expecting to pay, and because they were restricted to Guangzhou, they were unable to take their business elsewhere. As Barrow explained, 'the import and export duties, which by the law of the country ought to be levied ad valorem, are arbitrarily fixed according to the fancy of the collector'.[31] In 1731, Hosea Morse reported how one hoppo was imposing an additional 10 per cent charge on exports, which it was almost certain he planned to pocket. But when merchants appealed, they were simply fobbed off with excuses. 'Though the [hong] merchants talk of the mandarins fixing the prices, it is plain they themselves do it, and the mandarins only enforce its observance by their authority.'[32]

Hubus also imposed delays if they thought they might be able to make some more cash. In January 1782, one jaded merchant complained how 'from the caprice of one hoppo we have met with many impediments in loading our ships, particularly in sending raw silk on board, as he revived an old law of the emperors that [only] one hundred piculs [130 bales] can be exported on a ship; after much delay this difficulty was got over, and permission granted to export 250 bales, but not in time to take advantage of it as the ships were nearly loaded'.[33] Some mandarins with valuable commodities of their own to sell also tried to get in on the act, bypassing official channels entirely by selling to the merchants directly, leaving the supercargoes, factors and others scratching their heads in dismay. Nor were the British alone in finding such practices exasperating: 'The complaints of all nations against the extortions practised there have been loudly and frequently heard in Europe.'[34] So James Naish, an experienced EIC supercargo approached his French and Dutch counterparts and proposed sending a joint delegation to petition the Emperor. This might succeed in having some of the rules relaxed, and perhaps restore a couple of the other ports to trade, but it would also constitute an egregious breach of protocol. Indeed, when Captain Flint tried to make similar solicitations to Emperor Qianlong in 1759, he was promptly exiled to Macao for three years and then deported. Few were rash enough to want to risk repeating that experience, so the proposal was quietly dropped.

Moreover, their plight was not helped by the negative influence the Europeans had on the locals. Aeneas Anderson had observed that Guangzhou residents were very different 'from the people of every other part of China where we have been... I attribute this local character, which is knavish in the extreme, to their being the inhabitants of the only place where there is any communication with the natives of other countries.'[35] Evidently the European's less circumspect approach to commerce was totally at odds with the mindset of *mianzi*, causing many officials to 'lump us all together as "foreign devils" or "barbarians" from the West' explained British Consular official E. H. Parker, 'who have long noses and deep sunken eyes, mop-like hair... assume a bullying attitude... ogle women [and]... are prone to violence when misunderstandings occur'.[36] Nor, as John Barrow noted, was the contempt for foreigners 'confined to the upper ranks or men in office, but pervades the very lowest class, who consider them as placed in the scale of human beings, many degrees below them'.[37] Company servant Sir George Staunton's assessment of the locals was more magnanimous:

> Almost everything that is really vexatious and repressive on the part of the government towards foreigners at Canton arises not from its ill will, but its ignorance and its fears; their ignorance of our designs, and consequently precautionary restrictions which are harassing and vexatious ... [but] the position and progress of the English in India, can hardly be expected to be contemplated by the Chinese with indifference.[38]

The demonising of foreigners was not coloured by perception alone. When the port transformed into virtually a 24/7 operation, it became second home to thousands of raucous, high-spirited seamen. After months at sea most of them would head for Thirteen Factory Street, Old China Street and Hog Lane, where enterprising retailers did a brisk trade selling food, clothes and a range of knickknacks or 'chowchows' for crewmen to take home as souvenirs. Many preferred the services of the growing sex trade or to sample the cheap intoxicating rice liquor on sale. They would inevitably become drunken and rowdy, spoil for a fight and intimidate the locals, behaviour highly unlikely to endear them to officialdom. It also fed into the underlying sense of resentment, prompting the Governor of Guangdong Province to write a scathing denunciation to the EIC Board of Directors in 1781. He accused the English in particular of being 'a lying and troublesome people, for other nations that come to Canton act peaceful and do not hurt anyone, but you English are always in trouble'.[39]

An example of the kind of conduct that rankled with the locals occurred in November 1784. The gunner on the *Lady Hughs* recklessly fired a salute to a passing Dutch vessel, the blast from which hit a Chinese fishing boat, injuring three of its crew, two of whom later died. The authorities were naturally incensed and demanded that the man responsible be handed over to face justice. The captain initially refused to do so, but was led to believe that leniency would be shown and finally agreed to surrender him.

He was horrified to learn that instead he had been tried, sentenced and executed by strangulation. Not that it seems such harsh punishments served as much of a deterrent, because the EIC Board continued to be bombarded by complaints. In December 1785, it felt compelled to write a missive to its captains, berating them for the 'many irregularities and riots... lately committed... by the English seamen, among whom there at present appears a turbulent and uncontrollable disposition [as a result of which] much danger may befall our trade'.[40]

The risk to existing trade was bad enough, but businessmen from all countries were becoming impatient to sell more into China, not easy with so many of them living under such a cloud. As John Barrow explained, there was no great predilection on the part of the Chinese to open their markets in any case. This was primarily because 'the government is certainly averse to all novelties, and wishes to discountenance a taste for any foreign article that is not absolutely necessary'.[41] He calculated that as a result 'the total imports to Canton 'when summed up together, amount to about £200,000, and their exports from thence to between £600,000 and £700,000',[42] a massive trade surplus in China's favour. Essentially they were only interested in exchanging silver for their goods, not goods, and the result of this business model was that cash was only flowing one way. It was exacerbated by the conversion charges paid to buy silver on the open market, a situation the EIC in particular found unsustainable. Barrow was nonetheless optimistic, and believed that the answer lay in friendly persuasion. He was confident that by 'the proper management of the hong merchants at Canton [imports] might grow into general demand at Pekin',[43] and the dial finally shift in the Europeans' favour.

So in 1787, following negotiations with the British Government, the Board of the EIC appointed Lieutenant-Colonel Charles Cathcart MP to head a delegation to Beijing to broker a deal with Emperor Qianlong. His brief was to secure 'the relief of our present embarrassments at Canton by an extension of our privileges and a revision of the proceedings which have taken place to our prejudice and discredit'.[44] Tragically, his noble endeavour fell at the first hurdle, because the unfortunate man died mysteriously on the outward voyage, and more precious time elapsed before the news reached London. Then Lord

George Macartney was selected for the role, an Anglo-Irish diplomat and politician who had served as governor of Grenada in the British West Indies and Madras in British India. His standing had been further enhanced by his service as Envoy Extraordinary to Russia in 1764, where he negotiated an alliance with Empress Catherine II. He therefore had the bona fides and, crucially, the pedigree which the Company hoped would bode well for his venture. Ostensibly, he was making the trip primarily 'to convey the King's congratulations to the Emperor on the occasion of entering the eightieth year of his age, and [only] incidentally to discuss arrangements for conducting trade'.[45] Discretion and tact was therefore the order of the day and he was told to 'procure an audience as soon as possible after your arrival [but] conforming to all ceremonies which may not commit the honour of your sovereign or lessen your own dignity, so as to endanger the success of your negotiation'.[46]

Like his ill-starred predecessor, he was to seek a relaxation of the taxes, dues and other costs imposed at Guangzhou, secure more flexibility in their dealings with the hongs and hubus and secure the appointment of a permanent ambassador to Beijing, so more direct communications could be established. Because they had for many years been envious of Portugal's privileged status vis a vis Macao, he was also to seek permission for the use of 'a small unfortified island … for the residence of English traders, storage of goods, and outfitting of ships',[47] beyond the jurisdiction of Guangzhou. For this purpose, the rocky, inhospitable but conveniently sited island of Hong Kong, directly opposite Macao, would be ideal. Of huge significance for what was to come to pass, the Board agreed that 'our opium in Bengal must be left to take its chance in an open market or to find a consumption in the dispersed and circuitous traffic of the eastern seas'[48] if the concessions they sought were secured. He certainly led an auspicious enough entourage consisting, wrote Aeneas Anderson of 'every branch of arts, science, and manufacture',[49] including eminent botanist Joseph Banks, who had called for the mission partly so he could procure cuttings of tea plants. They also carried an impressive array of gifts and samples of British technical expertise such as clocks, telescopes, weapons, textiles and even camera obscuras.

Setting off confidently from Portsmouth on 26 September 1792, the eleven-month voyage finally brought them to Beijing on 21 August 1793. Although the delegation was greeted warmly enough, treated well and provided with food 'infinitely beyond the possibility of being consumed by those alone for whose use it was presented',[50] when they arrived in Beijing the main item on the menu was to be a large serving of humble pie. The main bone of contention was the kowtow, which he had already been instructed not to perform if it meant impugning the dignity of his office, and more importantly that of his king. This otherwise unforgivable breach of protocol was apparently circumvented by Macartney offering to undertake the full kowtow if a senior Court official did likewise to a portrait of the Prince Regent, a compromise to which the emperor agreed.

But this was to prove the mission's only diplomatic achievement. After his proposals were conveyed to the emperor, Macartney received a mortifying response. He was informed tersely that 'the emperor refused in the first instance to sign, and of course, to enter into any engagement by a written treaty with the Crown of Great Britain, or any other nation'.[51] This rebuff scuttled the entire mission in one fell swoop, leaving its members wondering what to do next. The meticulous planning, the long sea voyage and the equally arduous trek to the capital had all been in vain, and like many such delegations before them they were left high and dry. But a crestfallen Anderson felt there was more to their desperate plight that met the eye. He was convinced that the hand of some Machiavellian 'Tartar mandarin' was behind it all, exerting his influence from the shadows to 'prejudice the emperor against the English people by representing them as barbarous [and] inhuman'.[52] Even their gifts and samples were treated with indifference, the two camera obscuras in particular, according to one condescending mandarin were 'more suited to the amusement of children, than the information of men of science'.[53]

So the fruitless mission departed demoralised and almost completely empty-handed, apart from a casket of miniatures of previous emperors as a gift for King George. In the accompanying note, also probably drafted by a hostile 'Tartar' mandarin, Qianlong proceeded to scold the monarch for having the temerity to despatch the mission in the first place. He insisted that not only would Macartney's requests 'be utterly unproductive of good to yourself', they were inconsistent 'with our dynastic usage and cannot be entertained'.[54] He reminded the king:

> Our Celestial Empire possesses all things in prolific abundance and lacks no product within its own borders. There was therefore, no need to import the manufactures of barbarians in exchange for our own produce. But as the tea, silk and porcelain which the Celestial Empire produces are absolute necessities to European nations and to yourselves, we have permitted, as a signal mark of favour, that foreign hongs should be established at Canton, so that your wants might be supplied and your country thus participant in our beneficence.[55]

Instead of seeking further advantages he concluded:

> It is your bounden duty reverently to appreciate my feelings and to obey these instructions henceforward for all time, so that you may enjoy the blessings of perpetual peace [or] your merchants will assuredly never be permitted to land or to reside [here], but will be subject to instant expulsion ... do not say that you were not warned.[56]

This stinging reproof left its audience not only chastened, but convinced that it would be some time before anyone suggested repeating that gruelling experience again.

In fact, nearly twenty years would pass, during which time the trading conditions at Guangzhou continued along much the same unsatisfactory lines. So finally, in 1815, it was decided to make another attempt to tease out some concessions. This task fell to diplomat and governor-general of India Lord William Pitt Amherst, whose delegation arrived on 29 August 1816. By the time they reached Beijing everyone was exhausted and desperately needed to recover prior to meeting Emperor Jiaqing, but he demanded an immediate audience, which perhaps injudiciously Lord Amherst declined. He cited ill-health and asked to rest first but instead, as colleague Abel Clarke recorded, Amherst found himself subjected to a scathing rebuke. He was reminded curtly that 'the ceremonies of the Celestial Empire are unalterable [and the emperor,] incensed at the Ambassador's refusal to visit him ... commanded our immediate departure'.[57] Again, it is possible that scheming mandarins deliberately misrepresented his motives for requesting a deferral, but either way the ill-fated group packed their bags and made the long trip home. On the face of it, their hosts' obsession with saving face still outweighed any economic imperatives, although Sir George Staunton believed there might be more behind their brusque treatment than mere hubris:

> There is good reason to believe that any Chinese sovereign who should publicly renounce his absurd claim to universal dominion, and authorise free commercial intercourse between his own subjects and those of other states, would not long retain his sceptre.[58]

Certainly, there was strong evidence to suggest that such was the fragile foundations upon which the dynasty now rested, any sign of weakness might be eagerly seized upon by its enemies and detractors. On their journey the mission saw for themselves the parlous social conditions prevailing in the country. Staunton had also participated in the Macartney embassy, and was discouraged by widespread evidence of poverty and the neglect of important infrastructure. Fellow member Henry Ellis noted that in spite of the need for food' much land, from want of draining was left uncultivated',[59] evidently due to lack of funds. They sensed that with the mood so bleak if 'the discontent ... in the provinces were roused into action by external attack, or encouraged by foreign assistance, a change in the dynasty would not be an improbable event'.[60] Nor was this a hypothetical question. In 1796 the White Lotus Rebellion broke out in the mountains bordering Sichuan, Hubei and Shaanxi provinces, which Jiaqing was unable to suppress completely until 1804. This was a serious setback for the prestige of the dynasty and encouraged further uprisings. The most serious was that of the Eight Tigrams in 1813-1814, essentially an extension of the White Lotus rebellion, which spread throughout Zhili, Shandong and Heinan Provinces. On this occasion the rebels penetrated as far as the Forbidden City before they could be overcome, demonstrating just how fragile the foundations upon which the dynasty rested were becoming.

Yet, had either Qianlong or Jiaqing entertained the proposals presented to them, the consequences for the empire may have been profoundly positive. In spite of the deteriorating domestic situation, it remained strong enough to call the shots and manage the scale and speed of foreign penetration. The economy might have grown and the people prospered, removing any grounds for rebellion. Instead, obsessed with saving face and maintaining the chimera of invulnerability, the Imperial Court held its ground. Consequently, the British changed tack and followed a course of action in which a commodity once considered expendable was to play a pivotal role in the Middle Kingdom's downfall.

3

The Vile Dirt of Foreign Countries

Opium had been a staple medicament for centuries following its introduction by Arab traders during the Tang dynasty. Once its therapeutic properties had been identified by pharmacologist Su Dong, it became known as *Wuxiang*, or black powder, increasingly popular as a stimulant and male aphrodisiac. The Portuguese were among the first Europeans to grasp its commercial potential, and as its popularity increased so did its value. However over time, recreational use exceeded any other application, and growing numbers of addicts fell into a cycle of dependency and death. Therefore, in order to appreciate the part it would play in the disaster to follow, it is valuable to understand its pernicious effects on those who fell under its spell. Staunch abolitionist Charles Toogood Downing, furnishes this graphic description:

> It is delivered over to native brokers, who are usually termed Melters. From these men it passes into the hands of manufacturers, who subject it to a process of purification, by which an extract is obtained, the essential ingredient of which is morphia. The refuse of this process is sold to the poorer people, or made up with tobacco into cheroots ... the greater part of the opium is consumed by smoking... The opium pipes ... are so made, that the vapour is drawn down through water, or some scented liquid, previous to inhalation, in the same way as with the hookah or hubble-bubble of India. When the rich man has finished his pipe, the dregs which remain in the bowl are not thrown away as

useless, but are carefully collected for a second smoking by an inferior person... When the second smoking is completed, the ashes are again preserved, and sold with the scrapings and dirt of the pipe to the poor man, who mixes it with tobacco, tea, or some such material, and it is then a third time ignited.[1]

He then describes its effects on those who indulged in its intoxicating qualities:

When first taken in small doses it acts as a stimulant, exciting the action of the heart and arteries, and filling the mind with pleasant and agreeable thoughts. After a few hours this effect goes off, leaving a depression of spirits fully equal to the previous excitement. Gnomes and demons then take the place of the delightful visions which previously floated across the fancy, and despair is mixed with anguish for the past. To escape from the miserable state, another dose of the drug is taken immediately, when the same sensations are produced. With habit, however, the power of the stimulant diminishes, so that a larger quantity is required at each successive exhibition, until at last the fatal substance will no longer produce its wonted affect, and the deluded mortal is left with all the infirmity of mind and body which it has occasioned.[2]

The physical damage is recounted in detail:

Digestion is impaired ... followed by lassitude and a disinclination for all food whatever. In a short time the strength is wasted, and no inducement can rouse the drunkard to active exertion; he is completely absorbed in his own delusive revelries... The complexion then becomes sallow, and the body wastes away. The lower limbs become disproportionately thin and emaciated, and the gums separate, leaving the black and decayed teeth bared in their sockets. The mind at the same time suffers an equal deterioration; the memory and judgment fail, and the triumph of the animal over the intellectual faculties is indicated by a vacant and sottish expression of countenance ... premature old age, an almost constant state of trembling delirium, and then, lastly ... the opium smoker sinks into his untimely grave.[3]

The Vile Dirt of Foreign Countries

Those utterly within its grasp, explained fellow anti-opium campaigner Montgomery Martin, 'will steal, sell his property, his children, the mother of his children, and finally even commit murder for it'.[4]

Opium had been finding its way into China long before the Macartney and Amherst missions, although while the trade remained relatively modest it was tolerated. But when by 1729 it became more widespread, a ban was imposed, and the one product line from which the EIC could earn silver faced being lost. So a complex smuggling operation was initiated, which proved so successful that after a few years the price collapsed and consumption soared. Prior to 1767 about two hundred chests annually were being imported, but this leapt to 1,000 chests totalling sixty tons by 1780,[5] and following the failure of the Macartney Mission this virtually quadrupled again. Emperor Qianlong was moved to express his 'deep regret that the vile dirt of foreign countries should be received in exchange for the commodities and money of the empire',[6] and the government made further fruitless attempts to stem the flow. Steps taken in 1800 met with little success, so in 1809 the governor of Guangzhou instructed hong merchants to provide bonds of security certifying that the vessels they were handling were not carrying the drug. This measure too failed, and by 1816-17 over 3,000 chests were entering the empire annually, and with the acquisition of Singapore in 1819, the smuggling operation became even more sophisticated. Ships from India could now sail to the island and transfer their cargoes to vessels that completed the next leg to Lintin Island. From there, faster clippers raced up the delta to be met by even smaller craft, which found safe landing places up and down the coast. As a consequence, the amount finding its way through escalated exponentially, averaging 10,000 chests a year by 1826-27, and 24,000 by 1832-33. This was not all down to the smugglers however, for success also required the connivance of officials, who for a cut waved the cargo through under fake manifests. As one EIC official sarcastically observed, 'if opium was actually contraband, the hoppo could not levy duty on it, or even take cognizance of its existence'.[7] Although by far the worst offender, Britain was not alone. The Americans, for example, found that the proceeds from their furs, sandalwood and ginseng were eclipsed by what they could obtain from the drug, so they turned to smuggling Turkish as well as Indian opium. Similarly, the French and Portuguese saw a far higher return from bootlegging than legitimate commerce.

Understandably perhaps, few could resist the fantastic profits to be made from a drug which sold in Bengal for 500 rupees a chest and in China for five hundred dollars.[8] Annual turnover in Guangzhou was estimated to be 18,000,000 Mexican dollars,[9] and the emperors, too, were cashing in to the tune of $1,000,000 a year from the tribute sent by their officials. Even more profits were made through American and British run 'agency houses', which served as launderers for the proceeds, using the silver paid for the opium to buy tea on the legal open market. The illicit trade therefore benefited the British Government too, which at the time levied a tax on tea, of which Britain imported 30,000,000 pounds annually. It was estimated that in total some 9,000,000 taels of silver a year were being drained from the economy, and this meant its value against copper was rising and throwing farmers into destitution, because they paid their taxes in silver. Thus thousands more were becoming drawn into the spiral of poverty, turning to the very cause of their misery for relief. This simply increased demand and the subsequent profits to be made.

It had become such an indispensable item in the East India Company's ledgers that by the 1830s opium was accounting for nearly 15 per cent of its profits. But the organisation's future was seriously threatened when its monopoly of trade with China was removed under the 1833 Charter Act. After years of lobbying, the country had been opened to all comers, meaning margins would have to be cut unless some means could be found to shield the Company from the competition. There was some cause for optimism however, because as part of their reforms the British Government had created the post of Superintendent of Trade at Guangzhou. The role was essentially twofold, to oversee the new regime and to act as intermediary with the local officials. Further subtle approaches were to be made, to induce the mandarins to relax the rules and accommodate themselves to the influx of new merchants. The cherry on the cake for the EIC would be if the embargo on opium could be relaxed or better still, lifted entirely. This was a task that would ideally fall to someone cut from the same cloth as Lords Macartney and Amherst, but instead Royal Navy officer and veteran of Trafalgar Lord William Napier had been handed the responsibility. Having little flair for tact and diplomacy, his aloof and offhand manner immediately alienated the Chinese officials. He tried to cut through centuries of *mianzi*-inspired red tape and negotiate directly with the Viceroy, but he refused to receive this high-handed Englishman who had omitted to bring the required documentation and accreditation. Undeterred, Napier proceeded to push his case against an increasingly recalcitrant Imperial bureaucratic machine, finding himself frozen out and ignored. His feathers ruffled, he began to suggest to his superiors that armed force might be the only way to bring them round.

His blundering also caused increasing alarm among the merchants, who feared he would so anger the mandarins that they would simply throw them all out. Having suffered his arrogance for long enough, this is what they did, and trade was halted and a blockade imposed until Napier was removed. Under extreme pressure he reluctantly returned to Macao, following which a period of relative calm ensued. In his place, Captain Charles Elliott was appointed Superintendent in 1836, and although he shared the widespread disapproval of the opium trade, admitting it was 'staining the British character with deep disgrace',[10] he was nevertheless to seek some way of smoothing its passage through to the opium dens. This objective was completely at odds with the authorities' plans, for by now its use had reached such plague proportions the last thing they wanted was to have it made legal. Every lever was now being pulled to see that the law was enforced, regardless of the vested interests of foreign businessmen, hongs and hubus.

Instrumental in this crackdown was pugnacious Imperial Commissioner Lin Zexu, a respected scholar and highly effective administrator, who had taken a personal interest in eliminating the trade. Having authored a Memorial to the emperor on the subject, he was sent to Guangzhou in March 1839 with orders to put his theories into practice. One of these was to encourage people to turn dealers in, and within a few months 1,600 arrests had been made. Whilst the dealers faced execution, corrupt government employees were dismissed, faced banishment or corporal punishment. Addicts were given sixty days to surrender their smoking apparatus and eighteen months to quit their addiction, otherwise they, too, risked severe penalties. But although the campaign yielded 50,000 lbs of the drug and 70,000 pipes,[11] it was still only the tip of the iceberg, and the deterrents did not appear to be working. H. Hamilton Lindsay, a former employee of the East India Company, saw 'opium pipes, with all the apparatus for smoking, publicly exhibited for sale, not only in shops but by common hawkers in the streets'.[12] The British merchants were continuing to import chests of the product surreptitiously of course, and acting as if it was business as usual. So, to drive his message home, Lin decided that an unambiguous example needed to be made. One miscreant was tried, sentenced to death and publicly strangled in full view of the Factories and their European residents. The growing sense that this time Beijing meant business encouraged the Scottish firm of Jardine-Matheson to issue a profit warning to its shareholders, whilst American company Russell and Co. decided that the game was up and pulled out of the trade altogether. Lin also tried diplomacy to encourage the British to cooperate and penned an appeal to the newly crowned Queen Victoria. In it he explained that among her subjects

> ... there are those who smuggle opium to seduce the Chinese people and so cause the spread of the poison to all provinces. Such persons who only care to profit themselves, and disregard their harm to others, are not tolerated by the laws of heaven and are unanimously hated by human beings.[13]

With neither the measures he was taking nor the appeal to the Queen having much of an effect, he decided to take the nuclear option. He ordered that Elliott and the merchants be held under armed guard until the offending opium was surrendered. As a result, trade was brought to a virtual standstill, and as tensions increased a violent confrontation seemed inevitable. In an effort to break the deadlock Elliott persuaded the merchants to give in to Lin's ultimatum, and around 1,000 tons of the drug, worth $6,000,000, was finally handed over. Lin then promptly had the chests broken open and ostentatiously destroyed, but the entire exercise seemed like a pyrrhic victory for all concerned. With tensions still high and fearful for their lives, Elliott led a mass exodus to Macao, from where he instituted a blockade of his own. HMS *Volage* and HMS *Hyacinth* set up station a mile south of Chuenpi and on 3 November 1839 intercepted a British flagged ship attempting to break through. When twenty-nine war junks intervened, the Royal Navy ships' superior firepower destroyed four and damaged most of the rest. The British sustained only minimal damage and casualties.

When news of what was transpiring reached Britain, the issue of opium and the sanctity of private property became conflated with the broader question of British dignity and sovereign rights. Merchant H. Hamilton Lindsay charged the Chinese with breaching 'all international laws recognised by civilised nations for the protection of life and property ... for an alleged infraction of certain laws, which for years had been a dead letter, or rather, of which the chief violators had been those high functionaries who promulgated them'.[14] Fellow trader James Matheson put their behaviour down to 'a marvellous degree of imbecility, avarice, conceit and obstinacy',[15] which frankly called for them to be taught a severe lesson. Decades of frustration and resentment had finally boiled over and Lin had aroused a determination to make them pay 'for the insults and outrages offered to the British nation'.[16]

Foreign Secretary Lord Palmerston was among those hawks who saw in this affair a heaven-sent opportunity to achieve that which had eluded men such as Macartney, Amherst and a succession of other lobbyists. But whereas diplomacy had tried and failed, he proposed to use force, and under threat of war Britain was to present the Chinese with a list of demands that would throw the empire open to almost unlimited commercial opportunities. They were to put an end to the hongs and hubus and allow foreign merchants to trade with whom they pleased; instead of the ad hoc system of dues and taxes, properly fixed scales of charges were to be agreed; they must also end the monopoly at Guangzhou entirely and open more ports to foreign trade; diplomatic representation was to be established and a permanent ambassador appointed to the capital. Furthermore, a base must be established on Hong Kong Island, which was to be ceded to the British Crown in perpetuity to use as it wished. Not forgetting the root cause of the crisis, compensation for the opium that Lin had destroyed was also to be paid. As an incentive to comply, he proposed to send an expeditionary force. The icing on the cake was that none of this need cost the British taxpayer a brass farthing. All the expenses would be met by extracting a hefty indemnity from the humbled Chinese.

Riding high on the groundswell of jingoism stirred up by men like Lindsay and Matheson, he took his plans to his colleagues in Cabinet. Once they voted in favour, formal approval was granted by both Houses of Parliament in January 1840, and his Secretary of State for War set in train the necessary arrangements. A formidable land force would consist of around 18,000 highly trained and disciplined British, Indian, and Ceylonese troops with 7,000 Royal Marines, all equipped with the most modern arms and equipment, artillery, and rocket batteries. This formidable display of firepower was supported by a state-of-the art fleet of fourteen sloops of up to eighteen guns each, eight frigates with up to twenty-eight guns each, and three ships-of-the line of ninety guns. There would also be twelve miscellaneous support and troop-carrying vessels bearing down on an empire that had neglected its navy, much of its shore defences and its army for centuries. The repercussions were to prove catastrophic.

As early as 1435 the Chinese, seeing no threat from the sea, had begun scrapping warships, and in 1452 the Shenjamin naval base on the shore of Zhenjiang was abandoned completely. In 1524 a further edict commanded Dengzhou cease construction of warships altogether, so that by 1839 all that remained was a motley collection of aged, obsolete war junks unchanged in design or composition for centuries. Only the Dagu forts, built between 1522 and 1627 to protect Tianjin from pirates, remained an effective deterrent, having been upgraded in 1816 and with further improvements scheduled. Located on the Hai, or Peiho River Estuary, thirty-seven miles southeast of the city, they would prove a formidable challenge to any attacker, whilst Guangzhou was defended by the Bogue Forts of Chuenpi and Tycocktow located at the mouth of the Pearl River.

Much less prepared was its ponderous and outmoded army. As Henry Ellies had observed twenty years before, 'the army of China, sufficient ... for [the] purpose of policing, would not present much resistance to the irregular troops of Asia, and would certainly be quite unequal to cope with European armies'.[17] Although the British infantry could potentially face 16,000 or more Bannermen and over 205,000 Green Standard troops, both armies had long suffered from neglect. Many of the Green Standard units were at half-strength, some even at one-sixth of their official establishment, and consequently low morale pervaded most ranks, resulting in poor discipline and inefficiency. The Banner Army was now in effect the emperor's Praetorian Guard, and consisted almost exclusively of hereditary Manchu whose loyalty could not be questioned. Early Qing emperors made the training, arming, and provisioning of the Banner Army a priority whilst they engaged in wars of conquest and expanded the empire, but after 1644 they mostly guarded the capital or were garrisoned in Manchuria, the provinces and along the northern frontier. The Chinese Bannermen were largely discharged and incorporated into the Standard Army in order to retain the former's exclusivity, and in theory was double to two-thirds the size of the Bannermen. So, in part to offset any potential issues, it was scattered around the empire in small garrisons, and as Ellis observed, served primarily as a constabulary.

Although on campaign, elements of the Banner and Standard armies did fight together, great care was taken to ensure the latter remained subordinate. As a further check, the Government appointed most of their officers directly, and they were not allowed to serve in their native provinces to prevent any undue favouritism. Although both had once been well-equipped by the standards of the time, the adoption of new weapons and tactics was always patchy. Military technology in China had reached its high watermark with the acquisition of arquebuses in 1523, and by the 1550s they were in general use. In the latter half of the sixteenth century the breech loading cannon was developed, but advances stalled after the first flintlocks were acquired in 1636 and they failed to be adopted. As a consequence, most troops would be facing the British with their ancient matchlocks, bows, spears, crossbows, poleaxes and swords. Their shortcomings had already been exposed in wars conducted by Emperor Qianlong against Burma in the 1760s, and as recently as 1832 an expedition against rebels in the south had to be abandoned because so many men were affected by opium. As Zexu himself conceded, the omens were not good: 'Unless we have weapons, whatever help can we get now to drive away the crocodile and get rid of the whales?'[18] As events were to demonstrate, the answer was very little.

On 21 June 1840 a naval force commanded by Commodore Sir Gordon Bremmer arrived off Macao, moved north to Chusan and on 5 July shelled and occupied Tinghai. This early show of force appeared to do the trick and tentative negotiations started. But when the British demands as dictated by Palmerston were delivered to the Chinese they were horrified. They expressed their astonishment that such effrontery would even be considered and refused to discuss the matter further. In response the British renewed hostilities, capturing the Bogue Forts on 7 January 1841, and in an accompanying naval engagement captured ten of thirteen junks and sank another. A distrait Admiral Kuan Ti then asked for a ceasefire, and on 18 January handed over the keys to Hong Kong. This concession, however, went far beyond his authority and Beijing reiterated their resolute refusal to enter into discussions. After waiting for several more months a force commanded by Lieutenant-General Sir Hugh Gough proceeded up the Pearl River, capturing Guangzhou itself on 27 May. But when its governor promised to pay a £600,000 indemnity they agreed to withdraw, and Elliott proceeded to try and thrash out the elusive peace settlement.

His deal however, fell far short of what Palmerston wanted, so he was taken to task and replaced by Sir Henry Pottinger, who reiterated the Prime Minister's original demands, but still the Chinese demurred. In the face of their continued recalcitrance the British moved northwards, seizing Amoy on 26-27 August 1841, Ningpo on 13 October and Chinhai the following day. With winter closing in, further operations were suspended whilst a renewed round of discussions was attempted. On 10 March 1842, in the midst of these unproductive negotiations, the Chinese launched a counteroffensive which the British repulsed, losing Chapu in the process on 18 May. Despite their shortcomings in arms and tactics some Chinese troops proved more resourceful than expected. In one skirmish a ferocious rainstorm rendered the British muskets useless and forced them to rely on the bayonet. For once the two sides were more or less evenly matched, and in hand-to-hand fighting the Bannermen nearly turned the tables on the invaders and only when the British muskets became operational again were they able to regain the initiative. That minor achievement notwithstanding, Gough and Admiral Sir William Parker proceeded to Shanghai, which fell on 19 June. Next, they made their way up the Yangtse River capturing Chinkiang on 21 July. Finally, with the city of Nanking exposed and threatened with capture, the Chinese made renewed overtures, bringing the war to an end on 17 August 1842.

On paper at least, the subsequent Treaty of Nanjing, signed on 29 August satisfied all Palmerston's objectives and shattered forever the illusion of superiority that had sustained China for centuries. Having repeatedly rejected peaceful petitions because their bearers declined to adhere to archaic ritual or recognise assertions of global hegemony, the tectonic plates had been shifted irrevocably by force of arms. Despite Article I stating that the treaty would bring 'Peace and Friendship' between Queen Victoria and the emperor, no amount of *Mianzi* or Confucian guile could conceal the truth as every demand was grudgingly acceded to. Article II confirmed that British merchants were henceforth to be 'allowed to reside, for the purpose of carrying on their mercantile pursuits, without molestation or restraint, at the cities and towns of Canton, Amoy, Foochow, Ningpo and Shanghai... Consular officers [were to] be the medium of communication between the Chinese authorities and the said merchants'. Article III took the island: 'It being obviously necessary and desirable that British subjects should have some port whereat they may careen and refit their ships when required, and keep stores for that purpose, His Majesty the Emperor of China cedes to Her Majesty the Queen ... the island of Hong Kong to be possessed in perpetuity.' The pain continued. Article IV instructed the Chinese to pay $6,000,000 in compensation for 'the opium which was delivered up at Canton ... as a ransom for the lives of HBM Superintendent and subjects who had been imprisoned and threatened with death by the Chinese High Officers'.

Article V finally abolished the monopoly of the hong and confirmed that 'at all ports where British merchants may reside' they were to be allowed 'to carry on their mercantile transactions with whoever persons they please'. Succeeding Articles stated that $3,000,000 would be paid in lieu of debts owed by hong merchants who had gone bankrupt, and that $12,000,000 would be forthcoming to cover the cost of the expedition. Finally, Article X confirmed that the Chinese would establish 'a fair and regular tariff of export and import customs and other dues, which tariff shall be publicly notified and promulgated for general information'. On 8 September the supplemental Treaty of Bogue awarded Britain Most Favoured Nation status, giving its subjects any 'additional privileges and immunities' the emperor may see fit to grant. Furthermore, consuls alone would now be responsible for ensuring their nationals obeyed the rules, rather than the now defunct hongs.

The Chinese did succeed in extracting one concession in return. The treaty stipulated that these privileges only applied within the strict confines of the ports themselves, and foreigners were still forbidden to venture 'beyond certain distances to be named by local authorities'. Nonetheless, Beijing still had to suffer the indignity of having Royal Navy warships on standby in case another incident occurred.

It did not take long for China's helplessness to open the floodgates to other countries to demand similar concessions. France and the US compelled the Chinese to agree terms in 1844, followed by Sweden and Norway in 1847 and in 1851 Russia was permitted to open consulates in the Ili Valley of Chinese East Turkestan. George Staunton's prediction that such appalling loss of face would have disastrous consequences also came to pass. It became clear, recorded George Thin, that 'the prestige of the emperor's name is now almost useless for the practical purposes of government. It is openly defied in many parts of the country ... whatever treaty the Emperor of China may be brought to sign, it by no means follows it will be carried out in the provinces unless it meets the approval of the local mandarins.'[19] He was not only to be held accountable for the shame of defeat. The new ports that had been sanctioned meant that cheap foreign goods would flow into the empire with little restraint, undercutting domestic producers and throwing already impoverished and alienated peasants into destitution. Their distress was compounded by those still in work seeing the value of their incomes cut by the burdensome taxes levied to pay the indemnities.

Consequently, many people fell prey to demagogues and rabble-rousers eager to exploit their plight to their own ends. The revolts of 1796 and 1813 were to be mirrored by the Taiping Rebellion, which began in the southern province of Guanxi, and which would last from 1850 to 1864. Concurrently, the Qings faced the Muslim separatist Wienxu Rebellion in Western Yunnan, which ran from 1856 to 1872, and in Guangdong it fought to suppress the Red Turban Rebellion of 1854-56. To these would be added the Dungan Revolts of 1862 to 1877 in Gansu and Qinghai, stretching the dynasty's resources to the limit.

Arguably the most dangerous and immediate of these was the Taiping Rebellion, ruinously expensive to suppress and further damaging to the prestige of the Qings. By 1860, the proximity of the fighting to Shanghai brought both sides into contact with foreigners, and when their commercial interests were threatened the Western governments took action, supporting Beijing with both mercenary and professional troops. Men such as General Charles 'Chinese' Gordon were seconded from the British army, and at one stage he commanded the so-called Ever Victorious Army, which would prove instrumental in crushing the rebellion. It would finally come to an end with the recapture of Nanking on 19 July 1864, but nevertheless had far reaching repercussions. The fighting had increased the power of local mandarins, compromised central control, produced turf wars and created local power bases. Accepting help proved a double-edged sword. As French mercenary Prosper Giquel, recruited to help train Imperial troops, noted, 'in rendering the Chinese immense service for our help in battling the rebels, we augment our influence and create new obligations for Peking'.[20]

This state of affairs became more serious as Beijing attempted to resolve the empire's mounting economic problems. One solution was to frustrate the flow of goods being dumped on the country. Bitter at the treaty they had been coerced into signing in the first place, port officials either paid lip service to its terms, acted in bad faith or exploited the confusion which arose from ambiguities in the text. Those at Guangzhou, for example, insisted that the right of residency granted to foreigners was very elastic and indeed, only a temporary concession. They also delayed opening the new ports on the grounds that they were still 'unsafe' for foreigners. In fact, in the words of Paul Clements, a 'thousand petty exactions were religiously adhered to'[21] to make life for foreigners as difficult as irksome as possible, and as Robert Swinhoe noted, no opportunity was lost 'of humbling [them] before the eyes of the Chinese population'.[22]

Such an opportunity presented itself on 8 October 1856, when Chinese officials impounded the small boat *Arrow* in Guangzhou harbour and detained its crew. They suspected them of engaging in piracy, but being British-flagged with a British captain, acting consul Harry Parkes insisted that it enjoyed Crown protection. Steeped in *mianzi* and harbouring a visceral hatred of foreigners, Imperial Commissioner and Viceroy Ye Mingchen disagreed. When the two reached an impasse, Parkes sought the help of the Governor of Hong Kong Sir John Bowring. He added his voice to demands for the return of the vessel and an apology for infringing its owners' rights, but when neither was forthcoming Rear Admiral Sir Michael Seymour, commander of the Royal Navy's East Indies and China Station, waded in. True to the Imperialist playbook he seized a Chinese junk and initiated a blockade of the harbour. Only then did the implacable Ye appear to cede some ground, offering to give up all but two of the *Arrow*'s crew, who, he insisted, would have to stand trial. Dissatisfied with his response, skirmishes broke out and after nearly sixteen years the city came under bombardment from British naval guns for the second time. In consequence, a red mist came over the Commissioner, who promised a bounty of $30 for the head of every Englishman surrendered to him.

As the shelling intensified, a shore party was landed with instructions to arrest Ye and keep him under lock and key until he yielded. However, as the men approached his residence, they encountered stiffer resistance than expected and were compelled to withdraw under heavy fire. Enraged by the temerity of the foreign devils, Ye then called for the complete destruction of all 'red haired foreign dogs'[23] and increased the bounty on their heads. As the situation escalated, the British and French governments followed the crisis with growing interest. As Palmerston had realised in 1840, here was an issue which could be exploited to tie up some more loose ends and an ultimatum was sent to Ye demanding the release of the ship's crew, an end to the victimisation of their nationals, and the adoption of a more liberal interpretation of the treaties.

Ye still demurred, prompting more shelling and another, better planned assault, which resulted in his capture. The Chinese then offered to consider the Anglo-French demands, but delay followed delay, and once again the decision was taken to resort to force. In April 1858, a naval flotilla sailed north and seized the Dagu Forts, following which Tianjin fell and exposed Beijing to bombardment. Confronted with overwhelming firepower the Chinese grudgingly agreed to negotiate, and the Treaty of Tientsin was signed on 26 June 1858. Under its terms another indemnity had to be paid and six more ports with consuls, including in Formosa, on the Shandong Peninsula and in Manchuria, opened. The Yangtse was to be freed to British trade as far as Hankow, and Europeans permitted to travel without hindrance in the hinterland. Foreign missionaries were to be afforded protection and a Chinese embassy opened in London. The principle of extraterritoriality was defined, specifying that British subjects could only be tried by a British consul according to British law. Furthermore, the hated kowtow was to be dispensed with altogether, alongside the despised 'Yi' when referring to Europeans in official documents. On the face of it, this was another climbdown, but again the Chinese treated it with disdain and made no effort to ratify or implement its terms.

Accepting that Beijing had no intention of formalising the treaty, a second Anglo-French force was mobilised in May 1859, making another appearance at the Dagu Forts. However, in the intervening period, perhaps anticipating such an eventuality, the defences had been augmented considerably, and when the Allies arrived they were met by a wall of fire. Compelled to withdraw, the emboldened Chinese saw this as a massive victory and openly repudiated the terms of the treaty as 'insubordinate and extravagant'.[24] In response, another force 11,000 strong supported by 200 ships resumed the offensive. They finally closed on Beijing and envoys, including Harry Parkes, were sent ahead to parley with the emperor. A number of them were seized and those not killed outright were held captive. Ambassador Lord Elgin flew into a rage and demanded that the survivors were either released immediately and the emperor recant, or Beijing would come under immediate attack. He also ordered that as an object lesson the Old Imperial Summer Palace, built by emperors Kangxi and Qianlong, be ransacked. Faced with the imminent destruction of their capital the Chinese again reluctantly agreed, but then Robert Swinhoe and others claimed that the captives had been badly mistreated, and that some had their 'hands tightly bound with cords until mortification ensued and they died'.[25] When he learned of these abuses, Elgin's mood quickly changed to one of revenge.

Now, in a gratuitous act of spite, rather than just being looted the Old Summer Palace was to be completely razed. But first scores of soldiers descended upon the site like locusts, eager to grab what they could before it was put to the torch. Swinhoe saw men sweep up 'gold watches and small valuables ... with amazing velocity, and as speedily [they disappeared] in their capacious pockets',[26] whilst others helped themselves to strings of pearls, 'each the size of a marble [and] pencil cases set with diamonds'.[27] But as Sir Hope Grant watched men carry off 'piles of valuable rolls of silk and embroidered dresses',[28] he felt disgust at the 'way in which everything was being robbed'.[29] His verdict was shared by a French colleague, who condemned the proceedings as sheer 'barbarism',[30] but it nonetheless continued until there was little of value left. The pièce de resistance of this feeding frenzy was a dozen beautiful bronze animal heads, each representing a sign of the Chinese Zodiac, and once these were hauled away the second phase of the operation began. Men proceeded to make their way through the various buildings and put them to the torch room by room, Swinhoe witnessing with morbid satisfaction the 'crackling and rushing noise of fire [as] roof after roof crashed in'.[31] He was convinced that the sight of this devastation could not fail to be a blow to the emperor's pride 'as well as to his feelings [and] we could not help feeling a secret gratification that ... the murder of our hapless countrymen [was] revenged'.[32] It certainly did the trick, and with a gun held to their collective heads, the Chinese returned to the negotiating table.

Not only had they to hold their noses and fulfil the terms of the original Treaty of Tientsin, they were forced to agree to the so-called supplementary Convention of Peking. The emperor now had to express his 'deep regret' for the Dagu forts affair, pay a further indemnity of 8,000,000 taels of silver, add Tianjin to the list of treaty ports, recognise the rights of Chinese subjects to travel and work in British colonies, and permanently lease part of the Kowloon Peninsula to the existing colony of Hong Kong. As a final humiliation, and to ensure the Chinese honoured their financial commitments, Englishman Horatio Nelson Lay was appointed to head the Customs Service. It was opened in 1862 in Shanghai and was manned almost exclusively by Europeans, and under their purview revenues would increase from 5,526,435 Hong Kong taels of silver in 1845 to 11,970,000 by 1875.

News of China's latest prostration soon spread, reaching even the ears of Karl Marx. He predicted that the destruction of the Qings was now inevitable, 'as surely as that of any mummy carefully preserved in a hermetically sealed coffin, whenever it is brought into contact with the open air'.[33] His prophesy was soon realised, as once again other Powers followed close on Britain's heels to claim their piece of the atrophying corpse. The Americans took the opportunity to entrench their position, and not to be outdone, Germany signed the Sino-German Treaty of 1861. The Spanish secured treaty rights in 1864, Italy in 1866, and later Austria, Brazil, Mexico and the Congo Free State wrung similar arrangements out of Beijing. But the greatest beneficiary of the war, apart from Britain and France, was to be Russia.

Despite having been repeatedly rebuffed following the Treaty of Nerchinsk, the Russians had continued to extend their reach into Qing territory surreptitiously. In 1847, Count Nikolas Muravieff was appointed Governor-General of Eastern Siberia, and in the spring of 1848 he started sending out small parties to reconnoitre the area around the Amur. One reached the Sea of Okhotsk, whilst another surveyed the coastline and discovered its mouth. Captain Nevilskoi led a further expedition which established what would later be called Nikolaevsk on Kamchatka in 1851. In 1852 one of the Kurile Islands was occupied. The following year Alexandrovsk was founded in Castries Bay, and a settlement in Aniva Bay at the southern end of Sakhalin Island. Emboldened by the success of their operations, a post was also established at Dui on its western coast.

In 1854, Muravieff decided the time had come to seize the Amur outright. This was prompted in part by the outbreak of war in the Russian Crimea against Britain and France that had cut off access to the Black Sea, the usual route to the Siberian coast. It also appeared as if an Anglo-French fleet was going to threaten the area, so it was clearly more than ever essential to secure the region. In 1855 an advance party of 3,000 troops and colonists set off to establish a forward base, but when they reached the area they found that the Chinese were waiting for them. However, a lot of water had passed under the bridge since 1689, and they were far too few in number this time to foil their plans. Preoccupied elsewhere, the Chinese were in no position to open another front against the Russians, and could only look on as they began consolidating themselves and started constructing defences. Finally, and almost meekly, on 28 May 1858 they agreed to the Treaty of Aigun. This document ceded to the Czar suzerainty over some 600,000 square kilometres of territory, including the entire Maritime Province between the Ussuri River and the sea and the territory around Lakes Baikal and Issik Kul in Turkestan. The rivers Sangari and Ussuri were opened to trade and the new frontier between China and Siberia was also to be surveyed and mapped. The supplementary Treaty of Tientsin then conceded the right to an embassy in Beijing and the opening of ports to Russian trade. To further entrench its hold on the territory, Moscow established a chain of Cossack garrisons fifteen to thirty miles apart and began the construction of cities such as Khabarovka. The Treaty of Nerchinsk was now a dead letter.

This latest string of reverses may have hammered more nails in the dynastic coffin, but they also served to exacerbate the enmity felt towards Europeans in all their manifestations: 'Mandarin hatred of foreigners was as strong as ever.'[34] But with the country in its current state, there was little prospect that these sentiments could manifest themselves in organised rebellion. Instead, they continued to obstruct the merchants in the treaty ports whenever they could, whilst sporadic and isolated acts of resistance were possible through piracy or violence against individuals. One particularly conspicuous group against which they could vent their spleen were the Christian missionaries and their Chinese converts. They were a dangerously exposed group, working alone or clustered in small

The Vile Dirt of Foreign Countries

groups all around the country. To many Chinese they epitomised the insidious nature of foreign intrusion and had been present since at least 635 CE. In 1245, Franciscan friar John of Pian de Carpine was despatched by Pope Innocent IV to Mongolia to establish a diplomatic mission and Christian monk Rabban Sauma travelled from China to Rome via Constantinople. In 1556 Dominican Gaspar de Cruz travelled through China, and in 1582 Italian Jesuit Matteo Ricci arrived in Macao, in 1601 becoming the first European to enter the Forbidden City. He was followed in 1602-1607 by Portuguese Jesuit Bento de Grois, the first European to travel overland from India to China. They were not always guaranteed a friendly reception.

As early as 1664, Christians found themselves in the crosshairs of critics such as Confucian scholar and would-be astronomer Yang Guangxian. When he applied for a senior position in Court, he found that he and his compatriots had been beaten to it by Jesuits. Bitter at such rejection, he denounced them angrily for spreading apostasy and trying to indoctrinate the people with 'false ideas',[35] and conspired to have them exiled back to Macao. Yet despite such resentment, their fresh ideas in fields such as science and mathematics frequently attracted royal patronage and they kept coming. Hackles were raised nonetheless, when it was claimed that the Pope held a position supreme to that of their emperor, and the last straw came when in 1715 a Papal Bull by Pope Clement XI forbade Christian converts from either worshipping their ancestors or from adhering to the teachings of Confucius. Despite pleas that the two beliefs should be allowed to co-exist, the Pontiff refused to retract his Bull, and in 1721 Emperor Kangxi banned Christian missionaries from China altogether.

Even under this pressure, the push for the salvation of the Oriental soul continued, and the first Bible was published in Chinese in 1823, a shot in the arm for the missionaries but a red rag to the Confucian bulls. Other versions followed, including one believed to have helped inspire the Taiping uprising, because among its leadership were converts who planned to usurp the Qings and establish Christianity.

When this was added to more recent violations, dyed-in-the-wool Confucians and nationalists alike became convinced that their corrupting influence had to be stamped out once and for all. But, as George Thin observed, 'amongst the people of China, as distinguished from the mandarins, there is no natural dislike of foreigners'.[36] On the contrary, missionaries in particular were widely respected for their good works. A number managed orphanages for children abandoned by parents unable to care for them, and it would be difficult to persuade the average Chinese to turn their backs on such charity. However, they were also highly superstitious, and it might be possible to tap into such a mindset. It was therefore convenient that many peasants believed that by eating specific organs of the human body the user would be imbued with supernatural powers, and that those of infants were the most potent of all. It took no great leap of the imagination to conflate the two, and during the 1860s invidious rumours began to circulate. Resident A. H. Carvalho noted that the missionaries were now being accused of exploiting their young charges for 'nefarious means and... unholy practices'.[37] As these calumnies gained traction, the more credulous peasants decided to take the law into their own hands.

In August 1868, a group of Christians were accused of killing children for their hearts, eyes and livers to make love potions. They were attacked and fled for their lives, whilst their property was ransacked and set alight. On 25 June 1869, two priests anchored their boat for the night opposite a village thirty-five miles from Tianjin. When the locals became aware, frightened perhaps that they were scouting for children, a twenty-strong mob assaulted them and one was killed.[38] In April 1870, a Christian chapel at a place known as Peaou was destroyed and its occupants brutally murdered,[39] and by June 1870 it was estimated that as many as 400 foreigners had been killed.[40] As the campaign gained momentum, the menace moved from the countryside and crept into the towns and cities, where already resented Europeans found themselves dangerously exposed. In June 1870, a jurisdictional dispute between the French consul Henri Fontanier and Chinese officials in Tianjin had been causing ill-feeling for some time, and it would not take much of an excuse to bring the antagonism to a head. This was furnished by a serious epidemic that summer in which an unusually high infant mortality occurred, and when gossips implied that more lay behind the young deaths than met the eye, people started to grow suspicious.

As allegations spread during the middle of the month that missionary baby farmers were somehow responsible, admissions to the Catholic-run orphanage began to fall. As one European resident later explained, 'for several days ... parents had been coming by day and night to take away their children [from] the Jen-Tsze-Tang orphanage [until] out of 450, only about 200' remained.[41] Whereas in most other treaty ports the Chinese authorities largely sought to allay fears and call out the rumour mongers, that was not the case here. Instead, the Superintendent of Trade for the Three Northern Ports Commissioner Chonghou, was alleged to have actually published a proclamation 'that induced the people to believe that the reports were true'.[42] Increasingly concerned, the British Consul, a Mr Lay, wrote to Chonghou on 18 June 'pointing out the challenges to which the foreign community were exposed, and asking him to take means to calm the popular mind',[43] but he received no answer. This inaction prompted him to request that a warship be sent from Hong Kong, as anti-western gangs were now openly inciting the population to violence. Before any action could be taken, however, the French concession, being the location of the demonic missionaries and their orphanages, was targeted. At around 2.00 p.m. on 21 June, fires were observed in the French cathedral and consulate.

Fontanier sent an urgent message to the magistrate demanding protection, and when that elicited no response he went to confront him. After a heated and inconclusive argument, he left, to find himself being set upon by an angry mob in the street, where he died from his injuries. Elsewhere, more Europeans were being attacked, among them a newlywed sixteen-year-old Russian girl. The ferocity of the attacks were graphically described by a correspondent for the *Shanghai Evening Courier*, who claimed seeing one victim with their 'head and face cloven to pieces with sword cuts', another covered with 'spear wounds on the body' and a third who had suffered a 'sword cut through the back of the neck'.[44] A prime target for the mob was the orphanage of the Sisters of Charity, which was attacked, looted and where the nuns allegedly had 'their clothes torn off them, their bodies stabbed and ripped open, their breasts cut off, and their eyes dug out'. Their bodies were then piled in a heap and set on fire. 'All that is left of them are two charred masses.'[45] In all, eight Protestant chapels in and around the city were looted, sixteen other places of worship destroyed, and sixty foreigners lay dead. The violence only subsided after the rioters had exhausted their bloodlust and gunboats finally appeared to restore order.

Once the dust had settled, a funeral service was held for the victims on 8 July in the French Church, but it was not until three days later that the Governor-General of Chihli Zeng Guofan belatedly issued a proclamation instructing the Chinese not to 'interfere with foreigners coming to the city'.[46] This weak gesture fooled no one, and Carvalho remained convinced that 'there can be no doubt about the connivance of the authorities at this dreadful massacre, for even if it did not originate with them, it was perfectly in their powers to put down all display of bad feeling when they were first requested to do so'.[47] The ridiculous rumours that provoked the riot in the first place were soon debunked as utter fabrications. The *Peking Gazette* of 24 July confirmed that 'the hundred and fifty-odd male and female children found at the Jen-Tsze-Tang orphanage all state that they were sent by their parents to the establishment in question to be brought up, and nothing in the shape of being kidnapped has taken place'.[48]

The entire episode bore all the hallmarks of another *Arrow* incident, and British chargé d'affaires Thomas Wade was appointed to discuss the penalties to be exacted. As a man widely regarded as 'crafty and obstinate' by the Chinese and 'temperamental and extremely face saving'[49] by the French, in all likelihood these could be severe. In the event, they proved to be somewhat lenient considering the loss of life involved. Zeng Guofan agreed to send Chongho to France to apologise personally for his role in the affair and pay 400,000 taels of silver as compensation for the death and destruction inflicted. The prefect, magistrate, and twenty-five ringleaders were also banished, and a further twenty were sentenced to death. Despite these demeaning concessions, there was little sign of any real contrition among rank-and-file Chinese. As the condemned men were marched to their execution, some in the crowd were heard calling them 'brave boys',[50] and for some time afterwards specially produced fans showing the killing of the consul were brandished openly in the street.

Although the violence in Tianjin served as a graphic reminder of the loathing still felt towards foreigners, there were many other, more subtle ways in which officialdom sought to stymie the ambitions of the interlopers. Undertakings to allow Europeans to go about their business freely in the interior were constantly impeded by red tape and petty bureaucracy and, as before, the officials treated them with contempt. The rebellions had disrupted tax collection, causing local governors to try and make up the shortfall by imposing additional and often arbitrary charges on merchants exporting their wares. Any effort to raise these matters to higher authorities was frustrated because although ambassadors were permitted in the capital, they were unable to gain audiences either with the emperor or his representatives. Furthermore, contact through the usual diplomatic channels was hampered by the failure of the Chinese to open their own embassies in London and elsewhere. After years of hitting brick walls, the solution appeared to be simply to circumvent Beijing altogether, both politically and physically.

One option was for the British to travel eastwards from India to the interior rather than westwards from the coast, and several preliminary probes were mounted to check the feasibility of such an approach. Finally, a route via Bhamo in northern Burma on the Irrawaddy River through the Chinese Province of Yunnan to the north was decided upon. This could also open the door to markets further afield, but more detailed survey work was necessary before it could become a practical proposition. Despite the disconnect between Beijing and the outside world, and as a diplomatic courtesy, it was felt that Beijing should be consulted about the plan, and in May 1873 the Viceroy of India Lord Northbrook contacted Thomas Wade to sound him out. Wade was now Plenipotentiary Extraordinary and Chief Superintendent of British Trade, but when asked what the chances were of Beijing 'being induced' to open trade via this route he responded frankly, 'None [because] there is at this moment in many provinces as great [a] difficulty as ever in securing observance of [existing] treaty stipulations.'[51] So no further approaches were made to the government in Beijing, and that year Colonel Horace Browne was despatched with a force of Sikh and Burmese troops to undertake the necessary survey work.

The party found itself trekking through treacherous, unhealthy terrain, consisting of thick jungle, high mountain ranges and deep valleys, all intersected by swift river currents. These conditions alone rendered the passage of the expedition extremely slow and arduous, but it was also highly dangerous. The hostile environment concealed all manner of belligerent and suspicious Chinese traders and marauding bandits, both competing with Moslem anti-Qing rebels, and in these febrile conditions it was inevitable that by accident or design some sort of confrontation would occur. When one did, it resulted in the mysterious death of consular official Augustus Margary, who in February 1875 had been sent to act as liaison and ease the passage of the mission through to China. Due to the remoteness of the murder scene, and the reluctance of the local authorities to act upon or even inform them of the incident, it took six weeks for the news to reach the British. It was not until March 1876 that Legation Secretary Thomas Grosvenor arrived at Bhamo to try and find out what had happened.

Faced with a local governor bent on concealing the evidence and placing the blame on the Burmese, and with no real evidence forthcoming, the true culprits could not be properly identified. What was obvious, however, was that the Chinese had again failed in their obligations to protect British passport holders when travelling in the interior. Margary's death and the lacklustre response smacked of yet another snub, a further calculated insult to the British in general and of their treaty rights in particular. Fortunately for Beijing, this affair, like the massacre of its subjects in Tianjin a few years previously, was not one over which the British government was prepared to go to war. Instead, it was decided that the incident presented an opportunity to apply yet more diplomatic pressure and resolve a few more outstanding issues.

Thomas Wade again came into his own, given the job of extracting the required concessions. Under the shadow of threats of something worse, on 21 August 1876 Beijing agreed to the Chefoo, or Yantai Convention. A forty-nine-strong diplomatic mission was to travel to London bearing an apology for the Margary episode, and remain to establish a fully accredited embassy. In an endeavour to remove the constant problems of etiquette experienced by Westerners when dealing with their Chinese counterparts, they also agreed a code, whereby foreign officials in China 'may be treated with the same regard as is shown them when serving abroad in other countries, and as would be shown to Chinese agents so serving abroad'.[52] Viceroys and Governors-General were also formally obliged to afford all the protection to which they were entitled to foreigners bearing valid passports, and ambassadors in Beijing were to be granted proper access to the emperor and his representatives without the usual delays. The principle of extraterritoriality was also to be reinforced by the creation of a British Supreme Court and a Chinese Mixed Court in Shanghai. More ports were to be opened, greater access given for trade on the Yangtze River, and the border between Yunnan and Burma opened for commerce. The ongoing dispute regarding internal tariffs and dues, and particularly one known as the *Likin*, was also addressed, and imports from the treaty ports would be exempted from the tax. Hopefully, with these issues resolved the British would be placated for a while longer – but to the north the Russians were again on the prowl.

Beijing had been faced with troubling revolts among the predominantly Uyghur population of East Turkestan throughout the 1860s and 1870s, a situation Russia claimed challenged its strategic interests. Beijing was therefore pressured into admitting Czarist forces into the Ili Valley, St Petersburg promising to remove them once Beijing could furnish 'guarantees of an enduring re-establishment of its authority there'.[53] But when the Chinese re-occupied and pacified the territory in 1878, the Russians claimed that certain 'collateral questions'[54] remained unresolved. Commissioner Chonghou was sent to discuss these, but in the process managed to concede the one-sided Treaty of Livadia. This not only left the Russians with two-thirds of the valley, it granted them the right to establish seven more consulates in the territory. Chonghu had even agreed to Russian demands for an indemnity of 5,000,000 roubles to cover the cost of the occupation. When he returned to Beijing and the government was informed of the concessions he had made, it flew into a rage and ordered the governor of North-western China to mobilise his forces ready to re-occupy the area. The Russians, upon hearing that Beijing was planning to renege on the agreement, responded by stationing warships off the coast. As the weeks and months went by, the standoff risked escalating into a shooting war.

Fortunately, wiser heads prevailed, more plenipotentiaries were despatched to Russia, and after some tough negotiation the Treaty of St Petersburg was agreed in 1881. In exchange for another 4,000,000 roubles and the right to navigate some Manchurian rivers, Russia would return most of the valley and reduce its consulates to two. Although for once Chinese honour had been satisfied, this narrow escape reminded Beijing just how tenuous its hold on the territory had become. The decision was therefore taken in 1884 to solidify its presence by instituting a mass colonisation programme and renaming it the province of Xinjiang. At the conclusion of the exercise it was hoped that a permanent Han majority would be created and further Russian encroachments deterred. Although Beijing had now narrowly avoided war with both Britain and Russia, it was not out of the woods yet. To the south there were the French to contend with.

Interest in the southern tributary of Vietnam in South East Asia had been piqued in 1787, when King Nguyen Anh sought French assistance against rebels who had usurped his throne. This was agreed on condition that he grant them rights to the Bay of Tourane and possession of the Island of Poulo Condore close to the mouth of the Saigon River. Agreement reached, Louis XIV duly despatched a force from his Indian enclave of Pondicherry and restored Nguyen Anh to his throne. Then the French Revolution intervened, and plans for colonisation had to be shelved, but neither Louis nor his successors forgot about the particular 'interests and rights'[55] in Vietnam they had acquired as a result of the compact. However, due in part to domestic distractions and wars in Africa, it would be another seventy years before an opportunity arose for them to be reprised. Napoleon III exploited the growing tensions with Britain to impose French influence on the region, and in August 1858, with negotiations over a trade agreement at an impasse, Admiral Rigault de Genouilly used the murder of two missionaries as a pretext to force the Vietnamese to come to terms.

De Genouilly attacked and occupied Da Nang, but his understrength forces were then trapped there during a siege which lasted eighteen months. He also captured Saigon in 1859, but ended up evacuating both cities as he had insufficient forces to hold them both. Determined not to be humiliated, Napoleon reinforced de Genouilly and after he resumed the offensive the Vietnamese were finally crushed. In 1862 its king was forced to cede three of his provinces to the French, which were formed into the protectorate of Cochinchina and more territory was then extorted which doubled its size. In 1864 it was declared a colony. In 1874 the two countries then signed a treaty by which French protection was accepted in exchange for assistance against the numerous pirates who plagued the kingdom. A series of further commercial conventions were also agreed over succeeding years that offered greater commercial opportunities to French merchants.

China, still the de jure paramount power in the region, watched these developments with growing alarm. Although annual tribute continued to be sent to Beijing throughout the 1870s and into the early 1880s, Vietnam was clearly in the process of being drawn deeper into the French orbit. But as tensions increased between France and the Vietnamese, they called upon China for assistance, and troops were sent south to the border. When in late 1883 French forces penetrated up the Red River Valley hoping to add Tonkin to their growing empire, they encountered Qing forces advancing southwards from Yunnan. A series of inconclusive engagements led to negotiations, and the Tientsin Accord of 11 May 1884 was signed. An apparently conciliatory France agreed to 'respect and, in the case of need, to protect the southern frontier of China which separates the country from Tonkin', whilst for its part China undertook 'to withdraw within the Chinese frontier the Chinese troops garrisoned in Tonkin, respect the present and future treaties concluded or to be concluded between France and the Court of Annam [and] admit along the whole extent of her frontier bordering on Tonkin the liberty of commercial exchanges between Annam and France on the one hand, and China on the other'.[56]

The French underwrote this agreement with a separate Treaty of Hue signed with the Vietnamese, in which the latter formally renounced their tributary status to China. They then proceeded to pour troops into the country and began establishing themselves in the territory whilst they waited for Beijing to commence the process of withdrawal. However, no firm dates by which Chinese troops were to leave had been included in the Treaty of Tientsin, and even after some months they showed no sign of pulling out. Instead, when French forces advanced to take up position in Tonkin they encountered Chinese forces who fired on them. When news of this apparent perfidy reached the French authorities they insisted that Beijing not only implement the treaty provisions at once, but apologise for their actions and pay an indemnity. When none of these demands were met, a fleet was sent to Fuchou, where on 23 August 1884 the Qing navy was destroyed in a brief fifteen-minute engagement. Smelling blood, they sent another force to Keelung in Formosa with instructions to destroy its naval installations and occupy the town until the Chinese backed down. On arrival, the commander of the flotilla formally demanded the surrender of Keelung and the evacuation of the fort, and the Chinese commander just as formally declined to comply. Resident Scottish tea merchant John Dodd was living in the town at the time, and recorded what followed:

> The three men-of-war commenced operations precisely at 8.00 a.m. A deafening cannonade took place and ... the French gunners fired with excellent precision [and] silenced the large fort ... in a very short time it was a mass of ruins.[57]

The subsequent landing on 5 August met with less success. There was stiff resistance, and having been repulsed the French re-embarked the following day. A second attempt on 1 October proved more productive, and once Keelung was pacified the intention was to use it as a staging post from which to invest the rest of the island. Although numerous Chinese counterattacks were thrown back, the invaders were too few in number to press their advantage, and their position became more perilous when the Chinese reinforced their army from the Pescadores. So the French navy intercepted their troopships, instituted a blockade and landed more troops at Keelung. By 25 January 1885, they were ready to resume the offensive, but heavy rain brought fighting to a standstill until 4 March, after which they succeeded in pushing the Chinese back. With potential threats developing on their flanks from Japan and Russia, both of whom sensed an opportunity to exploit their plight, Beijing had to agree to terms.

By the protocol of 4 April 1885 it undertook to honour the previous accord, evacuate Tonkin and recognise the legitimacy of France's treaties with Vietnam. In 1887, Cochinchina, Annam and Tonkin, along with Cambodia would become French Indochina, joined a few years later by Laos, which had been acquired from neighbouring Thailand. They would also claim jurisdiction over the nearby Paracel and Spratly Islands, insisting that they fell within the territorial limits of Vietnam, something China strongly objected to. The French did return Formosa and the Pescadores however, and agreed not to pursue an indemnity, but all in all, China was left with little to show for another bruising encounter with the West.

Whilst the French had been slicing off more of its empire in the southeast, another dispute had been brewing in the northwest with Britain over Sikkim and neighbouring Tibet. In 1861, the British established a protectorate over Sikkim as part of a strategy to secure the northern border of British India. Both Lhasa and Beijing suspected it of being part of a larger plan to encroach deeper into the region, as in 1816 the EIC and the rulers of neighbouring Nepal had signed a treaty giving the British considerable rights there. These fears led to years of tension, which came to a head in 1886 when the Chinese began constructing physical barriers between the two states. The Indian authorities repeatedly insisted that these works were encroaching on its territory, but despite their protests the Chinese showed no sign of dismantling them. In 1888, having considered that they had exhausted all diplomatic avenues, the British mounted a military expedition, forcing Beijing to agree to the 1890 Convention of Calcutta. This recognised that Sikkim was an exclusively British sphere, and that the version of the border they insisted upon was correct. Nonetheless the outcome was thrown into doubt by the Tibetan government, which insisted that as the treaty had been signed over its head and without its approval, it bore no legitimacy. Although war was avoided in the end, this frustrating impasse would lead to endless litigation and leave the door open for more confrontations further down the line.

As if to add insult to injury, the British had also been annexing two other, albeit tenuously Chinese tributaries, Burma and Malaya. The former had begun to be absorbed into the Indian Empire in the 1820s, but by the 1880s had been annexed in its entirety. Similarly, the establishment of a presence in the Malayan Peninsula which had started in the 1820s, took on a greater momentum from 1874 onwards until it, too, was now firmly under the British flag.

This relentless cycle of foreign encroachment, confrontation and climbdown appeared to vindicate the prevailing view that the empire was in terminal decline. As Imperial diplomat Guo Songtao conceded, 'we goad them into acting with outrageous violence, then, once warfare has been resorted to, the military expense they incur will eventually be sought from us in an indemnity'.[58] This policy had seen Beijing surrender its sovereignty, its territory and even its tributaries, all compounded by an exponentially growing overseas debt. Yet despite the perception that the country was being salami sliced into oblivion, some remained firmly of the opinion that there was still time to stop the rot. But, they added, this could only be achieved if far-ranging reforms were implemented to turn the fortunes of the Empire around; the question was, did the will and the wherewithal remain to embrace such a challenge? The optics were not good.

4

Freedom of Trade for All the World Alike

By the 1880s, the aptly named 'Self-Strengthening Movement' had been ongoing in various guises for around twenty-five years. Its lodestar was the principle that the same competencies used by the West to crush China should be employed against them to defend it. This had long been the mantra of such luminaries as Zeng Guofan, Li Hongzhang, Zuo Zongtang and statesman Prince Gong. They had urged since at least the 1860s that unless China adapted to the new realities of the world, the country faced complete disintegration. Its sponsors nonetheless fully acknowledged that they were entering uncharted territory, one in which a great many obstacles lay in their path.

One of the government's most serious shortcomings was clearly in the diplomatic field, vividly demonstrated by Beijing's being outwitted for years by devious and wily European emissaries backed up by gunboat diplomacy. To address this deficit, in March 1861 Prince Gong set about root and branch reform of the foreign service by creating the Zongli Yamen, or Office of General Management. He then began implementing a programme of re-education in which the tactics and strategies usefully employed by the West would be learned and replicated. From 1862, interpreter colleges were founded in Beijing, Shanghai, Guangzhou, and Fuzhou, and students recruited to absorb Western practice in the field. Li Hongzhang urged a similar treatment for the civil service. Born in Anhui Province in 1823, he was a highly respected public servant and administrator who had been credited with suppressing the Taiping Rebellion. Although he had passed the civil service examination at the very young age of twenty-four, he nonetheless counselled that by adhering to the old Confucian principles, 'we are limited to the narrow compass of those qualified by passing the examinations [and] must introduce another system for their admission into the public service'.[1] To achieve this it was essential that the study of Western mathematics, engineering and science, disciplines essential to a modern state, should be included.

The empire's lamentable military performance was another crucial factor in its continued decline. Zeng Guofan explained in January 1861 that 'if China desires to make herself strong, there is nothing better than to learn about and use the superior weapons of foreign countries ... look for the machines with which to make the machines ... we must take warning from what has happened to prevent what has not yet happened'. His prescience was echoed in June 1863 by Li Hongzhang who, in the wake of the Second Opium War and in the midst of the Taiping Rebellion noted that 'all the foreign countries are willing to sell us foreign guns and cannon ... and also willing to send people to teach us the manufacture of all sorts of arms ... we should seize the opportunity to make a substantial study of all kinds of foreign machines and weapons in order to learn their secrets completely'.[3] This would require a total overhaul of both the archaic navy and anachronistic army, but would also prove much easier to advocate than to achieve.

In 1862, Prince Gong commissioned the British Inspector General of Customs, Horatio Nelson Lay, to travel to Britain and purchase seven steam cruisers and a supply ship to form the nucleus of a modern, state-of-the-art navy. Lay made his way back in February 1863 accompanied by a Captain Sherard Osborne RN, who had been appointed commander of the armada. They arrived to some fanfare in November, but then Lay insisted he should command the fleet and be answerable only to the emperor, whilst Captain Osborne claimed that he had been promised operational command. Beijing's mandarins not surprisingly balked at such unseemly demands and pointed out it was a Chinese fleet and would be under complete Chinese control. An almighty row ensued as the parties argued their cases, as a result of which Sherard left under a cloud and the obstinate Lay was sacked. Then, in what would prove to be a misguided fit of nationalist fervour, the ships were tetchily returned to Britain and the decision taken to build the new navy in China instead.

The project began promisingly enough and Chinese students were sent overseas to study shipbuilding at first-hand, whilst a shipyard was built in Fuzhou. Construction began in 1866 using French technicians, engineers and mechanics, whilst another yard and an arsenal was opened at Jiangnan. Naval bases were also begun at Port Arthur (Lushun) at the southern tip of the Liaodong Peninsula and at Weihaiwei (Weihai) on the northern end of the Shandong Peninsula in preparation for the spanking new navy. Work began in 1868, and by 1875 sixteen vessels were completed along with ten transports. However, on closer inspection the authorities were dissatisfied with the results. Many were of wooden design and had engines considered inferior to their French counterparts, leading to suspicions that they had deliberately been provided with old blueprints and obsolete equipment. Moreover, because the income from maritime customs revenues was insufficient both to pay indemnities and cover the yards' operating costs, the scheme was running low on capital. The whole enterprise was further dogged by the perennial problems of corruption, nepotism, and political infighting.

Nonetheless, when the Beiyang or Northern Fleet was created as one of four proposed regional navies, it appeared that the reformers had been vindicated. At its peak it contained seventy-eight men-of-war, eight armoured cruisers and numbers of smaller torpedo boats, but its shortcomings had been painfully highlighted by its battering at the hands of the French on the Fuzhou River in 1884. Then it began to suffer as the financial situation worsened. In 1888, resources were diverted to other projects or lost to corruption, and eventually the program hit the buffers. Underfunded, poorly maintained, equipped and crewed, the run-down fleet was soon overtaken by navies such as Japan's. It eventually became something of a white elephant, and when the French engineers and technicians left towards the end of the 1890s, their poorly trained Chinese counterparts proved inadequate. So the once-prized navy was left to languish, whilst the country faced the equally formidable challenge of bringing the army up to scratch.

As early as 1852, Zeng Guofan set about creating an entirely new Xiang Army in Hunan Province by recruiting 130,000 mercenaries and Chinese volunteers. His fresh approach to their training produced a more cohesive and coordinated force than either the Banner or Green Standard armies, and it soon became the template for similar forces, known collectively as the Yongying or 'Brave Battalions'. However, because they were created under the patronage of governors and viceroys, their officers and men would be bound to them rather than the emperor. Consequently, semi-autonomous armies with no accountability to the government were emerging, and although a cash-strapped Beijing had little choice but to sanction these new forces, they were to become the forerunners of the divisive warlord armies to follow. Moreover, the Banner and Green Standard armies would also remain, funded by the Imperial Government and leaving the empire with three distinct formations, none of which coordinated with the others. Moreover, in some units infantrymen were still practising with bows and arrows and ancient muzzle-loading muskets. There was also a dizzying array of modern weapons being used, ranging from Martini-Henrys, Winchesters and Schneiders. Likewise, the guns protecting key locations were often still old muzzle-loaders, completely useless against modern firepower, and the war in 1860 demonstrated the consequences of this dire situation.

Logistics and supply was therefore another issue the reformers sought to address, and by the 1870s the arsenal at Jiangnan could boast an impressive output of breech-loading cannons of British design. In the 1880s these replaced many of the muzzle-loaders but then Li Hongzhang complicated matters when he decided that he preferred German Krupp models for the larger field guns and cannons, and switched from the British ones. The production of small arms also proved problematic as these were found to be inferior to, and more expensive than, imported models. Moreover, the supply chain was compromised because throughout the entire empire there were still only seven arsenals and the one dockyard at Fuzhou. Whatever was achieved in the area of logistics and supply, it would prove of little avail if the armies continued to be poorly led.

This, British visitor Lord Beresford noted in the 1890s, was the root cause of their shortcomings. He was confident that the rank and file 'would make splendid soldiers if properly trained [being] sober, obedient, easily managed and very quick at learning', but when they were well-armed, they were badly led, and when well-led they were badly armed.[4] His conclusions were echoed by writer E. H. Parker: 'They have never yet had a fair chance in war… officers being almost invariably ignorant men – mere vulgar rankers masquerading as officers and gentlemen.'[5] Because the recruitment examination remained as outmoded as that for civil servants, relying upon physical prowess rather than mental acuity, when modern weapons did become available there were too few officers with the wherewithal to deploy them effectively. Consequently, two new military academies were established, one in Tianjin in 1885 and a second in Guangzhou in 1887, staffed by experienced German instructors. But starting from such a low base they faced an uphill struggle, and their students had a lot of catching up to do.

Despite the longevity of the Self Strengthening Movement, it met few of the metrics of success that its progenitors had set for it. It faced numerous obstacles, not only in terms of competence but also of apathy, indecision, and endemic shoulder-shrugging by mandarins absorbed by the teachings of Confucius. In such an environment, innovations like the Zongli Yamen were rendered largely ineffective, and any initiatives which threatened the status quo were left to wither on the vine. It explained why the overhaul of the traditional civil service examination never materialised, and meaningful progress in the army and navy stumbled at every turn. Li Hongzhang experienced this himself in 1877 when he visited Beijing hoping to get some railway projects underway. He was told by a mandarin that nothing would happen simply because no one would take responsibility for fear of failure and losing face. As E. H. Parker noted, 'the weak part of Chinese reforms is and always has been, the absence of continuity and sustained effort'.[6] Robert Hart, Inspector General of Imperial Maritime Customs concluded that 'the policy of the central government in China is not to guide, but to follow events … and strangle whatever comes before it in embryo'.[7] Whilst inertia continued to frustrate the efforts of the reformers, there were further threats looming, and they were much closer to home than Europe, they came from across the Yellow Sea.

Since around 400 BCE Japan had been a willing protege of its larger neighbour, absorbing innovations such as writing, pottery, bronze and ironworking. Contacts were at their height during the Tang dynasty when between 618-906 CE hundreds of Japanese scholars studied Buddhism, political science and architecture. Buddhist temples, Shinto shrines and the Royal Palaces copied Chinese styles, and roads were constructed along Chinese lines. Commerce boomed as Japan imported medicines, perfumes, silks, ceramics, spices, books, weapons, and armour. Thousands of Koreans, Chinese and Manchurians settled in Japan, many skilled in metallurgy, agriculture, and sericulture. By the middle of the sixth century CE there were as many as 100,000 living there, and within two centuries they would constitute a third of all noble families. Such was Japan's apparent dependence on them that they began referring to their acolytes as mere 'dwarfs',[8] subservient vassals on a small, insignificant chain of islands. However, as the centuries passed the two became increasingly estranged, especially so as their respective attitudes to foreigners diverged. Japan had become far more accommodating of the very modernising ideas the Self Strengthening Movement wanted to adopt but traditionalists opposed.

When the Meijis were restored to the throne in 1868, everything from European and American fashion to architecture, science and technology was copied. The first railway appeared in 1872, and major cities began to be connected by telegraph. Compulsory education was introduced, with ambitious plans for 50,000 schools, one for every 600 of the population. Taxation, coinage, the banking system, printing, newspapers and even cigars and cigarettes were adopted. Looking further ahead, whilst the Self Strengthening Movement continued to flounder, feudalism faced abolition, a representative assembly, cabinet government and a written constitution were being prepared and new criminal and civil codes drafted. A nascent middle class enjoyed the fruits of modernisation in an economy growing exponentially year on year. Between 1868 and 1897, imports of raw materials for its expanding industries would multiply by a factor of five, and exports of produce from those same factories by twenty. Instrumental in this revolution were men such as Sir Harry Parkes, now Britain's man in Tokyo, who had encouraged his compatriots to advise the navy and consult on infrastructure projects. Progress came at a price nonetheless, and the same system of treaty ports and extraterritoriality was imposed on the country as had been forced on China.

Freedom of Trade for All the World Alike

It was nevertheless inevitable that in the course of this transformation individuals began, as those in the West had done, to search for sources of raw materials and outlets for the country's products. Eyes again turned westwards, spurring attempts to establish closer ties with China. A start was made in September 1871 when the Sino-Japanese Friendship and Trade Treaty was signed, intended to 'restore that old friendship and forge closer diplomatic relations ... in order to obtain permanent security [and] treat each other's territory with due respect'.[9] To that end both parties undertook 'to aid and support the other in case of an attack by a foreign power', and to exchange ministers and appoint consuls in each other's ports.[10] In reality this was to prove little more than window dressing. Behind these fine words lay more sinister motives, a desire to emulate the European Powers' encroachment into their vast neighbour. Indeed, in April 1868 the Meiji Emperor himself pronounced that his empire's policy was to be expansion 'across the great waves ... proclaiming the national prestige everywhere'.[11]

One stepping stone towards realising this ambition was the Ryukyus, a chain of islands which stretched south from Japan to Formosa. Nominally independent, the islands' rulers nonetheless hedged their bets by paying tribute to both China and Japan. Since the 1850s, other powers had been showing an interest in the islands too, something the Japanese were determined to scotch, so they began flexing their muscles. When in 1871 fifty-four shipwrecked Ryukyuan crewmen were beheaded on neighbouring Formosa by hostile Paiwan tribesmen, Tokyo saw an opportunity. An emissary was sent to Beijing to insist that action be taken against the culprits, only to be told that the site where the incident took place was a grey area, outside direct Qing jurisdiction. So while the Chinese demurred, Tokyo made plans of its own, and on 2 May 1874 3,600 troops were landed on the island with orders to root out the perpetrators. However, in the course of the campaign Chinese-administered territory was also impinged, and it took until 11 May for Beijing to react. Even then it issued only the mildest of objections, claiming that Tokyo's actions were a breach of the treaty they had signed only three years previously. Preoccupied elsewhere, this was the strongest action Beijing felt able to take, but Harry Parkes was appalled. He insisted that if they 'had an atom of pluck they would demand the evacuation of Formosa very peremptorily',[12] but instead, the Japanese government made the running.

Not only did they want 500,000 taels of silver as compensation for the families of the murdered sailors, but also to cover the costs of pacifying the natives, to both of which proposals Beijing meekly assented. Parkes could not believe his ears. He thought that at the very least 'they might in the end agree to cry quits on condition that the Japanese retired from Formosa, but I certainly did not expect to find China willing to pay for being invaded'.[13] That was not the end of the matter, Beijing also had to undertake to protect marooned sailors from being attacked in future, and to construct a lighthouse to try and prevent more shipwrecks. This feeble response naturally encouraged Tokyo to go further. If they were so pusillanimous on the matter of an island as big as Formosa, they could hardly be expected to assert themselves over the Ryukyus. The Japanese proceeded to absorbed them even deeper into their orbit, forbidding the king to send any further tribute to Beijing, and in 1879 annexing his kingdom outright. Again, Beijing could only protest, Li Hongzhang insisting meekly that the action 'violated international law'.[14] Nonetheless, it did serve as another salutary lesson. As with Russian encroachment in Xinjiang, the Formosa incident and loss of the Ryukyus prompted a serious rethink of priorities. Having previously neglected Formosa as a backwater of little significance, it was now to be developed, properly protected and colonised by Han settlers.

Tokyo was not ready to make a move on the island yet, not when there was a much bigger prize nearby, Korea. Rich in the coal, iron ore, tungsten, lead and zinc Japan lacked, it had the potential to be, as diplomat Sada Hakubo described it, 'a gold mine'.[15] Although as long ago as the fifteenth century the Koreans allowed Japanese settlement in Busan on the southern tip of Korea, this toehold was lost when in 1592 Japan launched the first of many abortive invasions. Having captured Seoul and Pyongyang, they provoked Chinese forces into retaliating, who swiftly crossed the Yalu and drove them back to their starting point. Further failed incursions followed, although during a period of friendlier relations a port was opened to merchants on the island of Tsushima. Busan was also reopened in 1607, but the full potential of the peninsula could only be exploited properly by usurping its current overlords. Indeed, an uncharitable Lord Nathanial Curzon called its people 'supine and spiritless',[16] and not worth fighting over. Yet as a tributary, it still sent annually to Beijing the 100 oz of gold, 1000 oz of silver, 10,000 bags of rice, 2,000 pieces of silk, 300 pieces of flax cloth, 10,000 pieces of common cloth, 2,000 knives, 1,000 buffalo horns, 100 deerskins and 400 beaver skins, required of a vassal.[17]

Moderate Japanese politicians such as Chancellor Sanjo Sanetomi remained guarded, however. He weighed up the pros and cons of whether Japan should aim at restoring 'traditional friendship and improving neighbourly relations [or] make it ultimately into a dependent country'.[18] It was the latter policy that inspired the adherents of *seik-en-ron*, or 'subduing Korea',[19] and by the 1870s these hawks felt that there was no better time to act, encouraged by Chinese weakness over their actions in Formosa and the Ryukyus.

Domestic Korean politics was itself highly polarised, with one faction favouring liberalisation and reform and the other wanting to keep the country closed to foreigners entirely. The former school of thought was held by young King Gojon, but because he was only twelve years old when he ascended to the throne in 1864, his father Yi Ha-eung, or Prince Gung, had served as Regent. He was avowedly anti-foreign and used his powerful position to frustrate and thwart any reforms. In 1866 he exploited a diplomatic spat with France to orchestrate the persecution and expulsion of their missionaries, and he scotched an attempt in 1869 to establish closer relations with Japan. But when King Gojong achieved his majority in 1873, he and his wife Queen Min, backed by her powerful and influential clan, rowed back on Prince Gung's policies. When Japan despatched another envoy in 1875, proposing the establishment of formal diplomatic relations, clarification of Korea's constitutional position vis a vis Beijing and discussions for a formal trade agreement, he was more warmly received. Nonetheless, like Banquo's ghost the Chinese remained the conscience of the Seoul government, and in true Confucian style ensured that negotiations dragged on fruitlessly. In frustration, Tokyo recalled its envoy for further consultations, when by accident or design an incident took place which served as a timely opportunity to force Beijing's hand.

On 20 September 1875 a Japanese warship was undertaking survey work off the western coast of Korea when its captain decided to land a shore party on Ganghwa Island near Incheon. They were there ostensibly to ask the Korean garrison for water and supplies, but instead the shore batteries opened up, in response to which fire was returned, resulting in casualties on both sides. When reports of the skirmish reached Tokyo the government ordered the dispatch of more warships to Busan, claiming that they were needed to protect Japanese nationals. A blockade was also imposed as a show of strength, followed by demands for an apology from the Korean Government. The threat of force concentrated both Korean and Chinese minds and persuaded China to sanction renewed negotiations, the outcome of which was the Treaty of Ganghwa. Signed on 26 February 1876, it apparently acceded to all of Tokyo's demands. It defined Korea as an independent state, depending upon one's interpretation of its wording and increased diplomatic representation in both countries. It also opened more ports to Japanese ships, and the new arrangements soon began to bear fruit. Trade increased considerably and Busan developed as a key entry point to the Korean market. A regular mail service and commercial shipping vied between it, Shimonoseki and other Japanese ports, and by 1884 an undersea cable would be laid between the two countries. The effect of this would be to draw the peninsula closer to Tokyo and potentially further away from Beijing.

This possibility, and the fact that China had come so close to war therefore served as a stark warning, and prompted many in Beijing to toy with the idea of a preventive war before Japan became unassailable. Li Hongzhang shared these anxieties but with the Self-Strengthening reforms barely scratching the surface of its military shortcomings, this was not a feasible option. Furthermore, he was fearful of the wider implications of such a move: 'There is a probability that in the case of a conflict between China and Japan, foreign powers might side with Japan against us.'[20] He wanted to give the reforms more time, confident that 'if we only organise our resources and develop our army and navy ... Japan will not venture to carry out any hostile designs against us'.[21] In the meantime, diplomacy might buy them time, preserving Korea's integrity and protecting China's interests. Li believed that the answer lay in throwing the peninsula open to all foreign commerce, so that each of the Powers had an equal stake in ensuring it was not dominated by the Japanese. He commenced discussions first with the United States, and they signed the Korean-American Treaty of Amity and Commerce at Incheon in May 1882. Its fourteen clauses included mutual assistance in the event either party was attacked, extraterritorial rights for US citizens, most favoured nation status, the reciprocal payment of duties, the prohibition of opium, regulations regarding the importation of arms and ammunition, and labour rights. The following year, diplomatic relations were established and an American legation was opened in Seoul in May 1883. Similar agreements were swiftly made with Great Britain and Germany in 1883, Italy and Russia in 1884 and France in 1886.

Meanwhile, the Gujong-Gung factions were still at daggers drawn, with the king becoming increasingly unpopular. He faced accusations of nepotism and favouritism from his officers in the Joseon army, and charges of neglect from among an increasingly angry peasantry. In particular, his officers resented the appointment of a Japanese military attaché to form a new unit called the *Pyolgigun*, or Special Skills Force, which rivalled the existing army. The aim was to form the nucleus of an entirely new force equipped with modern arms and equipment, but at the same time the Joseon army was being neglected and its men paid in adulterated rice. The peasantry was angry, burdened by taxation to meet a growing balance of payments deficit and at the same time being priced out of the market by cheap imports. Facing ruin, many were being driven deeper into debt by loan sharks who charged extortionate rates of interest.

Tensions reached boiling point on 23 July 1882 in what would become known as the 'Soldier's Riot' (Imo Kullan), when disaffected troops stormed the warehouses and attacked those responsible for the bad rice. Then they were joined by civilians and together they ran amok, killing government officials, politicians and any Japanese they chanced upon. Their legation was also besieged by a baying mob and its staff barely escaped with their lives after fighting their way the seventeen miles to Incheon. From here they fled aboard the appropriately named British gunboat, *Flying Bat*. Prince Gung saw his chance to depose Gujong and reinstall himself in power, seizing the palace and holding the king and Queen Min under house arrest. But the Queen managed to escape, making her way to the protection of Chinese Imperial Resident Yuan Shikai. As soon as Li Hongzhang learned of the disorder he sent troops to suppress the mutiny and arrest Prince Gung, and once Tokyo was made aware, it, too, sent a force to protect its nationals. The rebellion was over by the time they arrived, although the short-lived but alarming implications of the attempted coup were not lost on Beijing.

Having arrested and executed anyone suspected of complicity in the rebellion, an Imperial Decree reclaimed Korea as 'a dependency of China [because] its Princes have for generations, been our feudatories and have ever been known to be reverent and respectful'.[22] Henceforth, Gujong had to allow Chinese advisers into his government and seek Beijing's approval before making any diplomatic appointments. Furthermore, a German was to head the country's Maritime Customs Service and Chinese merchants were granted extraterritorial rights and unobstructed access to Korean markets. To guarantee compliance, a 3,000-strong garrison would remain in the country and take over responsibility for training the army. In part to placate Tokyo, an indemnity of $500,000 was paid to cover the cost of its own expedition and as compensation for the deaths of its nationals. It also received a formal apology and was granted the right to station soldiers within its legation.

Nonetheless, the hawks surrounding the Meiji Emperor were far from satisfied, and felt that an opportunity to exploit the mutiny had slipped through their fingers, and their intrigues resulted in a suspected Japanese-backed coup in December 1884, when Conservatives tried to overthrow the government. The Royal Palace was attacked and members of the pro-Chinese faction killed, but again the Chinese garrison intervened, crushed the rebellion and drove the pro-Japanese faction into exile. Strongman Yuan Shikai was then appointed Resident-General and he provided an unmistakeably physical reminder that Beijing was firmly in charge.

In the meantime, Tokyo needed to be kept at bay, so on 18 April 1885 Li and the Japanese ambassador Marquis Ito signed the Li-Ito Convention in Tianjin. This document recognised that both powers should enjoy equal rights in the peninsula, but in the interests of peace withdraw their troops and military advisers. Korea would instead continue with its own army reforms in the hope that 'she may assure her public security',[23] without foreign involvement. If nonetheless either power deemed it necessary to send troops to protect their interests, they would first give advance warning and 'return after the matter is settled'.[24] With this arrangement in place, the two nations awaited developments.

Yet the peninsula continued to be unsettled by the desperate plight of the peasantry, increasing numbers of whom were turning to a Catholic-based movement called *Tonghak* or 'Eastern Learning'. Founded in 1860 partly in response to events in China, its teachings offered an alternative future of equality, freedom and democracy, but most worrying to the Japanese, it was vehemently opposed to foreign influence and modernisation. By 1894, the movement had spread across the country, and despite being met with increasing repression showed no sign of abating. In June, the government mobilised its army with orders to crush them once and for all, but when it encountered the rebels, its forces were humiliated. The king was then forced to appeal to Beijing for help in putting the rebellion down and 3,500 troops were despatched. Crucially, the Chinese had omitted to warn Tokyo in advance, a breach of the treaty which gave Japan the pretext it had been waiting for. Tokyo sent its own expedition, which landed on 9 June and marched on Seoul, although by the time they were ready to deploy the rebellion had petered out. Then, despite the crisis technically being over the Chinese refused to recall their own troops, so Tokyo would not withdraw theirs. Instead, they occupied King Gojong's palace and held him prisoner whilst a pro-Japanese government was installed. This regime then invited Tokyo to send more reinforcements to eject the Chinese.

On 25 July Japanese warships attacked Chinese troopships and accompanying naval vessels in Asan Bay, en route to reinforce their own garrison. Two were sunk and another was forced to flee, and on 28 July they launched an assault on the Asan garrison itself. The town fell quickly with the loss of 500 of the defenders, and the remainder fled to Pyongyang where the number of troops totalled around 15,000. In the meantime, the Japanese government had been preparing its casus belli, and on 1 August issued an official statement:

> Korea is an independent state... It has however, been the habit of China to regard Korea as a dependency of her own, and both

openly and secretly to interfere in her affairs... China secretly and insidiously endeavoured to circumvent and thwart Japan's purpose ... procrastinated and tried to make warlike preparations by land and sea ... opening fire on our ships in Korean waters... Such conduct on the part of China is not only a direct injury to the rights and interests of the Empire, but a menace to the permanent peace of East Asia. Under these circumstances we find it impossible to avoid a formal declaration of war.[25]

On the morning of 15 September, General Marquis Nodzu assaulted Pyongyang with 14,000 men, and it fell after only a day's fighting. Admiral Yugo Ito then sailed to the mouth of the Yalu River with ten cruisers and two gunboats, where on 17 September he attacked two battleships and eight cruisers of the Beiyang Fleet under Admiral Ting. Two ships fled immediately and two more were badly damaged, and after putting up a fight the remainder fled to Port Arthur. After the loss of Pyongyang and defeat on the Yalu River, the Chinese withdrew across the border with the Japanese in pursuit. On 24 October they broke into Manchuria, simultaneously landing troops on the Liaodong Peninsula and advancing on Port Arthur. On 21 November, after an initial naval bombardment, forces stormed ashore, the 9,000-strong garrison offering little resistance. They withdrew further up the peninsula, leaving the port to the tender mercies of vengeful invaders fired up by stories of atrocities committed against their nationals. A correspondent for the American Bible Society confirmed that the Chinese had indeed inflicted 'barbarities too revolting to mention',[26] but what followed served as a template for what was to be the experience of millions of ordinary Chinese for decades to come. American witness Trumbell White described

> ... scores of Chinese hunted out of cover, shot down, and hacked to pieces, and never a man made any attempt to fight ... many went down on their knees, supplicating with heads bent to the ground in kowtow, and in that attitude they were butchered mercilessly... Thursday, Friday, Saturday and Sunday were spent by the soldiery in murder and pillage from dawn to dark, in mutilation, in every conceivable kind of nameless atrocity, until the town became a

ghastly inferno... Women and children were hunted and shot at as they fled to the hills with their protectors. All along the street I could see bleeding storekeepers shot and sabred.[27]

The Japanese Ambassador to the UK, Takaki Koto, was unrepentant, maintaining that these claims were gross exaggerations and insisting that all the non-combatants, women and children, were removed to places of safety long before the battle began. Few were convinced by his account, particularly White who charged Japan with being 'disgraced before the world',[28] as its troops continued to sweep all before them. Massacres aside, *The Times* of London shared the incredulity of many that the war was becoming such a walkover, reporting how the 'most pessimistic prophet could hardly have predicted the utter ineptitude of the Chinese military'.[29] Much of this was evidently due to the failure of the Self-Strengthening reforms, the Japanese claiming that as few as sixty per cent of the troops that they confronted in battle had any kind of firearm at all. Faced with such a poorly equipped adversary, the drubbing of the Chinese continued, and on 4 February 1895 the Japanese cut the boom protecting Weihaiwei and their torpedo boats attacked the warships Admiral Ting had withdrawn there. Taking a relentless toll over successive days. supported by batteries of artillery set up on land, by 12 February he accepted that all was lost and ordered his men to surrender.

It was fortunate therefore, that peace negotiations were being undertaken amidst this carnage. Li Hongzhang led the Chinese delegation to Shimonoseki on the southwestern tip of the island of Honshu, and in anticipation of the inevitable outcome, on 29 March the Japanese Emperor declared an unconditional armistice. This time there was little Confucian procrastination and on 17 April the peace was signed, its terms arguably the most humiliating since 1860, and its ramifications perhaps even more so. China finally recognised 'the complete independence and autonomy of Korea'[30] and surrendered the Liaodong Peninsula, including Port Arthur, the Pescadores and Formosa. A $150,000,000 indemnity had to be paid with customs revenue and Weihaiwei pledged as security. The ports of Shashi, Chongqing, Suzhou and Hongzhou were to be 'opened to the trade, residence, industries and manufactures of Japanese subjects',[31] and be granted steam navigation on the Yangtse River between Yichang and Chongqing. Japanese subjects trading in China would also be exempt from all transit dues and taxes. A Treaty of Commerce and Navigation was to be negotiated at a later date, and this would also see the foreign treaty ports and extraterritoriality Japan had endured phased out within the next few years. Japan formally annexed the Senkaku Islands, which lay between Formosa and the southernmost island of the Ryukyus, Okinawa. Although they were uninhabited, Beijing considered them to be legally part of China and objected vehemently to the annexation.

Perhaps predictably, when news that China was so irredeemably prostrate became public, there was great rejoicing among many of its detractors. The *North China Herald* in particular could not conceal its delight over 'the soundest thrashing being administered to China that self-satisfied, ignorant, and unprincipled Empire has ever received'.[32] However, Tokyo soon discovered that it could not have everything its own way. Russia balked at the prospect of its presence on the Liaodong Peninsula and in Port Arthur in particular. It immediately proceeded to collude with other European Powers to make a 'friendly demand'[33] to Japan that it retrocede the territory and accept another 30,000,000 taels of silver in exchange. However it was couched, the demand was anything but friendly and was clearly intended to demonstrate the West's refusal to recognise Japan as a nation in any way equal to them. The slight was not lost on Tokyo, and such was the outrage that allegedly 'one hundred officers and men committed suicide ... preferring death to ignoble life under irreparable insult'.[34]

Japan's perceived dishonour paled in comparison with China's. To help meet the indemnity it had to borrow £16,000,000 in two Anglo-German loans in 1896 and 1898 secured against the proceeds of sales taxes, whilst a further 400,000,000 Franc loan from Russia came loaded with strings. The accompanying Cassini Convention of March 1896 gave Russia permission to construct a railway through Manchuria connecting the Trans-Baikal and the southern Ussuri sections of the Trans-Siberian Railway to their Maritime Provinces and Vladivostok, and it would be built, stocked, maintained and guarded by Russians. To save face, it would however remain under the nominal control of the Chinese, and for this purpose be known as the Chinese Eastern Railway. There was also a secret protocol which confirmed that China was 'willing'[35] to lease Russia the port of Qingdao (Tsingtao) in Kiaochow Bay on the Shandong Peninsula, and permit it to use Chinese ports for its warships. A fifteen-year military alliance was also signed in June 1896, ostensibly to provide against further Japanese aggression.

The shortcomings of the reforms to restore the ailing empire were now laid bare, leaving it practically helpless to resist further demands from other countries. Key among these was a power that had had long been eager to cash in on its difficulties, Germany. Like Japan, it was a relative newcomer to the world stage but was keen to secure its 'place in the sun' and was not slow in appreciating the potential China offered. Admiral Alfred von Tirpitz, long-time sponsor of the so-called 'China Project', especially shared Russia's eagerness for possession of Qingdao, which he found particularly attractive because

> ... there was not another single natural harbour along the whole of the neighbouring coast, and the possibility of a favourable railway connection was bound to make Tsingtao [sic] the outlet for Peking and indeed ... for the railway line to Moscow via Irkulsk, which was the best connection between Europe and Eastern Asia.[36]

Geographer Ferdinand von Richtofen agreed. He had surveyed the site as early as 1882, calling it the 'biggest and best ocean harbour in all of northern China'.[37] With this, it was believed they could give Hong Kong a run for its money, and in preparation the *Seminar fur Orientalische Spracken*, or Seminar for Oriental Languages, was opened in Berlin in 1887. This would give Sinophiles, potential businessmen and would-be administrators a firm grounding in the subject in preparation for the planned venture. Nonetheless, early, tentative approaches made to Beijing to secure a lease fell on stony ground because, as the other powers had so graphically demonstrated, Beijing only seemed to accommodate such requests if backed up by the threat of force. A war on the scale of that with

Japan was not an attractive prospect, even for Germany's verbose Emperor Wilhelm II, but an event occurred which would prove just as advantageous. As commentator H.C. Thompson wryly remarked, 'it is not necessary to follow step by step the various occasions on which the murder or ill-treatment of a missionary has been made use of as a pretext for political and commercial aggression'.[38] So it was that in 1897 providence sent such an opportunity when two German missionaries were murdered at a time when anti-Christian sentiments were again on the rise. The incident was eagerly seized upon to do some arm twisting, and warships and marines were rushed to the peninsula. Beijing was warned to expect terrible retribution unless it reconsidered its stance on Qingdao and, true to form, a ninety-nine year lease was duly negotiated.

Signed over on 6 March 1898, it was ostensibly 'inspired by the equal and mutual wish to strengthen the bonds of friendship which unite the two countries, and to develop the economic and commercial relations between the subjects of the two states',[39] but was in reality another nail in China's coffin. Beijing had to grant 'free passage of German troops at any time [and] abstain from taking any measures or issuing any ordinances therein without the previous consent of the German Government... The Chinese population dwelling in the ceded territory shall at all times enjoy the protection of the German Government, provided they behave in conformity with law and order.'[40] In effect, Chinese subjects and even their property had been signed over to a foreign power to do with as it wished. No wonder that for Weng Tonghe, scholar and Imperial tutor who helped to negotiate the one-sided arrangement, it proved the most bitter pill yet to swallow. He could ill disguise his resentment at being forced to sign away part of his beloved country to people he referred to as 'stinky foreigners'.[41]

The agreement raised eyebrows among the other Powers. British author and writer on China, Putnam Weale, believed Germany was not going to be limited to that small corner of the country. He saw it looking further south, like Japan, to the Yangtse Basin, and preparing to engage in 'a constant, deliberate, consistent pushing forward, in any possible way. No method is too mean; nothing is too small for the Berlin-Hamburg wire pullers.'[42] This interpretation of Berlin's tactics was shared by the British Government, and so to protect its own interests in the region it made further approaches to Beijing. These discussions secured an undertaking that the Basin would never be 'mortgaged, leased or ceded to another Power'.[43] The Russians, too, saw more sinister manoeuvrings behind the German's successful diplomacy.

With their nose out of joint having lost the option on Qingdao, they turned their attention to Port Arthur, now conveniently up for grabs following the ejection of the Japanese. Although they initially insisted that it 'has been lent to Russia only temporarily as a winter anchorage',[44] pressure was brought to bear for something more long-term. Faced with understandable reticence, they threatened to take 'hostile measures'[45] unless they got what they wanted. On 28 March 1898, the Emperor 'agreed to cede to Russia Port Arthur ... together with the adjacent seas' for twenty-five years. As usual, extraterritoriality was to be part of the deal and by Article IV, 'supreme civil administration will be entirely given over to the Russian authorities'[46] and 'no Chinese military land forces whatever will be allowed on the territory specified'.[47] The agreement also allowed them to construct barracks, defences, and a new port complex at nearby Dalny, on the southern tip of the peninsula. These projects, added to those already underway in Vladivostock where accommodation for 8,000 men was being built, potentially afforded the Russians considerable leverage.

The British in particular found themselves threatened by these developments. A German presence was worrying enough, but now a second major power had arrived to challenge its interests. They decided that they had no alternative but to increase their own presence in the area and so the government demanded access to the port at Weihaiwei, promising to 'give it up tomorrow'[48] if Russia quit Port Arthur. Once again, Beijing found itself between a rock and a hard place, and on 24 May 1898 they ceded the port 'to provide Great Britain with a suitable naval harbour in North China for the better protection of British commerce in the neighbouring seas'.[49] More importantly, it meant that it could keep an eye on its neighbours, placing them in a strategically advantageous position between the Russians to the north and the Germans to their south. As was now the practice, the lease also included a clause granting its residents 'sole jurisdiction'[50] within its confines, making it another part of the country within which its own people were second-class citizens. With Hong Kong also feeling vulnerable in the face of Russian and German shenanigans it secured a further lease on territory to the north of the colony, for its 'proper defence and protection'.[51]

With this sudden interest in Chinese real estate, it was inevitable that other countries would be keen to cash in. With Russia, Germany and Britain catered for, the French demanded a ninety-nine-year lease of Guangzhouwan near Guangzhou, opposite Hainan Island. The lease, signed on 27 May 1898, stipulated that it was to serve as a naval station and coaling depot, and although the French presence did not 'offset the sovereign rights of China over the territory ceded',[52] Article III specified that the territory 'shall be governed and administered ... by France alone'.[53] The Japanese also secured further concessions in Tianjin and Hankou, a town north of the Han and Yangtze rivers, whilst Austria-Hungary and Belgium were likewise accommodated. For Italy however, it was a different story. On 28 February 1899, Rome demanded the lease of Sanmen Bay on the coast of Chekiang as a coaling station and naval base, but this time Beijing refused and would only countenance a mining concession in northern Chekiang.[54]

Notwithstanding Italy's brush-off, many of China's provinces now had some form of foreign presence in them, whilst this undignified scramble saw the Powers agreeing unofficial 'spheres of influence' among themselves. Britain's became the Yangtse Valley, Germany's Shandong, Russia's Manchuria, Japan's Fukien (Fujian), and France the territory bordering on Tonkin. These machinations were also being watched with growing trepidation in the US State Department, which had not sought nor been granted such extensive privileges but was nonetheless mindful that its own interests might be compromised. So in September 1899, US Secretary of State John Hay sought clarification from the other powers that America's preferred 'Open Door' policy was not to be prejudiced by their manoeuvrings. To this end he presented each government with an undertaking along the lines of that agreed by London:

> The President ... understands it to be the settled policy and purpose of Great Britain not to use any privileges which may be

granted to it in China as a means of excluding any commercial rivals, and that freedom of trade for it in that Empire means freedom of trade for all the world alike.⁵⁵

The fact that the Western Powers and Japan were openly discussing China's internal affairs without proper recourse to the Zongli Yamen or any other organ of the government had once again brought into sharp relief its political impotence. Now more than ever, it was essential to mirror the strides that had been taken in Japan, and movements such as obscure lawyer Sun Yat-sen's 'China Revival Society', the 'Society for the Study of National Strengthening' and the 'Nation Protection Society' increased their activities. Kang Youwei, a longstanding and prominent political thinker who had led opposition to the Treaty of Shimonoseki, was among those who reiterated the need for radical change. He wrote to Emperor Guangxu in 1898 with a damning indictment of the status quo:

> Our present trouble lies in our clinging to old institutions without knowing how to change ... our present institutions are but unworthy vestiges of the Han, Tang, Yuan, and Ming dynasties, they are not even the institutions of the [Manchu] ancestors [but] the products of the fancy writing and corrupt dealings of the petty Officials.⁵⁶

As much as these fresh ideas resonated with the young emperor, for a clean sweep to be made the redoubtable Dowager Empress Cixi, nicknamed by some 'Old Buddha', had to be brought round first. She had been in effective control of the empire since 1861, when Emperor Xianfeng died without a legitimate heir and she managed to manoeuvre herself into the position of Regent, assisted by Prince Kung. When Guangxu succeeded to the throne in 1874 he was only four, so again she continued as regent. She only stepped down reluctantly in 1889 when he came of age, but remained a formidable presence, having entrenched her power by surrounding herself with a powerful clique of ultra-conservative yes-men. They were largely responsible for undermining the Self-Strengthening Movement, and during the first decade of his emperorship Guangxu faced a constant struggle to assert himself. The Grand Council and other ministers ignored him during the Sino-Japanese War and in their subsequent negotiations with the European Powers, but these setbacks served to convince him that such vocal exponents as Kang Youwei were right and that only radical change could save his empire. As the end of the 1890s approached, he finally grasped the nettle and on 11 June 1898 announced his intention to implement a complete retooling of the empire's institutions. He insisted that the current stagnation was 'a sign of grave internal sickness' and that he was determined to end the 'hopeless abuses bred from this palsied indifference'.[57] He optimistically believed that with the help of Kang and other likeminded supporters, he could achieve the complete transformation of government, economy, finance, and the military within a hundred days.

Among the 180 or so Edicts which were to serve as benchmarks for success, were orders to update the redundant civil service examination and build, along with other educational institutions, a university in Beijing. A Translation Department was also to be established so that standard foreign works on political economy and natural science could be included in their curriculums. The mining industry and agriculture were to be practically reinvented, and technical schools opened. A railway building programme was to be kickstarted through a new Bureau of Railways, and investment made available for the repair of 20,000 miles of roads. There were plans for new ministries to replace six defunct government boards, and for redundant governorships to be abolished. There were also proposals to dispense with the Manchu queue hairstyle or *towchang* – long seen as a sign of subservience – the kowtow, and the binding of women's feet. A move to constitutional monarchy and the creation of a national parliament were further indications of the emperor's radical agenda.

Once again, attention was focussed on the army and navy that had performed so badly in the recent war against Japan, and the improvements in which had been left unfinished. Lord Charles Beresford calculated that 'if a tenth part of the sum that the Chinese have had to pay as indemnity had been devoted to military organisation, such losses would not have taken place'.[58] Yet the armed forces were absorbing up to a third of the empire's audited revenue, paying, on paper at least, for the upkeep of nearly

1,000,000 soldiers. Some progress had been attempted when in 1895 Zhang Zhidong created the 'Self-Strengthening Army' in Nanking and Yuan Shikai the 'Newly Created Army' in Zhili Province, adopting western weapons, equipment and training, and their achievements prompted Guangxu to appoint Shikai to apply these reforms to the rest of the armed forces. A further decree attempted again to abolish the ancient military examinations and its emphasis on proficiency in archery, swordsmanship, and weightlifting, and place more importance on practical training programmes such as tactics and competence in modern firearms.

Funding for these ambitious reforms was going to be hard to find, however. The country was weighed down by indemnities and foreign debts of up to £60,000,000, much of which was owed to Britain, France, Russia and Germany at four to seven per cent interest.[59] Securities on these loans tied up revenue from customs, salt, railways and rolling stock, whilst as much as an astonishing eighty per cent of government income was calculated to be lost to corruption and inefficiency annually. Millions were also siphoned off funding sinecures and the perks enjoyed for generations by the Manchu elites. There also remained that omnipresent elephant in the room, a sycophantic Court eager to pander to the profligate lifestyle of the Dowager Empress and scupper any measures which threatened their own status and privileges. Her birthday in 1897 alone cost a million taels in silver,[60] and millions more was spent keeping her in comfortable retirement. As had been the case with earlier reforms, these vested interests immediately came into play to undermine the emperor. Among those intriguing against him was ultra-conservative xenophobe Kang Yi and the rest of the Old Guard, who had been feeding Empress Cixi regular reports of what was being perpetrated. Yi wrote a scathing Memorial complaining particularly that the old order was threatened by 'the establishment of schools and colleges [which] has only encouraged Chinese ambitions and developed Chinese talent to the danger of the Manchu dynasty ... the students should therefore be exterminated without delay'.[61] By the beginning of September, they were ready to strike.

A life-or-death struggle ensued as both factions fought for control of the government, but Guangxu could not overcome the solid wall of resistance which confronted him. He finally resigned himself to the inevitable and capitulated: 'The reactionary element deliberately misrepresents my objects, spreading baseless rumours so as to disturb the minds of men.'[62] On the morning of 5 September his fate was sealed when he received a Memorial from Cixi in which she admonished him for being nothing but

> ... an unsophisticated child. Return at once to your inner apartments. It is evident that I must resume control to save the empire, which you, in your extreme unwisdom and foolishness, seem to be doing your best to drive to perdition.[63]

To compound his defenestration, he was dragooned into recanting his actions publicly and putting his name to another Decree in which he confessed to having all along 'repeatedly besought Her Majesty to condescend once more to administer the government [and who] from this day [will once again] transact the business of government'.[64] Thus the experiment was over and the Hundred Days reforms annulled or reversed. Confucianism was among the many defunct practices, government posts and offices reinstated, with a Decree confirming that 'for the future, the old system shall be restored, and ... public examinations shall henceforward consist of themes and extracts from the classics'.[65] To ensure that there would be no revival of Guangxu's heresy, reformist newspapers were shut down and dozens of his supporters arrested, tortured and imprisoned. Many more sought sanctuary in foreign legations or fled abroad, Kang Youwei choosing to live in Canada. Here he founded the 'Chinese Empire Reform Society' as a platform from which to continue his campaign for a modern constitutional monarchy.

Yet despite the repression carried out against the reformers, outside of the immediate circle of the Forbidden City there was widespread consternation. Movements sprang up demanding Guangxu's reinstatement and newspapers in Shanghai denounced what amounted to a Manchu coup. But their remonstrations were in vain, and the Hundred Days would prove to be the last chance to stave off disaster. Instead, the blind obstinacy of Cixi and her coterie of reactionaries had set in train a series of events that doomed the Qing dynasty to oblivion.

5

A Piece of Stupidity Which Will Be Remembered for All Time

Military humiliation and the failure of the Hundred Days were just two among a litany of misfortunes to bedevil the empire as the century came to a close. Famine or severe shortage was also affecting Shanxi, Zhili, Henan and Shandong Provinces, where nearly 10,000,000 perished from hunger. A correspondent for New Zealand's *Bay of Plenty Times* was one among many foreigners who saw at first hand the suffering endured by ordinary people. He recounted the sight of 'living skeletons walking about, begging in the streets',[1] as thousands resorted to eating tree bark, the roots from plants and even, it was rumoured, one another. Their misery was compounded by monsoon rains of biblical proportions, which in August of 1897 caused the Yellow River to burst its banks. Nearly 2,000 villages were overwhelmed leaving their inhabitants homeless and clinging to dykes as they waited months for the flood water to subside. American missionaries calculated that as many as 2,000,000 people were affected and pleaded with the US Government for help with food relief. They were told that all its ships were needed for the upcoming invasion of the Philippines and could not be spared for humanitarian work. More to the point, had attempts at reform not been repeatedly sabotaged, investment in efficient irrigation networks could have allayed much of this suffering, and there might have been reserves of grains had the funds allocated to such schemes not been misappropriated by venal officials. One example of their corruption was described in the Government's own *Peking Gazette*:

The Censor Chang-Chao-Lan denounces the practice, prevalent among the magistrates, of speculating with the cereals stored in public granaries, with the result that they become bankrupt and are unable to settle their accounts with the government... They are authorised ... to sell a certain portion of old stock and replenish it with the fresh harvest. Instead of doing that, the Censor accuses them of allowing the old grain to mould in the granaries and of selling the fresh for their personal profit.[2]

Yet although responsibility for these disasters rested largely upon the shoulders of officialdom, missionaries and others once again found themselves lightning rods for those pursuing their vendetta against all things foreign. The hatred which had provoked the events of 1870 had only been suppressed, never eradicated, and as the conditions worsened anti-foreign organisations spread vicious calumnies. It was claimed that Christian churches and cathedrals were disrupting the empire's *feng shui* and arousing the wrath of the Earth Dragon, who in turn was chastising their wrongdoing by sending apocalyptic weather. As had been the case thirty years before, it was a sentiment that tapped into the wellspring of the average superstitious Chinese, compounded by the distribution of salacious propaganda. One example came as a refrain along the lines of: 'No rain comes from heaven / the earth is parched and dry. And all because the [Christian] churches / have bottled up the sky.'[3] More disinformation came in the form of placards, one of which claimed that 'on account of the Protestant and Catholic religions the Buddhist gods are oppressed and our sages thrust into the background. The law of Buddha is no longer respected, and the Five Relationships are disregarded... If the foreign religions are not destroyed there will be no rain.'[4] The willingness of many peasants to accept such specious reasoning was exacerbated by sixty years of pernicious foreign influence.

Although Lord Curzon had once cynically remarked that 'you might as well try to convert a Chinaman as a coconut',[5] by the late 1890s there were around 4,000 missionaries and 700,000 converts in the country. Approximately 500,000 were Roman Catholic, and of these 110,000 were in Shandong Province alone. The Catholic publication *Monitor* of March 1898 naturally rejoiced at these once lost souls, now 'models of Christian life [who] go to Mass everyday [and] say their morning and evening prayers ... in their poor little churches'.⁶ But as much as traditionalists seethed with resentment, their own government was at least in part culpable. A devious Jesuit interpreter had reworked the terms of the 1860 Beijing Convention to afford missionaries certain rights, of which the Chinese negotiators were unaware until it was too late. In their version had been inserted the clause 'It shall be lawful for French missionaries in any of the provinces to lease or buy land and build houses',⁷ and, fearful of losing face if they raised objections afterwards, they were forced to let it stand. The events of 1870 and the repercussions that followed also served to underpin their privileged status, giving them added leverage many exploited shamelessly. Some assumed titles and ranks comparable to those of mandarins, which gave them a temporal authority which they exercised to their own advantage.

Furthermore, they routinely manoeuvred among themselves to gain the upper hand. When the French Roman Catholics heard of plans to establish a Chinese Embassy in the Vatican they feared coming under the authority of Italian priests, and had the plan scotched. German Bishop Johan Baptiste Anzer, who had worked in China since 1881, ruffled feathers when in 1884 he built a mission in what was purported to have been Confucius' birthplace in Zou in Shandong. Angry at such sacrilege, the local Chinese burnt it down, and when he appealed to the local mandarins they proved decidedly unsympathetic. He was reportedly warned that 'this is a holy city and we cannot have a Christian Mission here'. He then appealed to the French ambassador, who was told that 'this is the cradle of our holy Confucius and therefore no foreign religion can be tolerated'.⁸ Nonetheless, the Germans waited and when the time was ripe Kaiser William II overruled their protests and opened the town to foreign missionaries anyway. For good measure, the site of a former Buddhist temple in Liyuantan was also appropriated and a church built in its place. Bishop Anzer had also established a seminary for the ordination of Chinese priests, and when the first two graduates emerged in 1896, he and his colleagues were delighted. Not so devout Confucians and Buddhists, who raged at these further acts of sacrilege. As the bitterness spread, they plotted their retaliation, and what was to follow would, in the words of one European, be the understandable distillation of the 'concentrated wrath and hate of sixty years'.[9]

In north and central China this polarisation manifested itself in the creation of both anti-Western and anti-Qing groups such as the *I-ho Chuan*, the Righteous and Harmonious Fists. Steeped in traditional superstition, they were described as fanatically brave but 'badly armed and utterly untrained and undisciplined'.[10] Instead of guns or fieldcraft, they put their faith in the pugilistic calisthenics that earned them the epithet Boxers, and which they believed created invisible 'iron shirts' rendering them impervious to bullets. These, alongside their battle cry of 'Sha! Sha!' kill, kill!'[11] gave full expression to their zealotry. As more disaffected peasants flocked to their colours, they became emboldened and targeted the Chinese converts they saw as traitors and turncoats. Many suffered 'the most cruel martyrdom, rather than recant'[12] as a climate of fear increasingly stalked the hinterland. Doctor Hykes of the American Bible Society recounted stories of 'persecution, sometimes confined to one man alone, and in other cases whole families and whole villages suffering loss of life and destruction of property'.[13] In central Szechuan alone, rebels burnt over 4,000 houses in thirty missions, causing £850,000 damage and leaving over 20,000 converts homeless. However, whilst the Dowager Empress was not particularly perturbed by attacks on foreigners, she was not prepared to tolerate insurgents running riot over the countryside calling for the overthrow of her dynasty. Orders were issued to subdue the rebels, and on 18 October 1899 a force of 1,500 Boxers encountered Qing troops commanded by Governor Yuan Shikai in Pingyuan in northwest Shandong. In the subsequent skirmish they were successfully repulsed by comparatively well-trained and equipped Imperial forces. Although the twenty-seven who died demonstrated that their 'iron shirts' afforded them no protection from firearms, that did not deter the diehards, who ascribed their deaths instead to 'lack of faith'.[14]

In neighbouring Zhili Province, the Viceroy executed a hundred equally faithless Boxers who were captured after killing a missionary, calling them 'robbers and malcontents',[15] but such punitive measures did little to deter the growing rebellion. In December 1899, one Mr Brooks of the 'Society for the propagation of the Gospel' was murdered near Tainan-Fu, and the following spring further disturbances took place in Shandong and Zhili. These culminated at the end of May 1900 in the murder of missionaries, mining engineers and converts at Pao-ting and Lang-fang. In the German concession in Shandong meanwhile, angry peasants were also objecting to the construction of the railway line, refusing to cooperate and spurning demands to sell their land. When the Germans ploughed on regardless, they turned violent, burning down railway stations and tearing up track, their rage stoked by rumours that children were being buried in the foundations of buildings for good luck. Faced with this growing militancy, the German governor Paul Jaeshke decided to 'teach the peasants a lesson'[16] and sent out troops to deal with the unrest. In one such foray twenty-five Chinese were killed, the town of Gaomi occupied for two weeks and its renowned academy and library destroyed along with its books. Another column deployed 'for the purpose of restoring order and peace'[17] burnt down two villages because their inhabitants had allegedly attacked an army lieutenant and an engineer. A further detachment marched to a village where a Catholic priest had been assaulted and held several headmen hostage until suitable financial restitution was forthcoming.

In Beijing, soon to serve as the crucible for the approaching firestorm, the atmosphere was becoming increasingly tense. In September 1898 at the annual mid-autumn festivals, the Dean of the Diplomatic Corps reported: 'The father of a member of the Legation of the United States was severely wounded, and a member of the British Legation and an English lady, a French citizen and two Japanese subjects were wounded or attacked or insulted.'[18] The British Ambassador Sir Claude Maxwell MacDonald was in no doubt that there was a strong link between the deterioration in law and order and the suppression of the reform movement:

> There has been, since the so-called *coup d'etat*, a very considerable amount of unrest in the city, more especially since the execution of six of the reform party. These men were supposed by the common people to have been put to death by order of the Empress Dowager because they had dealings with foreigners. It was, therefore, considered safe to insult foreigners in every possible way.[19]

Lord Charles Beresford noted that 'never before has [central] authority been in so weak or so helpless a condition, the financial position of the Empire hindering the government from maintaining a force adequate in either numbers or efficiency, to prevent disturbances and rebellions'.[20]

In fact, hard-line anti-foreign factions at Court were learning of the violence with growing satisfaction, tempered only by the fact that the rebels also wanted to see the end of the Qings. This left them in a quandary. The Boxers represented an ideal conduit through which to achieve their dream of sweeping 'the foreign devils back into the sea',[21] but they could not afford to ally themselves with traitorous revolutionaries. So Prince Duan was charged with negotiating an understanding with them. As a man the American ambassador described as 'malignantly anti-foreign [and] a patron of the Boxers',[22] he was ideally qualified for such a task. To smooth the way to this Faustian pact, Cixi issued a Decree endorsing the existence of 'militias' and provided funding to encourage recruitment. Yuan Shikai had by now also begun cultivating rather than opposing the insurgents, and enrolled them into his own forces, changing their name to the 'Righteous and Harmonious Militia'. The regular army, too, was being primed, including the 10,000-strong Gansu Braves, commanded by General Dong Fuxiang, who had developed strong Boxer sympathies. They had been transferred to the outskirts of the city in 1898 and were ideally placed to be committed to the inevitable confrontation that was being surreptitiously prepared.

An early sign of what was to come occurred when some of its men assaulted the Assistant Chinese Secretary to the British Legation, prompting Ambassador MacDonald to demand that the 'uniformed brigands' responsible be apprehended and a 'thorough investigation and punishment of the offenders' conducted.[23] Although the Zongli Yamen glibly apologised and promised to have the unit moved, sympathisers in the government ensured that only two of those responsible were brought to book.

As the mood became more corrosive, demands were made to the authorities to assign guards to protect the legations, but when these failed to materialise the decision was taken to have troops sent instead from Tianjin. This naturally elicited strong objections from the Zongli Yamen, the Chinese ambassador in London informing the British Foreign Office that it constituted 'a slur upon the Chinese Government'.[24] Such faux outrage cut little ice with a foreign community now feeling extremely concerned for their safety, and MacDonald responded that they would have to 'accept the inevitable, and accept it graciously',[25] if the Chinese Government was not prepared to do anything. The arrival of friendly troops certainly served as a welcome fillip, and American missionary Reverend Gilbert Reid was among those reassured by the sight of '459 officers and men of different nationalities [who] came to Peking as our foreign guard'.[26] They only remained until early spring 1900, by which time a period of relative calm appeared to be descending on the city, but it proved to be the lull before the storm. Outside the capital, the Boxers were moving to escalate the crisis.

On 5 June they severed the railway line between Tianjin and Beijing, but according to a reporter for the *Shanghai Mercury*, 'the Chinese troops sent to guard the line have failed to accomplish anything and even if not in sympathy with the present anti-foreign movement ... there is every reason to believe that they have secret instructions not to resist or punish the Boxers'.[27] Such reports heightened the fears of the legations, and on 9 June MacDonald cabled Vice-Admiral Edward Seymour, commander of the Royal Navy's Chinese Squadron requesting more help. He set off the next day by train with 2,000 men but met with constant delays due to the Boxers and the need to keep stopping and repair the track. The correspondent for the *Shanghai Mercury* reported on 15 June: 'The railway to Peking is more seriously damaged than was at first supposed and very slow progress is being made. No news whatever came from upline yesterday, and some people were fearing that the line had been destroyed in the rear.'[28]

Meanwhile, back in the capital the risk to foreigners was escalating exponentially. On 11 June the secretary to the Japanese legation, Sugiyama Akira, encountered a group of Gansu Braves who started to harass and jostle him. As he struggled to extricate himself from the situation the officers suddenly drew their swords and disembowelled him, prompting Prince Duan to tell Fuxiang admiringly, 'You are indeed a hero.'[29] The regular forces were now being reinforced by around 20,000 Boxers who had reached the city, and on 16 June this farrago began setting buildings ablaze. When firefighters arrived to try and put out the conflagration they were denied access by the arsonists, who told them, 'This year the gods are angry at water.'[30] They were forced to let the fires spread, destroying at least 4,000 shops and houses. Now allied with the government, the Boxers could be heard screaming 'Elevate the Manchus, kill the foreigners'[31] – music to Cixi's ears but a terrifying refrain for those trapped in the legations, whose only hope of salvation now lay in rescue by Vice-Admiral Seymour.

Fourteen ships and 2,000 soldiers had been dispatched to seize the Dagu Forts in support of Seymour's laborious advance, and a sustained bombardment followed by landing parties soon captured the stronghold. It had been a perfect opportunity to avenge some of the excesses committed against foreigners and converts, with eyewitness Mrs James Jones noting 'rivers of blood with headless and armless bodies everywhere, which the blue jackets were gathering together and cremating in heaps'.[32] Despite the Dagu victory, on 18 June Seymour's column confronted and was nearly overwhelmed by a considerable force of Imperial and Boxer troops. They managed to fight them off, but low on supplies, ammunition and with growing numbers of wounded to care for, their position was becoming precarious. The prospect of further, even heavier attacks forced the decision to return to Tianjin, and then try again with a larger force. The news of the retreating foreigners soon reached the capital where the Boxers and Imperial troops were naturally elated. Reverend Reid observed that they were now more than ever 'inspired with jubilation and self-confidence', adding with some understatement that it 'rendered our position in Peking one of extreme peril'.[33]

On 19 June, the foreign ministers were handed their passports and given a day to depart with their staffs and families, promised safe passage and protection if they did as they were told. MacDonald and the other envoys had, however, also heard the news and were busy fortifying the diplomatic quarter. There were altogether around 3,000 in the compound, two-thirds of whom were Chinese converts and their families. More foreigners and Chinese had taken refuge in the cathedral. Their 400 or so defenders were armed with a variety of modern weapons including rifles, a Maxim gun, a one-pounder field gun, and in an inspired piece of improvisation, someone uncovered an old British gun barrel in a Chinese shop. In a piece of Heath-Robinson creativity it was fitted to an Italian carriage, supplied with Russian shells and served by a US Marine.[34] Nonetheless, a smug Empress Cixi, boosted by news of Seymour's predicament and the overwhelming numerical superiority of her forces, remarked that they were now 'like fish in a stewpan',[35] and on 20 June bet the house when she issued a decree appealing to her people to back the rebels and support 'the loyal and patriotic object they have in view, and render it convenient for them to attack and exterminate [the foreigners and Christians]'.[36]

On 21 June, another decree finally crossed the Rubicon and war was declared, using the attack on the Dagu forts as a pretext. It announced: 'It was not of our beginning or choosing ... even if China [would] rush into war, was it likely or reasonable that she would of her own accord elect to fight all the Powers at once?'[37] A reasonable defence perhaps, but however worded or phrased, the declaration horrified the more levelled-headed among her subjects. One, the ever faithful Li Hongzhang, learned of the suicide note with dismay, and seeing his life's work in tatters, he did not mince his words:

> My blood runs cold at the thought of events to come. Under any enlightened sovereign these Boxers, with their ridiculous claims of supernatural powers, would most assuredly have been condemned to death long since... Your Majesties ... are still in the hands of traitors, regarding these Boxers as your dutiful subjects, with the result that unrest is spreading and alarm universal.[38]

Even Jung Lu, a favourite of Cixi and a central figure in suppressing the reform movement, reminded her firmly that 'foreign envoys were inviolate within the territory of any civilised state ... this attack on the legations is worse than an outrage; it is a piece of stupidity which will be remembered against China for all time'.[39] The empire may have been staring into the abyss, but dissent was not an option, to disagree exposed those who voiced their doubts to the most merciless retribution. One Censor who 'Memorialised the Empress Dowager praying her to behead Prince Duan, Grand secretary Kang Yi and General Fuxiang'[40] had his entire family slaughtered by the Boxers in revenge. On 24 June, unmoved by the entreaties of even her most senior ministers, Cixi placed Prince Duan in overall command of the Boxers. To these he contributed his own 'Tiger and Divine Corps' and began launching heavy but uncoordinated and ill-timed assaults on the legations, his men doubtless eager to collect the bounty of fifty taels for a foreign male, forty for a female and thirty per child.[41]

With such rewards on offer, it was not surprising that anyone reckless enough to venture outside stood little chance. One man was decapitated and his head displayed on a pole, prompting Ching Shan, a minister in the Zongli Yamen to brag that 'the face has a most horrible expression, but it is a fine thing, all the same, to see a foreigner's head hung up at our palace gates'.[42] *The Times* described similar scenes, perhaps embellished for their readers, of 'women and children hacked to pieces, men trussed like fowls, with noses and ears cut off and eyes gouged out'.[43] On 20 June, the German chargé d'affaires Baron von Ketteler had been shot at point blank range in his sedan chair when he was caught trying to make his way from the German Legation to the Palace to reason with the government, and when he heard, a livid Kaiser Wilhelm telegraphed his grandmother Queen Victoria with the news. With unusual understatement he advised her that 'this means serious business',[44] and immediately issued instructions for an expeditionary force to be dispatched. On 27 July he went to see his initial contingent of 4,000 troops off from Bremerhaven, where he produced a more typically bravura performance. In language incendiary even for this warmonger, he announced:

> You must know, my men, that you are about to meet a crafty, well-armed, cruel foe! Meet him and beat him! Give him no quarter! Take no prisoners! Kill him when he falls into your hands! Even as a thousand years ago, the Huns under their king Attila made such a name for themselves as still resounds in terror through legend and fable, so may the name of German resound through Chinese history a thousand years from now, and may you so conduct yourselves that no Chinaman will ever again so much as dare to look crooked at a German![45]

A Piece of Stupidity Which Will Be Remembered for All Time

He sent off its commander, Count von Waldersee, with 200 bottles of Champagne, fifty bottles of spirits and two bodyguards,[46] demanding that Beijing 'must be stormed and levelled to the ground'.[47] But by the time the expeditionary force reached China six weeks later, the fighting would be over. In the meantime, on 4 August the second relief column of 19,000 soldiers, mainly from Japan and Russia but including British, American, French, Austro-Hungarians and Italians, was ready to march. In addition, Germans stationed at Kiaochow and the coast and British troops in Hong Kong were held in reserve. As reports of the advancing column reached Beijing, one of Cixi's army commanders, General Liu, boasted that he would finish off the foreigners in three days, and that when the relief column learned of their victory it would give up and return to Tianjin. He proved incapable of making good on his promise, as one assault after another was repulsed. Diehard Ching Shan was among those now distancing themselves from the debacle, remarking bitterly and far too late in the day, 'The Boxers have proved themselves utterly useless. I always said they would never do anything.'[48]

Sharing this evaluation of the situation, Cixi realised that she had overplayed her hand and left fall guy Li Hongzhang to face the music before fleeing with her entourage to Xi'an in Shanxi Province. It was not a moment too soon, as the column was making good progress and on 14 August Reverend Reid 'heard the first glad sound of relief from beyond the city from the east. In the afternoon of the fourteenth came the first appearance of the relief force at the British Legation. They were the Sikhs who were cheered lustily by men and women of every nationality.'[49] Captain J. Boyce-Kup, commander of the Tientsin Volunteer Corps and now on the staff of expedition commander Major-General Alfred Gaselee, was also surprised to find that the appearance of the legation 'was anything but what we had expected, as everyone looked well and all (especially the ladies) had donned their best bib and tucker in honour of our arrival'.[50]

A triumphal procession on 17 August emphasised the scale and extent of the victory, and afterwards the officers were allowed to inspect the Forbidden City, where, as Boyce-Kup observed, they 'availed themselves of the opportunity to do a little looting'.[51] French novelist Pere Loti betrayed some sympathy for the losers, finding this former symbol of Chinese Imperial power, once the exclusive preserve of generations of demi-gods now 'violated even unto its innermost secrets'.[52] But English explorer and artist Henry Landor Savage felt it proved that finally, 'The spell was broken. The deed was done. What celestials had kept secret for 500 years, foreign devils desecrated in two seconds.'[53] Nonetheless, the desecration of the seat of the rebellion was considered apt retribution for the roughly 400 foreigners who had perished, including 200 orphans and eighty soldiers. In addition, around 3,000 Boxers, Imperial troops and other rebels lay dead before the walls of the legation, testament to the suicidal tactics that achieved nothing at such high cost. An estimated 100,000 civilians also died in the fighting and in the subsequent campaign of revenge.

Count Von Waldersee landed at Shanghai on 21 September, too late to lead the liberation of the legations or share in the quashing of the Boxers. Although he lamented that having been entrusted with leading the capture of Beijing, 'that dream was over ... Pekin had been taken without much loss of life',[54] he was still determined to leave his mark. True to his Kaiser's exhortation to behave like the Huns of old, terror was to be employed to exact revenge and also resolve the associated problem of resistance to the railway. After a brief conference on 6-7 October, Waldersee and Governor Jaeshke concluded that naked intimidation was the answer, and Waldersee ordered his troops to start things off by shooting 'all the headmen of every village for hundreds of miles around Peking'.[55] Then between 23 October and 1 November a number of villages were shelled without warning, killing 450 civilians, many of whom were women and children. Nationals from other countries in the coalition were appalled at such brutality, British pacifist and philosopher Goldsworthy Lowe Dickinson recalled seeing 'the corpses of murdered men and outraged women and children ... the innocent mingled indiscriminately with the guilty'.[56] Waldersee's own countrymen, too, felt such excesses could prove counterproductive. One admitted that their 'acquiescence in the German policy of vengeance has alienated us from both America and Japan',[57] but terror was proving too expedient a remedy to Chinese resistance to be abandoned.

A Piece of Stupidity Which Will Be Remembered for All Time

On 29 June, whilst their compatriots were helping defend the legations, the Czar used Boxer attacks as a pretext to send 100,000 Cossacks into Manchuria, overwhelming the Bannermen and sending them reeling southwards. As they advanced, they demonstrated an appetite for bloodshed equal to anything the Germans were capable of. The terror culminated with the Military Governor of the Amur Region, Lieutenant-General Konstantin Nikolaevich Gribskii, ordering that approximately 15,000 or so Qing subjects still living in Blagoveshchensk and sixty-four surrounding villages be rounded up. They were to be expelled from the entire north bank of the Amur, and his men eagerly set about burning their homes and herding them towards its banks. Finally, between 3,000 and 9,000 innocent people were forced into the river, their tormentors mocking them as they struggled in the raging torrent. Any that managed to avoid drowning were shot and killed like ducks in a shooting gallery until, in the words of one eyewitness, 'the progress of the Amur River was choked by the bodies of 5,000 unoffending Chinese civilians who had been driven into the water by the Russians at the point of the bayonet'.[58]

Whilst Russian and German soldiers were satisfying their bloodlust, Cixi's hapless scapegoat Li Hongzhang had thrown himself on the mercy of the Allies. One crucial mitigating factor was that the fighting had been largely confined to the capital and its immediate vicinity and had been disavowed by much of the country at large. The Imperial Viceroys in south and central China largely defied the government and refused to countenance the war, and instead used their provincial forces to suppress any anti-foreigner outbreaks within their jurisdiction. This meant that if blame could be shifted to the Boxers and the perfidy of the Empress offset, it might help in ameliorating the peace terms. In fact, having worked in lockstep to crush the rebellion, the allies proved far less of one mind when it came to seeking redress. Although Russia's Count Vladimir Lamsdorff fairly represented the general mood when he insisted upon 'the punishment of the leaders of the movement',[59] men like Kang Yi, a more pressing issue was the inevitable indemnity which many looked forward to collecting for their respective governments. On this subject there was little consensus, however. Commentator H. C. Thompson admitted that although

China had long proved to be 'a milch cow, if the milch cow is bled violently after an exhausting illness she will die; and surely what is wanted for China now is nourishment and considerate treatment'.[60] His de haut en bas magnanimity was broadly shared by the Americans, and on 23 July Hays sent a circular reminding his colleagues that the sole purpose of the war was to 'protect all rights guaranteed to friendly powers by treaty, and safeguard for the world the principle of equal and impartial trade with all parts of the Chinese Empire',[61] not to bleed it dry. Conceding nonetheless that some reparations were due, the State Department felt that at most, Beijing could afford $150,000,000.

This cake was far too small for Berlin's avaricious tastes. Not only did they want the costs of their expedition covered, they hoped to milk the cow for several more millions on top. Its motive was, as German General Helmuth von Moltke frankly admitted, 'pure greed. We want to ... get money, make railways, get mines going ... we're not an atom better than the English in the Transvaal'.[62] The other powers also wanted their share, so after much haggling the final amount included in the so-called Boxer Protocol, signed on 7 September 1901, was set at $333,900,000,[63] more than twice what the Americans thought reasonable. Its thirty-eight annual portions were subject to four per cent interest, commencing on 1 January 1902 and all going well, the final slice would be served up in 1940.

The rest of the Protocol was no less crushing. It included Article VII, in which 'the Chinese Government has agreed that the quarter occupied by the Legations shall be considered as one exclusively reserved for their use and placed under their exclusive control, in which Chinese shall not have the right to reside and which may be made defensible'.[64] This clause, according to Putnam Weale, gave the foreigners a blank cheque to behave with callous disregard for the feelings of the locals. He noted how as a result of its strict application, 'Chinese officials are forbidden to go openly through the foreign quarter, and many have been quite recently dragged from their carts and brutally treated by the common European soldiery'.[65]

Under Article VIII the troublesome Dagu forts, so often a source of problems for campaigning Western armies, were to be destroyed once and for all, and under Article IX legation guards and garrisons were established to protect land and river communications between Beijing and the sea.[66] France, Germany, Britain, Italy and Japan had also established a provisional government in Tianjin, and the Chinese were forced to agree not to station or march troops within seven miles of the city. Foreign jurisdiction was to extend two miles on either side of the railway, and troops used to enforce this were to be provided with summer quarters.[67] As a consequence, by 1908 France and Japan would have 1,200 troops each and Germany 700 stationed at strategic points on Chinese soil.[68] Eventually, the British alone would have 11,000 soldiers stationed across northern China, supplemented by gunboats operating on the Yangtze River to safeguard its commercial interests.[69] For the Germans, this was still not enough. A grovelling apology for the murder of Baron von Ketteler also had to be delivered to Berlin personally by a representative of the Empress. Prince Chun Zaifeng drew the short straw, and the humbling letter assured the Kaiser of their contrition:

> We regret most deeply that Baron von Ketteler met so terrible an end among us. The fact that we were not able to take due protective measures was painful to our feeling of responsibility ... we have sent to Germany with this our letter the Imperial Prince who is our own brother, [who] will assure Your Majesty how deeply events of the past year have grieved us, and how deeply the feeling of penitence and shame animates us.[70]

Wilhelm, never one to pass up an opportunity for theatre, replied in his usual verbose way, warning the Prince and his entourage sternly that his countrymen

> ... must not delude themselves into believing that by an expiatory mission alone they will have made atonement and obtained pardon for their guilt. This can only be done by the future attitude, in conformity with the prescriptions of international law and usages of civilised nations. [Then] peace and friendly relations will again prevail, and conduce to the benefit of the two nations and the whole of human civilisation.[71]

For Li Hongzhang, who died two months after the signing of the Protocol aged seventy-seven, it was to prove his swansong. But it was not that for which he would have wished to be remembered. His other achievements, for which he was once lauded as the 'Bismack of the East', would be overshadowed by his participation in this final climbdown, and it tarnished his reputation in the minds of generations to come. He was blamed for the fact that sixty years on from the first Opium War, China continued to be subjected to the whims and caprice of foreigners, its abortive attempts at reform insufficient in scope or breadth to fend off repeated extortions, land grabs and massacres. In what was hoped to be a watershed moment, it had tried to stop the rot with an ill-judged rebellion, but shown itself badly wanting when confronted by the combined power of an international cartel. Having relegated the country to the status of a virtual vassal, its unwelcome guests resumed their traditional roles, picking over the remains and jockeying for position amongst themselves.

6

They Would Never Try to Fight Us

To many observers, Russia was the one power to have emerged best strategically enhanced from the recent turmoil. Britain's H. C. Thompson calculated that its prestige, having increased 'in proportion to the decline of Britain's',[1] was 'the only Power which will profit from [the] chaos into which the north of China has been plunged'. At the terminus of the South Manchurian Railway he noted, they were now 'pushing hurriedly on with the erection of her new commercial town of Dalny which she confidently anticipates will become the Chicago of her Eastern Dominions'.[2] John Birch, travelling through the north and central belts, saw evidence of ' Russian activity on the Yangtze Basin, which our government says is our sphere'.[3] Furthermore, Thomas Cowen realised that having built up its military assets in Port Arthur, Dalny and Vladivostok, Russia was more than ever well placed to menace the other powers with 'the whole fighting force of the most feared power in the world'.[4]

These developments were not lost on the Japanese either, and they now regarded Russia as their 'White Peril', threatening Tokyo's interests in the region. The *Weekly Gazette* of 22 October 1900 predicted that 'unless Russia evacuates Manchuria, England and Germany will consider what other part of China they shall seize in compensation'.[5] Germany was also watching with a wary eye, and in the spring of 1901 Baron von Eckardstein, German chargé d'affaires in London, discussed the issue with Japan's resident minister, Hayashi Tadasu. He raised the prospect of a combination of powers against St Petersburg, confident that 'nothing would prove more effective for the maintenance of peace in the Far East than the conclusion of a triple alliance between Japan, Great Britain and Germany'.[6] The following year Hayashi told British foreign secretary Lord Lansdowne pointedly that his country 'considers as its first and last wish the protection of its interests in Korea, and the prevention of interference by another country',[7] whilst Marquis Ito added: 'We have had our eyes on Russia all the time, and shall know what to do when the time comes.'[8]

Arguably, of all the powers Japan had most to lose from Russian expansion. Since opening up to modernisation, its population had grown from 34,000,000 in the 1860s to 45,000,000 by 1900,[9] and by 1903, with just 3.33 per cent of the land under cultivation, the country would be spending the equivalent of US$80,000,000 annually importing food.[10] This situation could not be sustained indefinitely, and it was unacceptable to have to compete with a third party for its resources at the same time. Men like Marquis Ito were nonetheless well aware of the risks involved in resorting to force and remembered the ignominy of having to back down over Port Arthur when confronted by a hostile coalition. He concluded that before taking any irrevocable steps, Japan needed some form of insurance: 'We have ships, we have guns ... we need an alliance too.'[11]

Was it really feasible for Japan and Germany to combine with isolationist Britain against Russia? It was certainly something that would have been inconceivable a few years before, but Russian designs on Afghanistan, and by extension India, had long been a cause for concern. With its resources stretched and budgets tight, the British government was certainly anxious to share the burden. As a candidate, Japan, having emerged from the Boxer rebellion as a strong and reliable ally, was fast becoming the front runner.

Tentative discussions in London were nonetheless tempered by suspicions of Japan's wider agenda, and the prospect of Tokyo exploiting any alliance to underwrite military adventures. But following Hayashi's assurance that even with an alliance 'the Japanese government has no intention of using that freedom as a means of aggression',[12] such fears were largely allayed. Furthermore, Germany was now out of the equation, as there was no prospect of including an increasingly anti-British Berlin in any arrangement. Consequently, in January 1902 the two parties signed the Anglo-Japanese Treaty, in which they recognised the independence of China and Korea, but crucially included the caveat that they both had interests 'to a peculiar degree',[13] which they were prepared to protect. To this end, they undertook to come to one another's aid if they were separately or severally attacked by a third party. Although the agreement was made without consulting Beijing, the London *Times* believed that the respective strengths of the two empires actually protected China's territorial integrity and furthermore, 'delivered a weighty lecture on the opportunity the alliance afforded [the country] to set her house in order'.[14] Predictably perhaps, St Petersburg did not share so sanguine an interpretation. A communiqué of 20 March reminded the two countries pointedly that 'Russia insists on the independence and integrity of China – a friendly neighbouring country – as well as that of Korea',[15] where it, too, had 'special interests'.

Its presence in Manchuria was perhaps of greatest concern to Beijing, too, and following lengthy negotiations it was led to believe it had obtained a guarded undertaking to withdraw its troops by October 1903 at the latest, 'provided that no disturbances arise'.[16] However, as the clock counted down towards the deadline, Japanese agents were sending disquieting reports back to Tokyo. On 28 July 1903 came warnings that 'Russia must have abandoned the intention of retiring from Manchuria ... her increased activity upon the Korean border is such to raise doubts as to the limits of her ambition'.[17] Once the railway line from St Petersburg to Port Arthur was completed in August 1903, further reports were received that they were bringing more troops into Manchuria, not taking them out. Then further sightings followed in October, which revealed that 10,000 to 20,000 men were marching across Liaotung towards the Korean border. Shortly afterwards, intelligence revealed that a Russian contractor had secured the rights to log timber in the Yalu Valley, joined by an influx of armed Russians who were constructing a defended settlement at Yongampo on the Korean side of the river. On 2 February 1904, all pretence was dropped when Russian forces crossed the Yalu River into Korea, after which matters took on a momentum of their own.

Tokyo had been processing these reports with increasing alarm. Frequent enquiries had been made for clarification but were met with silence, so when news of the movement into Korea was received the emperor summoned his president of the Privy Council, Prince Ito Hirobumi, for consultations. This produced a terse note, which was despatched to Moscow on 5 February: 'The obstinate refusals of Russia to respect China's territorial integrity in Manchuria ... have made it necessary for the Imperial Government to consider what measures of self-defence they are called upon to take.'[18] Diplomatic relations were severed and the Russian ambassador was presented with his passports. Unfazed, a certain General Wogack was confident that Japan had no plans to use force. He believed their protests were all bluster and was sure that 'there will be no such war. They would never try to fight us.'[19] He was quickly disabused.

Hostilities commenced with a coup de main against Port Arthur on the night of 8/9 February 1904 by Admiral Togo. Without an official declaration of war, torpedo boats sped into the harbour, badly damaging three ships, and when one ventured out both it and 600 of its crew was sent to the bottom. Novelist Thomas Cowen was among those stunned by the audacity of the attack, admitting, 'Few people seriously thought Japan would dare, even in self-defence, to strike the first blow... A puny Asiatic people could not think of such a thing.'[20] It had, an act that not only shocked the Russians but caught Beijing off-guard. So in order to allay its fears Tokyo promised on 17 February that it had 'not the slightest intention of acquiring territory as a result of the war at the expense of China. [Any] measures to be taken in the field of action... arising as they will from military necessities, will not be of a nature to infringe the sovereign rights of the Chinese Empire.'[21] Japanese Prime Minister Count Katsura followed the script when he assured visiting missionaries that 'the object of the present war, on the part of Japan is the security of the empire and the permanent peace of the East'.[22]

Such undertakings were academic in any case. Beijing could only look on as five divisions of infantry were landed above Port Arthur on 5 May, launching numerous assaults on the vital Mount Nanhan. Faced with stiff resistance, they were pulled back and the Russian positions were instead subjected to a ferocious bombardment. This was followed by a further assault on 27 May, which overwhelmed the shattered defenders. The Russians were now surrounded by land and sea, and by 1 June 80,000 Japanese had taken up positions whilst the fleet maintained a constant bombardment. Under this sustained pressure the Russian fleet attempted a breakout, but they were intercepted and sent back. Further Japanese assaults took 203 Metre Hill, which had a commanding view of the port and from here the Russians came under sustained artillery barrages until the garrison surrendered on 2 January 1905.

With this potential threat removed, 40,000 men were landed on the west coast of Korea and swiftly moved north. The Russians had concentrated their forces near Liaoyang thirty-five miles south of Mukden in southern Manchuria, leaving 7,000 troops on the Yalu River to prevent the Japanese from crossing. But these were far too few in number and on 1 May they were swept aside as the reinforced Japanese advanced northwest. On 25 August, 100,000 Japanese encountered roughly the same number of Russians at Liaoyang and a vast battle ensued, played out across an extended front. Finally, on 1 September, the exhausted Russians were halted and forced to withdraw northward towards Mukden, leaving 16,500 casualties behind to Japan's 23,500. Fighting resumed in mid-October, only stopping when the autumn rains made manoeuvre impossible, so both sides dug in and settled down for a long, cold winter. The Japanese used the lull to build their forces up to 300,000 men, and on 5 February 1905 launched a massive offensive towards Mukden along a forty-seven-mile front. They had hoped to encircle the Czarist forces but they managed to extricate themselves in brutal fighting that cost the Japanese another 50,000 casualties and the Russians twice as many.

Caught completely off-guard by the effectiveness of the Japanese naval forces, the Russian Baltic Fleet was ordered to steam halfway round the world in the hope that it would tip the balance. The forty-seven-strong armada, which included seven battleships and six cruisers, did not arrive at Tsushima Strait until 27 May 1905, and it immediately encountered Admiral Togo with a fleet of comparable size and was completely outmanoeuvred, outgunned and outclassed. In a brief half-hour engagement the Japanese sank one battleship, crippled another and scattered the rest. Togo followed closely as the Russians sought the protection of Vladivostok, sinking three more battleships en route. By 28 May, every ship save twelve of the once vaunted Baltic Fleet had been sunk, damaged or run aground for the loss of only three Japanese torpedo boats.

Despite winning on all fronts, the horrendously expensive war had nearly exhausted the Japanese treasury. Russia, on the verge of revolution following the fall of Port Arthur, now had domestic problems to address, so needed to bury its pride and agree to negotiate. When talks stalled, US President Roosevelt intervened and sugared the pill for the Japanese in July 1905 when the Taft-Katsura Agreement was signed recognising Japanese pre-eminence in Korea in return for Tokyo's acceptance of US dominance in the Philippines. Britain also undertook to renew the 1902 Alliance, further underpinning the country's new-found status. With Tokyo persuaded to return to the negotiating table, the two sides finally agreed to the Treaty of Portsmouth, signed on 5 September 1905.

This was the first defeat of a European power by an Asiatic one since China humbled Russia in 1689 and was a humiliating climbdown by a vast empire that had so blithely dismissed a smaller nation's claims to parity. For Japan, it was also sweet revenge for its put down by Russia in 1895. On the face of it, China, too, had been restored some self-respect, because both parties agreed under Article III to 'evacuate completely and simultaneously Manchuria except the territory affected by the lease of the Liaotung Peninsula ... and to restore entirely and completely to the exclusive administration of China all portions of Manchuria now in the occupation or under the control of the Japanese or Russian troops'.[23] However, unknown to Beijing, Articles V and VI transferred to Japan Russia's former leased territory on the peninsula, the city of Dalny, Port Arthur, and the southern portion of the Manchurian Railway. Tokyo also established the long-coveted protectorate over Korea and gained southern Sakhalin and the Kurile Islands. Russia did, however, refuse to pay an indemnity and the Japanese were persuaded not to press the matter.

Whilst the wider international community digested the scale of Tokyo's victory with some reservations, others were more upbeat. Japanophiles such as American academic Sidney Gulick naively welcomed the outcome of the war and, beguiled by Tokyo's claims of benign intentions, claimed that 'empire for the sake of glory is the last consideration in the Japanese mind',[24] endorsing instead its 'wholly altruistic motive of goodwill to Korea and China and her desire to stand for honest straightforward diplomacy'.[25] He would live to 1945, dying at the age of 85, by which time he would have had years to reflect upon the irony of these words.

Having been relegated to the status of virtual spectator, Beijing had no role to play other than rubber stamp the decisions made at Portsmouth, and on 22 December 1905 signed a document consenting to 'all transfers and assignments by Russia to Japan'.[26] A few days later Tokyo extracted from Beijing a further concession by which 'all materials required for the railways in South Manchuria shall be exempt from all duties, taxation and *Likin*'.[27] China also agreed not to construct 'any main line in the neighbourhood of, and parallel to that railway, or any branch line which might be prejudicial to the interests of the South Manchuria Railway'.[28] They even had to consult the Japanese if they planned to open any more towns to foreign trade.

The following year the South Manchuria Railway Company was officially formed to oversee Japanese interests and to supervise the Railway Zone. Here they set to work transforming the network, which had been started by the Russians in 1900 but had been done cheaply, was poorly equipped and inadequate for their needs. The lines were rebuilt and double tracked using the standard US gauge, curves straightened, grades reduced, tunnels and bridges built. The number of stations was increased from fifty-four to 114 and new workshops, roundhouses and warehouses constructed. The rebuilding of the Mukden-Antung line alone cost £12,000,000,[29] but the Japanese would consider it money well spent, as it was in preparation for their next step. That same year the Kwantung Army was formed to garrison their concessions in Manchuria, giving Japan rather than Russia a permanent military presence on Chinese soil. It would protect Tokyo's ambitious plans for colonising their zones of interest, relieving the population pressures becoming more acute at home. Count Goto Shinpei, the first Director General of the South Manchuria Railway and then Director of the Colonial Bureau, would devise a scheme for 500,000 settlers to colonise the areas around the railway, and in 1906 he founded the 'Aikawa Village' near the port of Dalny, now renamed Dairen.

At the same time, Tokyo was eager to mend fences with Russia, unprepared yet for another expensive conflict and keen to keep their new neighbour on side. An agreement was signed on 10 June 1907, containing the usual clichéd niceties, and promising mutual support for the preservation of peace and security in the 'regions' of China 'with a view to maintaining the respective situation and the territorial rights of the two contracting parties in the continent of Asia'.[30] These platitudes masked another, highly secret protocol which divided Manchuria into spheres of interest, followed on 4 July 1910 by a further treaty guaranteeing the exercise of special powers and the protection of increasing special interests in those areas not covered by the 1907 treaty.[31] These undertakings ignored Beijing's insistence that Manchuria remained its sovereign territory, but there was little it could do but protest.

Japan was also consolidating its hold on the Korean Peninsula. In 1905 it laid the foundations for a complete takeover when King Gujong was forced to accept a Resident General, who assumed responsibility for external relations. Whilst successive Residents were preparing the ground to absorb the country completely, in 1907 Gujong tried to escape their stranglehold by appealing to the second Hague Convention. When the Japanese discovered his plans, he was forced to abdicate in favour of his son Sunjong. Tokyo then forced the new king to sign a treaty giving it the right to intervene militarily, and to appoint Japanese ministers in his government. His army was disbanded and in 1909 the state's judicial power was dissolved. Finally, on 29 August 1910 he was coerced into making 'complete and permanent cession to His Majesty the Emperor of Japan of all rights and sovereignty over the whole of Korea'.[32] This was ostensibly done in the name of 'maintaining peace and stability [and to] promote the welfare and prosperity of Koreans'.[33] The new regime embarked upon a campaign of ethnocide.

The country's official name was changed to Chosen, the teaching of Korean was banned in schools, Buddhism and Confucianism was replaced by Shintoism, and to eradicate their cultural history entirely some 200,000 books were destroyed.[34] Even physical reminders were removed, the royal palace was almost entirely destroyed and thousands of native trees were replaced by Japanese varieties. Farmers living on the most fertile land were evicted and replaced by Japanese settlers, facing bleak futures as itinerant labourers in Manchuria and Japan. Those who resisted faced imprisonment and torture, and between 1905 and 1912 alone approximately 20,000 of those brave enough to resist were killed.[35]

Whilst Japan proceeded with its acquisitions, other powers were pursuing their own self-interests, and in 1903 the British mounted another expedition to Tibet. Still under nominal Chinese suzerainty, they agreed to evacuate after Beijing undertook to prevent any other power from establishing itself in the country. China itself then invaded in 1908, forcing the Dalai Lama to flee to India, but when in 1911 the Chinese garrison mutinied the Tibetans staged a coup and the Dalai Lama returned. A treaty led to the withdrawal of its garrison, but when Beijing planned another invasion the British intervened again. To guarantee future stability they sponsored a further treaty in 1914, which divided the country into Inner and Outer Tibet. Inner Tibet was to remain part of China and Outer Tibet become autonomous; any disagreements between the two were to be subject to British arbitration.

These and the other disasters that characterised the early 1900s had at least galvanised reformers into renewing their calls for change, but they were still confronted by the irreconcilables within the Forbidden City. As Governor Jaeshke explained in a cable to Berlin, 'at the moment there is a fierce struggle between two different ideologies in China; the national Chinese *Weltanschauung*, which rests on centuries-old traditions, and the cosmopolitan occidental *Weltanschauung*'.[36] However, Empress Cixi had been among those who underwent a Damascene conversion, finally accepting that the reforms so often scuppered in the past offered her dynasty its only hope of salvation. In April 1901 the Administration Office was established to produce 'New Policies', and missions were despatched to Japan, the US and Europe to glean best practice. Their findings would form the nucleus of a raft of reforms in areas such as education, the military, public administration and the constitution, to be implemented over a rolling nine-year period.

They began in 1902 when the binding of women's feet was finally abolished, and in 1904 the centuries-old system of civil service examinations was abandoned at last. The cumbersome sexagenary cycle would also give way to the Gregorian calendar, to bring the country in line with most of the rest of the world. In 1905 the diplomatic corps was overhauled, and in 1906 the old six boards system was replaced by eleven new ministries created to run key areas such as commerce, posts and communications. The same year a Supreme Court was established to reform the law and remove foreign justification for the right of extraterritoriality. Chambers of Commerce were also created and Port cities known as *Zikai Shangbu* established, which would compete with the Treaty Ports. In these, foreigners would be able to buy land and open businesses but unlike places such as Tianjin, they were under Chinese administration, not European control. They would also make possible the development of the hinterland and, it was hoped, bring prosperity to the countryside by connecting it and the ports by rail, road and canal. The study of sciences was opened to schools, eleven new colleges established across the country and curriculums modernised. These included the study of writers such as Aldous Huxley, John Stuart Mill and John Smith, and Japanese textbooks and professors were also imported.

Many modernisers believed that overseas education, particularly in the US, was key to the reformation and advancement the country needed. Diplomat Ying Huqinq explained in 1905 that this would allow students to become 'the interpreters and expositors of America to our own people [in a way] that no explaining in books by Americans themselves could accomplish'.[37] Such sentiments were echoed by influential bodies in the United States, and in 1907 Yale, Cornell and Wellesley Universities set up scholarships for ten men and three women, attracting 600 candidates for the exams arranged in Nanjing. Behind such altruism there lay more pragmatic ulterior motives. Edmund J. James, President of the University of Illinois, shared with President Wilson his belief that 'the nation which succeeds in educating the young Chinese will reap the largest possible returns in moral, intellectual and commercial influence'.[38] Perhaps the US Congress had this in mind when it voted to return its $10,800,000 share of the Boxer Indemnity on condition that the money was used to finance a university in Beijing. The offer was duly taken up, and in 1912 the Tsing Hua Imperial College was opened.

Mandarins were also despatched to Washington to study the American constitutional model, and in October 1909 elected provincial assemblies were formed. But when plans were set in play for a National Assembly, concerns were raised that they were going too far too fast. Liang Qichao, a former imperial adviser and reformer who had visited the United States and Canada in 1903, demurred at the prospect of full democracy. Seeing first-hand the workings of government there, he was more than ever convinced that his own country was not yet ready for such a leap of faith. 'If we were to adopt a democratic system of government now, it would be nothing less than committing national suicide ... the Chinese people of today can only be governed autocratically; they cannot enjoy freedom'[39] Oriental scholar and linguist Sir Edmund Backhouse concurred. He asserted that democracy simply would not work, and that it would only herald the return of 'throne and court'.[40]

In the meantime the military again came under the spotlight, as it seemed that even the humiliation of 1900 had failed to convince the anti-modernisers. Returning from covering the war, correspondent George Lynch saw troops still 'practising with bows and arrows at targets when riding on horseback at the full gallop and taking apparently as much interest in this as they did in rifle practice'.[41] So, determined once and for all to force meaningful change, Yuan Shikai incorporated the Self-Strengthening Army into the newly created Beiyang Army. The last remnants of the Yongying, Lianjun and Green Standard forces were also broken up to form provincial standing armies, or 'Changbeijin'. The best men were recruited to these, the second best to reserve or constabulary formations and the rest were pensioned off. In 1901, the old entry examination was finally abolished and military academies were created in every province, while some students were also sent to Japan. In 1903, a Commission for Army Reorganisation was set up to centralise policies and standardise organisation, and in 1904 it began a plan for a nationwide system of education by opening military primary schools in every province, secondary schools in four key cities, and officer and staff colleges in the capital. By 1911 the New Armies overall had seventeen out of the planned thirty-six divisions and twenty independent or mixed brigades in place. Nonetheless, these measures did little to reduce the power and influence of those forces who remained loyal to warlords in key provinces.

Any reforms, no matter how enthusiastically they were embraced, were too little too late for many. The optics therefore did not look good, especially with men such as Kang Youwei using their influence abroad to spread the cause of revolution and seek help wherever it could be found. One such sponsor was Japanese Tayama Mitsuru, an ultra-nationalist and avowed expansionist who saw in revolution his country's best chance to extend its own power. He warmed to one particularly promising disciple, Sun Yat-sen, who in 1904 published his credo of nationalism, democracy and socialism within a republican system. He brought various dissident groups under one umbrella organisation, the Revolutionary Alliance, later the Kuomintang (KMT), which from 1906 mounted a concerted campaign against the Qings. At one stage, he even courted Li Hongzhang, urging him to join his movement and declare the independence of Guangdong and Guanxi Provinces. To men like Mitsuru, he seemed the ideal candidate for fulfilling his plans.

Their chance seemed to have come when Dowager Empress Cixi died in 1908, one day before Guangxu. Their passing left only Cixi's nominee for the throne, the three-year-old Henry Pu Yi, on whose behalf his father Prince Chun was appointed regent. Lacking even the discredited authority of the old guard, the tattered threads began to unravel quickly. Although he tried to bring constitutional reform forward, his clumsy handling of it produced even more problems. His creation of a ministerial cabinet was a wise enough move, but he caused friction right away when he appointed eight Manchus, one Mongol Bannerman but only four Han Chinese. Regional and provincial jealousies also clashed with the reform's contradictory attempts to devolve powers in some areas but promote a stronger central government in others. Reforms to education and the army were among the measures most resented by governors and emerging warlords, and when in 1910 a decree was issued announcing the nationalisation of the railways, many of which had been funded and built provincially, there was an outcry. Furthermore, the money to pay for both the nationalisation and further modernisation was to be secured with more loans from foreign banks, a move seen as an egregious sell out to foreign interests.

Riots broke out in Szechuan which spread quickly, sparking an army mutiny in Wuchung in October 1911. The dominoes then fell with incredible speed, and by the end of November fifteen provinces had seceded from the Empire, their delegates proclaiming a republic on 29 December. This, the Xinhai Revolution, finally swept away 2,132 years of imperial rule and 276 years of the Qing dynasty, heralding a great new era under Sun Yat-sen who returned from exile as leader of the KMT. He was elected Provisional President, but immediately faced so much internal bickering that he agreed to step aside in the interests of unity in favour of Yuan Shikai. He was then elected Provisional President by the Nanking Provisional Senate in February 1912 and plans were put in place for the country's first democratic elections. In February 1913, the KMT won the elections with its *Minguo*, or 'People's Nation' slogan, and the National Assembly opened in April 1913. But Shikai soon demonstrated that he shared none of the democratic aspirations of the KMT, and Liang Qichao's prediction would prove prescient.

In May 1913 trouble flared after Shikai was accused of purging anyone he saw as a threat to his position. Matters came to a head when he replaced KMT governors in the provinces with his own placemen, provoking renewed declarations of independence to which he responded by sending his Beiyang Army, freshly equipped with the proceeds of a £25,000,000 'Reorganisation Loan' secured from Britain, France, Russia, Germany and Japan. The rebels were soon crushed and Sun Yat-sen fled to Japan, leaving Shikai free to be appointed president for life. Having secured international recognition, he dissolved the fledgling Parliament in January 1914 and replaced it with a pliant sixty-six-man junta. This immediately approved a 'constitutional compact' in place of the Provisional Constitution and granted him dictatorial powers. American academician Frank Johnson Goodnow, who had ironically been appointed his constitutional adviser in March 1913, soon became disenchanted with the turn of events. He concluded that the chaos and anarchy was proof that the regime had lost control and that 'the old ideas of Chinese absolutism are now in the ascendancy ... the prospect of adopting a constitution on western lines has been set back for perhaps twenty-five years; indeed such a constitution may never be adopted'.[42]

These were troubling times, but for now at least the turmoil engulfing the nascent republic could be observed with relative detachment by the country's 70,000 or so foreign residents. Secure behind their extraterritorial privileges, for them it was pretty much business as usual.

7

A Place of Dingy Dilapidation

Life for the early Portuguese residents in the modest enclave of Macao had been perhaps the most settled of all. It had not been acquired by extortion or coercion and was therefore relatively free of the antipathy felt towards foreigners in other parts of the country. So as long as its residents observed the by-laws and paid their dues to Beijing, they were left pretty much to their own devices. By 1583 there were around 900 Portuguese nationals out of a total population of 2,000. By 1622, this figure had increased to 2,000 Portuguese, 20,000 Chinese, and about 5,000 slaves imported from Angola and Mozambique. There appears to have been little mixing however. When Aeneas Anderson dropped by on his return from Beijing in 1794 he noted that the locals still observed their customs 'with a rigid preference, nor has the long intercourse they have had with Europeans ... induced them to deviate in the least article from the long established and, as it appears, invariable usages of their country'.[1]

The Chinese were not alone in wishing to keep the rest of the population at arm's length. The Portuguese had instituted a strict pecking order based on race, with themselves at the top, forming the colony's aristocracy. They were headed by the governor who took charge of defence and external affairs, and below him sat the town council or *Camara*, handling finances and the day-to-day running of the territory. Then came the ordinary merchants, and at the bottom those of mixed race and the native population.

A Place of Dingy Dilapidation

One other layer in the territory's hierarchy was its missionary community. They had established themselves early on, founding a college in 1562 and the *Hospital dos Probres* in 1568, the first in China, for the care of lepers. The *Santa Casa da Misericordia*, or House of Mercy followed in 1569, treating the sick and later serving as an orphanage and sanctuary for the wives of sailors lost at sea. In the early 1600s, Clarissa nuns travelled from the Philippines to found the Santa Clara Convent, grounding the territory's reputation as a centre for religious devotion and good works. It was created a diocese in 1576 and a city in 1586.

Its size certainly belied the role it played in the Portuguese economy. From its inception, merchants enjoyed a virtual monopoly not only through the China-Macao-Japan triangular trade, but with Vietnam, Thailand, the East Indies and the Philippines. As we have seen, it was able to preserve this position through its unique relationship with Beijing, and its determination to prevent anyone else from sharing its good fortune. But from about 1639, stagnation began to set in. First, Japan closed itself off from foreigners entirely, and the coast was sealed in the 1650s in response to the anti-Qing rebellions. Even the liberalisation of trade in the 1680s was a double-edged sword as the new ports brought unwelcome competition. Although the restrictive terms imposed on them by Beijing were advantageous to Macao for a while, they would ultimately seal its fate. By the end of the eighteenth century it was on the wane, and when Aeneas Anderson visited he was singularly unimpressed by its modest size, especially compared to Guangzhou: 'The whole extent of the Portuguese possession does not exceed four miles in length and one mile and a half in breadth.'[2] He also found its buildings unprepossessing, noting that although they were made of stone, 'and constructed on the plan of European architecture [they were] without exterior elegance'.[3] Its small size meant that 'the streets[were] very narrow and irregular',[4] making traversing them something of a challenge. Nor was there very much chance of expansion because 'a fort prevents strangers from passing the limits of it ... no one is suffered to walk on the neck of land, nor is any boat permitted to approach their side of the shore'.[5]

Business revived somewhat during the French Revolutionary Wars of 1792 to 1802, because Portugal was neutral and largely immune from the interruptions which affected other European nations. Then in 1802 and 1808 during the Napoleonic Wars, Britain attempted to seize the island on the pretext of protecting Portugal's interests. The two countries did have a longstanding treaty, and this was used to justify the action, but the Chinese saw through the ruse and ordered them to leave. Thereafter, the territory was left to its own devices and following Britain's possession of Hong Kong the British no longer had any interest in it. But the competition was seriously affecting its trade, and by this stage an average of just ten ships a year were calling in. English panoramic painter Robert Burford, saw that with its declining trade 'the desolation becomes more apparent every year [and although] the inner harbour is spacious and capable of affording anchorage to a large number of ships of three or four hundred tons, larger ships must be lightered before they can come in'.[6] He blamed this state of affairs in large part on the Chinese themselves: 'The jealousies which have always led them to endeavour to curtail the few privileges granted have all tended to depress their trade.' Although they had originally granted permission for twenty-five vessels to enter the harbour at any one time, this number had never been revised and consequently, 'the same number only can receive that indulgence at present ... all others must lie in Macao roads'.[7] Because, noted Burford, 'no vigorous efforts have been made to redeem their losses ... decay is visibly stamped on everything, both civil and religious'.[8]

Things began to look up the 1840s, when the Portuguese were able to take advantage of China's misfortunes. A tough new governor, Joao Ferriera, was installed, who proceeded to dispense with many of the restrictions still being imposed. In 1845 he declared the territory a freeport, and in 1849 cancelled the rent payable to Beijing and closed down the Chinese customs house. He also ordered the construction of a road from the walled city north to the border post. These measures understandably incurred the displeasure of Beijing, but it emerged the loser from the resulting spat when the Portuguese kept their reforms and annexed two more islands for good measure. Still more control was gradually clawed back until in 1887 a Treaty of Friendship and Commerce finally recognised Portuguese sovereignty and its right to permanent occupation. Beijing's ongoing problems then encouraged the seizure of Ilha Verde in 1890, a kilometre offshore, along with some other smaller islands. Nonetheless, Lord Curzon, who passed through a few years later, thought it was still a place of 'dingy dilapidation... illustrating so eloquently the decline and fall of a once conquering race'.[9]

When James Dyer, author of *Cantonese Made Easy*, visited in 1908, he was rather more upbeat. The number of foreign residents was now only around 3,800, but the Chinese population had grown to 60,000.[10] He found the streets 'beautifully clean ... public and private buildings are often gaily coloured'.[11] Indeed he added, 'One of the most striking features about the public buildings in Macao is the clean state in which they are kept, affording a striking contrast to those in Hong Kong.'[12] He also encountered major infrastructure projects. Although many streets were still 'exceedingly narrow and tortuous ... newer roads and the boulevard [had been] recently formed on what used to be the Campo without the city walls and below the Guia fort and lighthouse'.[13] Some of this was due to the extensive land reclamation which was being undertaken, including the outer avenue of the Inner Harbour, and to the north the *Portos do Cercos* started in the 1880s. Ilha Verde would eventually be entirely subsumed by such schemes.

Although the outer harbour remained too shallow for larger vessels and the inner harbour was still silting up, the port enjoyed another renaissance. In 1906 it hosted a total of 1,782 steamships grossing 819,340 tons and 4,283 junks which imported wood, bricks, medicines, rice, oil, coal, wine and sugar cane to the value of $26,846,825.[14] They were serviced by Deacon and Company, which operated as agents for the P&O Line, and there were also a few shipping merchants and commissioning agents. Some junk building and sail making survived, and there was a cement works, a flour mill, shoe, tea, fruit and cigarette factories, a silk filature and an opium boiling facility, which alone accounted for $334,000 in revenue.[15] Despite this, the territory had come to rely increasingly on fantan gambling, of which the government enjoyed a monopoly. This yielded $456,000 in 1906, added to which were various lotteries bringing in another $222,000, a third of all the colony's revenue.[16] When the authorities in Guangdong outlawed gambling altogether and the dens moved to Macao, the industry really took off, and following the introduction of casinos it earned the epithet of the 'Monte Carlo of the East', a reputation it enjoys to this day.

Macao's nemesis Guangzhou continued to prosper and had a population of around 3,000,000 by the 1890s, 50,000 of whom still lived on the omnipresent junks. The Foreign Office report for 1903 revealed that trade valued at £14,568,000 had been carried in and out by 2,589,000 tons of shipping. Imports consisted of socks, towels, flannel and other cotton goods, plus clocks, umbrellas, oil from Sumatra and wines and spirits for its burgeoning middle class. Silk was still big business, and some 99,000 hundredweight had been exported that year. In addition, it sold tea, cassia, chinaware, jade, brown sugar and eggs. A more curious export was human hair to Japan, where it was processed and turned into rope and wigs.[17] Acting Consul-General C.W. Campbell was nonetheless highly critical of his compatriots' persistent inability to learn the language. He found it exasperating that 'there is not a single member of an important foreign firm who can converse with a native in decent Cantonese, or who can attempt to check a simple correspondence in Chinese writing'.[18] This he explained put them at a considerable disadvantage when it came to commerce, and even after all these years the compradors remained a key element when conducting business.

It also appeared to have changed little physically. Visitor Arnold Wright remarked in 1908 that much of it remained 'a labyrinth of some 600 evil-smelling, simply lighted stone-flagged streets ... so narrow that in the widest of them four men would find it hard to walk abreast'.[19] Little had changed twelve years later when C. A. Middleton Smith passed through. Although steps were being taken to demolish its restrictive walls and build roads wide enough for vehicular traffic and trams to be introduced, he found that 'only a sedan chair can pass between the shops, and only at certain places can one chair pass another'.[20] Modernity was slow in coming on the river, where 'wooden stern-wheel passenger boats propelled by a dozen men who appear to be walking the treadmill' still plied their trade, curious reminders of a bygone age.[21]

Such relics however, had long been overshadowed by the march of modernity in other areas. There was now a state-of-the-art telephone network that had 11,000 subscribers paying $5.00

a month for its services, plus modern banks, merchant houses, schools, clubs and libraries. Some of these however, shared the Bund with 'tempting gaming houses with their gaudy Chinese signs and other garish attractions [where] the gay life never ceases',[22] drawing the curious foreigner and seasoned local alike to risk their shirts. It was in part at least to deter impressionable young people from succumbing to their allure that high-minded citizens had opened a YMCA. This offered rather more conventional pastimes such as a swimming pool and science lectures, although whether or not they succeeded is not recorded.

Both Macao and Guangzhou had long lain under the shadow of Hong Kong, which in 1842 was still a modest fishing and pastoral community of around 15,000, an inauspicious island eleven miles long east to west. Here fishermen lived cheek by jowl with pirates, their nefarious activities now rudely interrupted by the march of progress. Nonetheless, despite the inevitable disruption the newcomers brought they appeared sanguine enough. Indeed, a British military surgeon found them 'industrious and obliging ... very peaceably disposed'. They did not exhibit 'any marked approbation or disapprobation on their transfer to British sway'.[23] In any case, those arriving from places such as Guangzhou were not much interested in competing for fish or booty. They looked to the potential profits to be made from the harbour, which Scottish Botanist Robert Fortune described as

> ... one of the finest which I have ever seen: it is eight or ten miles in length, and irregular in breadth; in some places two, and in others six miles wide, having excellent anchorage all over it, and perfectly free from hidden dangers. It is completely sheltered by the mountains of Hong Kong on the south, and by those of the mainland of China on the opposite shore; landlocked in fact, on all sides, so that the shipping can ride out the heaviest gales with perfect safety.[24]

Apart from its potential as a seaport, there was not much else to recommend it. In what was to become Victoria, the waterfront on the northwest of the island, visitor Arnold Wright found only a few dilapidated ruins 'scattered about the foreshore, either quaint improvised huts [or] ramshackle habitations constructed out of junks'.[25] Neither did it appear to the casual observer to be a particularly well-appointed site for development. It consisted of a rugged slope of sheer rock shelving, which led precipitously down to the water's edge, with just a narrow pathway winding along the cliff. Indeed, Queen Victoria herself is reported to have referred to this latest addition to her empire as little more than 'a scarcely populated, barren granite rock', not really worth her time.[26]

Not surprisingly, business was initially slow to pick up, and early speculators feared having backed the wrong horse. Nor did its fetid and unhealthy water and the diseases it encouraged help to sell it as a place of business, one trader condemning it as being in 'a condition of extreme decay'.[27] Montgomery Martin's verdict was particularly damning: 'There does not appear to be the slightest probability Hong Kong will ever become a place of trade.'[28] He recommended that they cut their losses, abandon the entire enterprise and transfer all business to Guangzhou. A House of Commons Select Committee reached a similar conclusion: 'We cannot be said to have derived directly much commercial advantage, nor indeed does it seem to be likely by its position to become the seat of an extended commerce.'[29] Nonetheless, as merchants, stonemasons, bricklayers and carpenters arrived, the colony witnessed something of a boom, with the construction of government buildings, post offices, warehouses, shops, wharves and piers. Altogether, the early colony assumed the appearance a frontier town, and it was these early pioneers, armed with incredible self-belief and determination, who helped to confound the critics.

The population quickly jumped from 5,000 in 1842 to 24,000 in 1848, by which time approximately 229,465 tons of shipping were using the port annually, growing revenue from £9,500 to £31,000 over the same period.[30] The creation of joint stock enterprises and the establishment in 1864 of the Hong Kong and Shanghai Bank proved an added fillip to growth. This massive vote of confidence meant that it was no longer necessary to draw on the resources of Indian banks for capital, the bank could finance further improvements to port facilities and other important projects itself. This created steamer and cable links to San Francisco, Singapore, Malaya, Indo China, London, New York, the Dutch East Indies

A Place of Dingy Dilapidation

and Japan. The opening of the Suez Canal in 1869 attracted more shipping and served as further stimulus to trade. The discovery of gold in America brought thousands of Chinese prospectors through the island seeking their fortunes across the Pacific Ocean, and many of those who struck gold returned to the colony to set up more businesses. Likewise, the Taiping Rebellion and other upheavals produced thousands of refugees, those who remained adding further to the growing population and becoming more or less productive members of the community.

In 1898, the harbour was utilised by Commodore George Dewey as a staging post in his preparations for the invasion of the Philippines, and by 1907 it was handling over 6,000,000 passenger arrivals and 5,300,000 departures a year.[31] By the 1890s more than 15,500,000 tons of shipping were also passing through annually, of which over 8,000,000 was British. In 1897 alone, the total value of trade handled in the colony was £50,000,000.[32] There were also ship repair and building concerns employing 12,000 workers, sugar refining, cotton-spinning and weaving industries, flour mills, soap factories, timber traders, ginger factories and engineering companies. Some of these were Chinese businesses, such as Kwong Hip Lung and Co., established in 1877, and Tung Tai Shung Kee and Co., established in 1897. A sizeable German presence in the colony was represented by Siemssen and Co. and Arnold and Co., and there were Germans on the board of the HSBC Bank. By the 1890s German merchants were involved in about half of all trading and re-exportation business, commentator Middleton Smith attributing such success to their more gregarious and outgoing 'hail fellow, well met'[33] demeanours, in contrast to the more staid and conservative Britons.

Among the less legitimate traders were the pimps who managed its many brothels. *Mui Tsai*, young girls bought from families too poor to keep them and often sold into lives of servitude and prostitution, would service their clientele both aboard junks and on terra firma. Alongside these came the inevitable opium dens which also prospered, twenty having been opened by 1844,[34] and to ensure that the government remained the sole legitimate beneficiary, fines ranging from $100-150 could be levied on anyone operating without a licence.[35] More income was derived from bhang, an edible concoction made from the leaves of the cannabis plant.

But by the 1860s it was risking becoming a victim of its own success, the already unhealthy climate exposing the population to plague and other diseases. Visitor Robert Swinhoe observed that it was developing a reputation for being 'one of the most unhealthy places on the earth's surface, owing to the settlement being completely shut in from the gentle southerly gales by the towering rocks that rise behind it, [which] retain for hours long after sunset the violent heat'.[36] The best solution to this problem was expansion, and beginning in 1851 the first of a number of land reclamation schemes was started along Victoria, a process which continued into the next century. This alone was not sufficient and, as Swinhoe explained 'the opposite peninsula of Kowloon has been for years looked to with longing eyes by the community as a spot that ought to become British property, where merchants might build their bungalows and enjoy the evening breeze'.[37] This ambition was realised after the 1860 Treaty ceded eight square miles of the southern portion of Kowloon and Stonecutters Island, resulting in another spate of development, including the Royal Navy depot.

No amount of judicious real estate acquisition could protect the colony from the frequent typhoons. One in particular, which struck on 22 September 1874, left in its wake such destruction that eyewitness Doctor Eitel thought it looked 'as if it had undergone a terrific bombardment. Thousands of houses unroofed, hundreds of dwellings in ruins'.[38] The cost of the damage was estimated to have been as much as $5,000,000. Another in 1904 killed 10,000 people and required more millions of dollars to repair. The compact layout of the city made frequent fires an added peril and particularly serious conflagrations broke out in 1851, 1867, 1878, and 1904, all of which called upon the valour of the volunteer fire service. But not plague, wind or fire could stop the entrepreneurialism of the colony's residents.

In 1865 gaslighting was introduced in Victoria, Kowloon following suit in 1892. Trams were brought into the colony in 1888 when the Peak Tramway was finished, a funicular railway that provided access to the top of the 1,774-foot Victoria Peak. Dominating the colony, it not only dispensed with the need for visitors to endure an uncomfortable sedan chair ride but opened the area up as a prestigious residential district with houses and villas built in the English style. From here wrote one visitor, the colony's elite could quite literally 'look down on everything and everybody'.[39] In addition to English style homes, there was the Happy Valley racecourse opened in 1845, the Hong Kong Club founded in 1846 from which 'shopkeepers, Chinese, Indians, women and other undesirables' were excluded,[40] and the Jockey Club, founded in 1884. The educational and health needs of the population were not neglected, and in 1862 many of the existing village schools were amalgamated and the Central School for Boys opened. Its original aim was to educate only Chinese scholars, and qualify them for employment with European firms, although later it broadened its appeal to attract Indian, British, Japanese and Thai pupils.

In 1872, the 244-bed Tung Wah Hospital was opened, funded by wealthy Chinese benefactors for those who did not trust Western notions of health care. In 1887, the Hong Kong College of Medicine was founded, allowing Chinese students to study for medical degrees, followed in 1912 by the University of Hong Kong.

All well and good, but it had long been recognised that its continued viability was compromised by being constrained to Hong Kong Island and part of Kowloon. As we have seen, it was also feeling vulnerable to encroachment by the other Powers as they scrambled for similar concessions. Such considerations compelled the authorities to look north to the largely rural land lying temptingly between Kowloon and Guangdong Province. Its acquisition would also furnish food and additional supplies of much needed fresh water. Unlike their compatriots fifty years before, however, its residents found the prospect of falling under British dominion less attractive and feared for their traditional way of life. Village elders were uneasy about loss of personal power and prestige, and when news of the proposed transfer leaked out there was resistance, both violent and non-violent. Arson, vandalism and attacks on strangers were committed but all was in vain; once the British had made their minds up, opposition was to little avail.

Led by redoubtable Ambassador Sir Claude MacDonald, a convention was agreed, leasing the so-called New Territories for ninety-nine years with effect from 1 July 1898. This increased

Britain's footprint by a factor of ten in one fell swoop, adding 365 square miles of real estate, which included 235 outlying islands and 300,000 people. There remained the issue of its recalcitrant locals, but reassured that their lifestyles would go on pretty much as before, with the elders left to keep order and make sure taxes were paid, they largely accepted their lot. There were inevitably some changes, and between 1899 and 1901 eight new harbour master offices were opened for the issuing of licences and permits and the collection of fines and dues. To maintain order, two NCOs and twenty-two other ranks of the Royal Welsh Fusiliers were temporarily seconded to serve as Special Constables, and three new police stations were opened. It also lived up to the hopes that it would enhance the colony's water supply by providing an additional 100,000 gallons a day, and in 1902 the construction of a reservoir with a capacity of 350,000,000 gallons was begun.[41] The New Territories soon became a popular and very healthy escape from the confines of Kowloon and the island, a destination for excursions. As a result, the death rate due to illness, which stood at sixty-four in every thousand of the foreign population in the early days, would plummet to just fourteen.[42] By the turn of the century Hong Kong had earned much praise from those who had come to see it for themselves, among them the usually critical Lord Curzon. He was proud to admit that to him it epitomised the far-flung British Empire, being the 'furthermost eastern link in that chain of fortresses which from Spain to China girdles half the globe'.[43]

Some 1,200 miles to the northeast lay Shanghai, a thriving city port which would eventually earn the accolade 'Paris of the East'. However, the waterway upon which it sat was no Seine, Middleton Smith observing that the approach to it was 'as ugly as that to Hong Kong is beautiful. It is thirteen dreary miles from the sea up to Shanghai, and the country is as flat as that of the Thames near Tilbury.'[44] Nonetheless, it was worth the ennui of the journey to find, as the *Twentieth Century Impressions of Hong Kong, Shanghai and Other Treaty Ports of China* explained in 1908 that 'from Woosung to Shanghai the river is alive with shipping ... a constant succession of tenders, lighters, junks and sampans is met at all states of the tide'.[45] Through such frenetic activity the port had prospered pretty much from its inception in 1844, when it was already exporting 1,500,000 pounds of tea and 4,000 bales of silk a year. In return nearly 500,000 items of British manufactures were pouring in, yielding £488,000 in revenue, turnover that grew exponentially until by the turn of the century 7,696,674 tons of shipping was providing trade worth over £14,500,000.[46] Adding to its wealth were such concerns as the successful Indian firm of textile exporters Tata and Sons, and shipbuilding and engineering giant Farnham Boyd and Co. Ltd. Founded in 1865 as one of the earliest ship repair facilities in China, by the turn of the century its workshops, offices and docks covered sixteen acres of prime real estate. Other businesses included cement making, cotton spinning, silk filature, match and paper making, packing and flour milling, so that within a decade the city would account for a third of all the customs revenue raised by the treaty ports and 63% of their trade. By the 1930s, 75 per cent of all British investment would be funnelled through this one port.

A foreign population of just 276 in 1864 had grown by the end of the century into a cosmopolitan blend of 4,465 British, 3,361 Japanese, 1,495 Portuguese and 940 Americans. There were also 317 Russians, 113 Danes, eighty-three Turkish, forty-nine Persians, eleven Egyptians and seven Brazilians.[47] At the heart of this bustling metropolis sat the 5,584-acre British concession, the residents of which had come to refer to themselves as Shanghailanders. A French concession followed in 1849, and a US one in 1854, but in 1863 the Americans and British merged to become the International Settlement. By 1918 another nineteen nations had joined, abiding by the rulings of its governing body, the Shanghai International Settlement Municipal Council. Elected annually on a property-based franchise of 2,700, it managed nearly every facet of the International Settlement's life. This included the sale of opium, control of prostitution, gas and electricity and postal services, its police and fire brigade. By the 1900s, the police force of European Superintendents and Inspectors and 604 Chinese and 167 Sikh constables presided over what had become an apparently law-abiding town. Figures for 1902 recorded a mere fifty-two cases of larceny from the person, six of robbery and just three murders. Of all the 10,000 arrests made, the vast majority were for petty offences, such as loitering, letting off fireworks or keeping a dirty rickshaw.[48] More serious misdemeanours could be tried in the Mixed Court, opened in 1863 for cases in which foreigners were also involved. Presided over by a Chinese magistrate and one American, French or British assessor attending in rotation, if found guilty the miscreant could be sent to prison or sentenced to wearing the cangue, the awful wooden block which was secured around the neck.

The fire brigade was an all-volunteer organisation formed in 1866 and proved indispensable in such a tight-packed and volatile city, fighting 102 fires in 1902 alone.[49] The Shanghai Volunteer Corps was formed hastily during the disruptions of the Taiping and other upheavals, and also served during the Boxer conflict. It consisted of representatives from most of the foreign concessions and if necessary, could supplement the police. The stability and continuity this arrangement delivered almost uninterrupted progress and modernisation, with the first telephone company setting up business in 1881 and electric lighting being installed in 1883. Not surprisingly in such a racially diverse city there were seventy-three Chinese and twenty-five foreign language newspapers for sale, including the English language *North China Daily* and *Shanghai Mercury*, the French *Echo de Chine*, *Der Ostasiatische Lloyd* for German readers and the Chinese *Sin Vung Pao Kway*.[50]

Architecturally avant-garde offices, trading houses and banks lined the sprawling waterfront, or Bund, which ran along the western bank of the Huangpu River. The massive Customs House would dominate the skyline from 1927, sitting alongside the Imperial Bank of China built in the 1890s and the Hong Kong and Shanghai Bank built in the 1920s. The *Banque de L'Indo Chine* catered for the French, the *Deutsche Asiatische Bank* for German customers, the Netherlands Trading Society the Dutch, and the Russo-German Bank and the Sino-Belgian Bank served their respective nationalities. The meteoric rise in real estate values is illustrated by the example of Jardine-Matheson, whose offices were the oldest on the Bund. When the land was purchased in 1852 it cost just $500, but by the turn of the century was estimated to be worth over $1,000,000.[51] In fact, the total value of all the real estate in the city had been valued in 1881 at £14,250,000,[52] but by the 1920s it had increased three thousandfold in seventy-five years.

A Place of Dingy Dilapidation

Its merchants' and businessmen's lifestyles naturally reflected this wealth. They returned home each evening to houses that could have been plucked straight out of the Home Counties of England, or Renaissance or Palladian Italy, distinguished only by their Chinese servants, gardeners and chauffeurs. Leaving their loyal retainers to their labours, those seeking relaxation and entertainment could take a trip to the cinema or the Lyceum Theatre. For the more energetic there were yacht, cricket, baseball and rowing clubs and a swimming baths, fox hunting or pheasant shoots. American correspondent Eliza Scidmore described the social life as 'formal, exacting, elaborate and extravagant',[53] and this self-indulgence grated on those excluded from such affluence. One Chinese critic saw them as people who 'only care about the value of gold and silver and do not know the origin of elegance'.[54] He may have had in mind, too, the opium shops which could be found in Foochow Road, but long-time resident Reverend C. E. Darwent disputed such claims as a calumny. He instead proudly cited the existence of the Shanghai Library, founded in 1849 and stocking 12,000 books. This equated to three per British resident, comparing very favourably with London's total of 4,000,000 works, or just two-thirds of a volume per head. This he asserted with evident pride, 'gives the lie to the ridiculous taunt that people in the treaty ports are a set of brainless pleasure seekers'.[55]

The number of churches which ministered to the spiritual needs of the population also suggested that its residents did not only worship mammon. These included Holy Trinity Anglican Church, the American Episcopal Church and a synagogue. The less spiritual could avail themselves of social clubs such as the St George's Association, the American Association, the *Deutsche Vereinigung*, the Swiss Community, the Club Concordia, *Club Portuguez*, and the YMCA. Their sons' and daughters' educational needs were met by a number of institutions, including the Shanghai Public School founded in 1886, the *Ecole Municipale*, and the *Deutsche Schule*. There were also mission schools such as the Mary Farnham Girls School for Presbyterians, founded in 1861, and St Xaviers College for Roman Catholics, established in 1864.

A number of steamship companies offered regular sailings to Southampton, London, Seattle, San Francisco, Nagasaki,

Yokohama, and Vladivostok. Arrivals could stay at the Astor House in Whangpoo Road, or the Central Hotel on the Bund. Hunger might be sated at the Restaurant Milan in Szechuan Road or the Grill Room in Canton Road, which offered breakfast for $35 and dinner for $30. Friends and relatives back home could be kept up to date with postcards despatched from any of the French, German, Japanese, Russian and American post offices in the city. They might wish to describe their experience of riding on one of the city's 5,000 rickshaws, fares ranging from five to fifteen cents, but they would be well advised to heed Reverend Darwent's warning that 'Coolies frequently attempt to extort exorbitant fares from newcomers. The visitor must not let himself be imposed upon.'[56] Likewise the avid souvenir hunter had to take care not to be duped. He knew of many a canny shop owner who 'having observed that the foreign devil wants brasses from the Ming dynasty ... has promptly supplied them in unlimited quantities'.[57]

As elsewhere, the indigenous Chinese were virtually excluded from participation in the everyday life of the Settlement. Under title deeds of 1848 no Chinese national could legally own land or property within it and foreigners were not allowed to let or rent land to them. A particular source of resentment was that Huangpu Park at the northern end of the Bund was reserved for foreign nationals. A 1913 Methodist guidebook entitled 'What the Chinese in Shanghai Ought to Know' described a sign at the entrance which stated, 'Unless accompanied by a westerner, Chinese are not allowed to enter. Dogs and bicycles are definitely forbidden to enter.'[58] This soon allegedly became simply 'No dogs or Chinese allowed'. Those who could gain access were not even entitled to use the chairs in the park when a concert was playing. When the city became home to stateless White Russians in the early 1920s, Chinese lowly status was highlighted further. Not only were the refugees treated better than the Chinese residents, the newcomers soon adopted the same discriminatory attitudes towards them as their hosts. Nonetheless, the *North China Daily News* of 1913 expressed little sympathy for their plight, one editorial claiming bluntly that 'they knew what to expect when they came to live in the Settlement'.[59]

Although banned from parks reserved to foreigners, in 1890 the authorities sought to compensate by providing the Chinese

Gardens on Soochow Road for their exclusive use. In the meantime, traditional festivals provided experiences which foreigners could share without risking too much of a scandal, with New Year, the Feasts of Lanterns and Tsing Ming, the Dai Wong Festival and the Dragon Boat Festival in the calendar. The native population also benefited from the good offices of the American Episcopal Church, which founded a hospital in 1869 for 100 Chinese men and fifty women, and in 1900 an isolation hospital was opened for 150 patients. Schools had been established, such as St John's College and the Anglo-Chinese School, in which it was hoped Western knowledge could be imparted to the children. Nonetheless, it was only after more liberal attitudes became acceptable in later years that there was any noticeable increase in interactions between the races.

Tianjin, over 740 miles to the northwest, appears to have put its unfortunate history behind it, and was turning over around £8,000,000 a year by the 1890s. Imports mainly consisted of cotton goods, yarn, sugar, railway material, flour, paper, kerosene oil and cigarettes. Exports were primarily of sheep, camel and goats' wool, goat- and sheepskins, bristles and ground nuts.[60] The 1,326,663 tons of shipping which carried this trade also yielded further income from duties and charges, which had grown from £85,500 in 1888 to £139,000 by 1897.[61] Various businesses had made their homes there, engaging in maize distillation, salt, coal, wool, goatskin, and fur processing.[62]

Its population of 1,984 Japanese, 600 British, 500 Germans, 250 French, 150 Americans, fifty Russians, forty-five Austro-Hungarians and twenty-five Belgians lived among its million or so Chinese in their traditional concessions.[63] These sat to the southeast along the banks of the Hai Ho River, on the west bank resided the Japanese, French, British and German, and on the eastern the Austro-Hungarian, Italian, Russian and Belgian. They were, noted Burton St John essentially 'miniatures, with modifications, of the countries they represent. As we come into the German concession we find German architecture prevailing, the streets with German names, and even the Chinese coolies trying to speak German'.[64] The neighbouring British concession gave way to the French concession which, noted St John, housed 'the YMCA, the Chinese Post Office, the Arcade, the Imperial Hotel, and the

Roman Catholic Church of St Louis. A number of the Protestant missions, American and British, are situated in Taku Road, in territory formerly Chinese, but acquired by the French in 1900.'[65] What impressed him most though was the Japanese enclave, the growth of which 'has far outrun that of any ... Japan in Tientsin has had the largest growth in trade, in population, and in building'. He remarked upon the large number of stores and small shops and an electric tramway which ran 'from the Chinese city through the Japanese ... and the French concessions across International Bridge to the railway station'.[66]

In fact, there was a total of eight miles of tramway, the first in China, as well as a water works, pumping station, steam rollers and sprinklers for the streets. Its residents also benefited from a health department, telegraph, telephone and fire departments. There were no financial institutions at all in 1880, but by 1897 there were four, among them the ubiquitous Hong Kong and Shanghai Bank. The British, French and Austro-Hungarians had their own markets and post offices, and an Indian Field Post Office for the British military. For entertainment St John told his readers, there were numerous theatres, touring companies, concerts and dances, as well as a 'new school for foreign children, the Union Church, All Saints Church, Astor House, Victoria Hospital ... a Masonic Temple; Temperance Recreation Grounds, swimming baths'.[67] Charitable organisations looked after the welfare of those locals who fell on hard times. A rescue home gave refuge to girls aged between 7-15 who had escaped slavery but who were then married off to men too poor to pay a dowry, but only if he could show himself 'able to support a wife'.[68] He also mentioned the Magdala Home – Chi Nua Soa – where 'girls are fed, clothed and cared for',[69] whilst the Chou Ch'ang porridge kitchen helped feed 300 to 400 beggars a day.

By the turn of the twentieth century other treaty ports were also experiencing various degrees of success. For example, Chefoo's merchants were turning over £3,000,000 a year and handling 2,385,301 tons of shipping[70] and Wuhan, optimistically labelled the 'Chicago of the East', traded in tea, hides, wood, and sesamum seeds worth around £18,700,000 a year. All of this aggregate trade was overwhelmingly dominated by the British, who enjoyed around half by the early 1900s. The Chinese by comparison were running a distant second with 17 per cent, the Japanese 13 per cent and Germany 12 per cent, with the few remaining crumbs picked up by other countries.[71] Much of this was due to the sheer scale and scope of Britain's presence, with its nationals running 398 of the 773 mercantile houses operating at that time.[72] Such statistics testified to the extent to which the opportunities opened up by war, intimidation and coercion had been grasped by ambitious entrepreneurs who knew how to turn a profit.

Uniquely however, the empire's most recent acquisition, Weihaiwei, about 849 miles from Wuhan to the northeast, had only ever been intended to serve as a stopgap and not a commercial enterprise. Described by District Officer Reginald Johnston as the 'Cinderella of the British Empire',[73] it felt like something of a backwater. Despite its strategic importance, he lamented, 'the lords of commerce despise it, the traveller dismisses it ... the sinologue knows it not ... the ethnologist ignores it'.[74] At least its name fairly represented the purpose for which it had been acquired, not for commerce or as a tourist destination, but as a fortress. The first 'Wei' meant august, majestic or imposing, the 'hai' stood for the sea, and the second 'wei' could be interpreted as guardian or protector. Together they could be read as 'City of the August Ocean', and it was for this purpose the British Government wanted it. Until 1901 its administration was the responsibility of naval and military officers, but it then came under the Colonial Office and was administered by a civil commissioner appointed by the Crown.

Nestling in the easternmost Shandong Peninsula, it consisted of Liugong Island, dominated by the 498-foot High Hill, or Signal Station. Known to the locals as Liu-King-tao, the island of Mister Ling, it was named in honour of a long-gone benefactor to whom local fishermen and other seafarers still made offerings at Ling Temple, in exchange for good luck and fortune at sea. Two-and-a-quarter miles long, seven-eighths of a mile at its widest point and with a circumference of five-and-a-half miles, it commanded the two-mile wide eastern harbour entrance, and the three-quarters-of-a-mile wide western entrance. Within lay an eleven-square-mile harbour, since 1899 the summer home of the Royal Navy's China Squadron. The island also contained the permanent headquarters of the Royal Naval Establishment, a naval canteen, United Services

Club, bungalows for summer visitors, a hotel, the offices of some shipping companies, several streets of shops run by locals and Japanese, tennis courts and a golf course. The island was connected by ferry to the seat of government at Port Edward – Ma-t'ou – meaning landing place, on the southwest side of the harbour where it was sheltered from storms. Here was another hotel, more bungalows, sulphur baths run by Japanese, and a golf course. There were also some schools which had been founded and managed by missionaries, including the government-funded and managed Huang Jen school for boys, with 200 day pupils costing $3,600 a year to maintain.[75] Close by stood the original battlemented city of Weihaiwei, protected by formidable gates and consisting of a few streets, three or four temples and home to around 2,000 people. Excluded from the lease, it stood as a virtually autonomous city-state, where gambling and prostitution thrived beyond the jurisdiction of the British.

A total of 285 square miles of land surrounded the bay with approximately seventy-two miles of coastline and a land frontier of forty miles. Within this the British Government exercised sole jurisdiction, but beyond was a much larger area of approximately 1,500 square miles extending from about halfway between Chefoo and Weihaiwei in an easterly direction to the Shandong Promontory. Here, the British had the right to erect fortifications and garrison troops, but for the sake of goodwill it was agreed that within the zone Chinese administration would not be interfered with, so long as they did not admit any other foreign troops. The land was mainly hilly, barren and rugged, dissected by extremely fertile and well cultivated valleys supporting a population scattered through 315 villages. The principal crops were wheat, millet, barley, maize, beans, sweet potatoes, ground nuts and cotton.

The 1911 census put the total population at 147,177, rising by 1921 to 154,416 and by 1927 it would have grown again to 175,000. By then, the permanent foreign population was still only 101, seventy-two of whom were British and thirteen Korean,[76] but according to a correspondent of the *Army and Navy Illustrated*, everyone seemed to be getting on well enough. He wrote encouragingly that the inhabitants 'are a comfortable set, easy to deal with'.[77] This was most probably because life inside

A Place of Dingy Dilapidation

the relative safety of the leased territory protected by the Chinese Regiment spared them the turmoil raging outside. But it was an expensive insurance policy, costing £30,000 a year to maintain,[78] around £3,500,000 in today's money, and with little to do to justify its cost it was disbanded in 1906. Thenceforth, the territory relied upon a police force consisting of just three European Inspectors, nineteen Chinese non-commissioned officers and 142 constables.[79] This decision left Johnson concerned that the territory was 'without a permanent garrison ... practically at the mercy of any band of robbers that happened to regard it with a covetous eye'.[80]

This was not the only example of the territory's Cinderella status. Even by 1927 there were no phones outside of the Port Edward area and the island was instead dependent upon telegraphic communication from a Chinese-owned land line to Chefoo. A temporary wireless was installed by the military in the summer of 1927, but apart from that there was only a regular steamship service to Tianjin and Shanghai, and irregular ones to Hong Kong, Qingdao, Chefoo and Dairen. Post to London took up to forty days to arrive.[81] One reason for this lack of investment was the fact that once the naval squadron and the European visitors left each September, the place was left to its own resources until the month of May or June the following year,[82] and therefore was not deemed to warrant any greater expenditure.

As the British presence grew however, so did its financial health. Whereas in 1900 revenue from licenses and internal revenue, court fees and rental income from government property was only $4,077, by 1901 it had grown to $21,188 and by 1903 had totalled $58,364. This was largely the result of a steady growth in maritime traffic. In 1902, just 146 merchant ships had entered the port, with a total tonnage of 151,809, realising shipping dues of $1,067. In 1927, 858 merchant ships with a total tonnage of 1,029,478 tons called,[83] realising income of $340,000.[84] There was also a sericulture industry with 85,000 acres of land planted with scrub oak, the leaves from which fed the silk worms. The raw silk was then sent to Chefoo to be turned into Shantung ponge and to manufacture stockings. There were also prosperous sea fishing and salted fish industries, and by 1927 salt manufacturing had become big business. The saltpan area grew from thirty acres in 1902 to

1,000 in 1927, 70 per cent of which was exported to Hong Kong, Shanghai, Korea and Japan. Other industries included lace making, and brick and tile manufacture. These businesses created good employment opportunities for the locals and by 1927 two-thirds of males over nine years of age worked either on the land, in the harbour or in the building trade.

Less successful was an enterprise to extract gold. The Weihaiwei Mining Company was formed with capital of $300,000 in 1904 and installed a twenty-stamp mill with capacity of 2,500 tons a month. At its height it employed 400 locals, but proved a very short-lived venture when the gold dried up and the company went broke. Even with all the accrued income from its various enterprises plus revenue from harbour dues, the territory could not make ends meet all the time. Grant-in-aid of £144,500 was needed until 1916-17, after which it returned to the black for a couple of years. From 1921 it again became self-supporting,[85] bolstered by total trade valued in 1927 at $17,650,100.[86] The economy was also helped by the civil war of the 1920s, because its relative safety encouraged merchants from Chefoo to cut their losses in favour of Port Edward. This increased prosperity considerably, leading to higher property values and rents, and stimulating a building boom. Land selling on the outskirts of Port Edward for an average of $20 for one-sixth of an acre (one mu) in 1902 changed hands for $200-800 in 1921 and $1,300 by 1927.[87]

Nonetheless, Britain's days in the territory were numbered. At the Washington Conference of 1921 it had announced its intention, as per its original undertaking, to vacate the territory and return it to China. A Rendition Agreement had been prepared to that effect in 1924, but with the chaos and anarchy still taking place there was no recognisable government to hand the cession back to, so it postponed the decision. Indeed, according to the 1928 Annual Colonial Report on Weihaiwei, the local Chinese made 'no attempt to disguise their hope that the British flag may long continue to afford them the peace and protection which they know they could not hope to obtain under the present government of Shantung'.[88] Nevertheless, in 1930 the Union Flag did come down for the last time and off they went, one might assume to the disappointment of many of the local inhabitants.

Above left: 1. Emperor Shi Huang, who vanquished the Warring States and cleared the way for the founding of the Qin dynasty.

Above right: 2. The Heavenly King's throne in the former capital of Nanjing, symbol of Imperial power for centuries.

Right: 3. Emperor Quianlong, whose obstinacy in the face of European calls for more open trade ultimately led to the Century of Humiliation.

4. Commissioner Lin Zexu destroying the foreign traders' opium in Guangzhou harbour, igniting the fuse that led to war with Britain.

5. The Taiping Revolution Seal, representing one of many rebellions that served to weaken and undermine the Manchus.

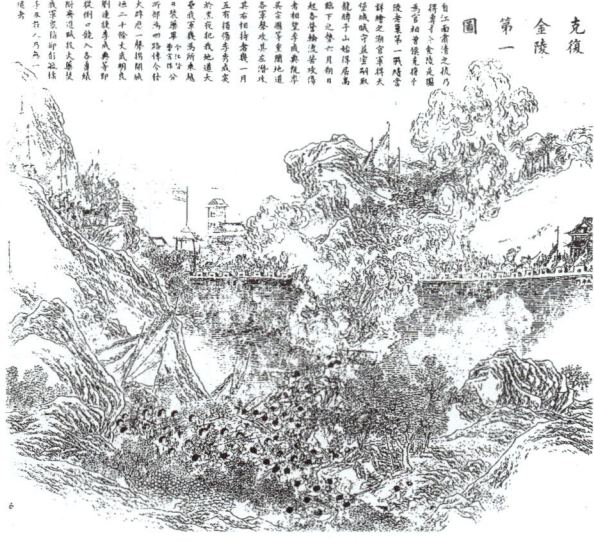

6. The retaking of Jinling (Nanjing) during the Taiping Rebellion.

Above: 7. The looking and destruction of the Old Summer Palace in Beijing by the British and French in 1860. Today its ruins stand as mute testament to the indignities suffered during the Century of Humiliation.

Right: 8. Zeng Guofan, one of the architects of the ill-starred Self-Strengthening Movement, which floundered in the face of incompetence, corruption and self-interest.

9. Zeng's tomb in Hunan, since designated a National, Historical and Cultural site in his honour.

10. Sir Robert Hart, Inspector General of the Imperial Custom Service, who prophesied a day of reckoning for the Europeans in China.

11. A depiction of British naval guns zeroed in on the distant city of Tianjin, one of many cities to have suffered widespread damage at the hands of invading Europeans.

12. A fanciful rendition of British, US and Japanese troops assaulting Tianjin during the Boxer uprising.

13. A stylised depiction of European troops engaging with Boxers as they fight their way to the Foreign Legations in Beijing during the uprising.

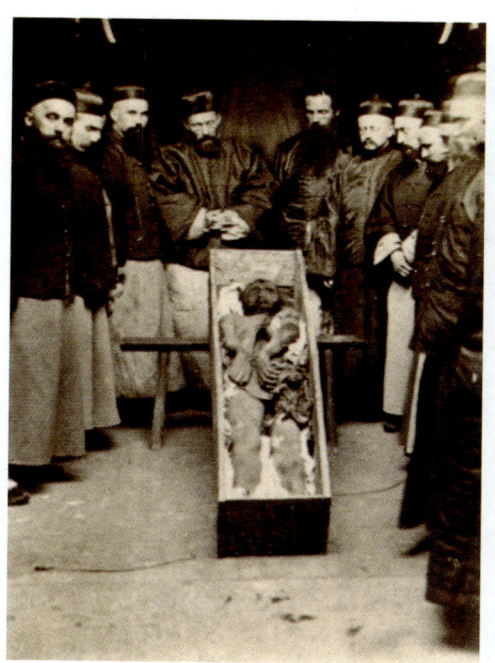 

Above left: 14. Suspected remains of one of the European victims of Boxer atrocities committed on the hated foreign missionaries.

Above right: 15. To the victors the spoils. Britain, Germany, Russia, France and Japan eyeing up the Chinese cake in the wake of its defeat in 1900.

Below: 16. Bloody reprisals. A captured Boxer is publicly executed as European troops and Chinese witnesses look on. Similar excesses were committed in the vicinity of the capital.

Above: 17. As part of the Boxer Protocols, Chinese are excluded from entering the Foreign Legations in Beijing, another indignity heaped on them by the hated 'foreign devils'.

Below: 18. Sun Yat-sen together with founder members of the Singapore branch of the Tongman Hui, one of many precursors to the Kuomintang.

Above left: 19. Ikki Kita, a Japanese intellectual and philosopher whose writings helped to create a right-wing fascist mindset among many of his compatriots.

Left: 20. A graphic example of the hundreds of thousands of atrocities committed against the Chinese by members of the Imperial Japanese Army during their long and bloody occupation of the country.

Below: 21. Joe Biden with Xi Jinping before the 2022 G20 summit in Bali.

A Place of Dingy Dilapidation

Just over 164 miles to the southwest was the German concession of Qingdao (Tsingtao), known as 'Azure Island' to the Chinese. When its 214 square miles came into their hands in 1898, it comprised the 8,000-strong fishing community and garrison, along with around 275 smaller communities totalling 83,000 people. Although legally still under Chinese jurisdiction, it was categorised as a *Schutzgebeit* or Protectorate, and the German Imperial Naval Office which was responsible for its administration conducted themselves as if it was sovereign German territory. Its most enthusiastic servant was undoubtedly Admiral Oskar Truppel. who served as governor from 1901 until 1911.

Soon after its acquisition, parcels of land were auctioned off so that its grand centrepiece, the city of Qingdao, could be constructed. The native residents were unceremoniously dispossessed and a new metropolis, emulating Berlin's leafy district of Dahlem, began to take shape. Once completed, it served as the European quarter, sprawling majestically along the banks of the Clara and Qingdao Bays with panoramic views of the Yellow Sea. Some civic buildings such as the governor's mansion and the military hospital were prefabricated in Germany and then shipped out, and as was the custom all street names and signs were in German, honouring rulers or other notaries. One, *Iltis Strasse*, or Polecat Street, was named after a torpedo boat which played a role in the Boxer Rising. B. L. Putnam Weale noted how they were all 'well made, broad and properly attended to ... including thoroughly German shops, where nothing which is not made in Germany is placed on sale'.[89]

It also had its own telephone network, schools and hospitals, currency and the neo-gothic Catholic St Emil's Cathedral, completed in 1902. A railway station was opened in 1901 and by 1904 it was possible to travel from Germany to Qingdao in twelve to fourteen days via the trans-Siberian railway, crossing Russia and northeast China. On arrival weary travellers could choose to recover in either the *Prinz Heinrich* Hotel, completed in 1899 with forty ensuite rooms, the thirty-one-room *Strandhotel* opened in 1903, or the *Logierhaus* or Lodging House, all offering the most modern amenities. Because, as von Tirpitz wrote 'the climate was comparatively good'[90] residents could indulge in a leisurely stroll or take the fresh air of one of its parks. They could sit in the shade of the numerous trees imported from Germany and watch the world go by. To protect the wellbeing of its inhabitants, the admiral explained how fever and typhus were successfully combatted 'by erecting waterworks, and the pestilences which devastate China from time to time were kept in check by the sanitary cordon along the Boxer Wall'.[91] This meant that bathing became a popular pastime for many, earning it the moniker, the 'Brighton of the East'.[92]

Apart from unique architecture and a model town, they left one other enduring legacy. This was the world-renowned Tsingtao Brewery, founded in 1903 by German and British merchants as the *Germania-Brauerei Tsingtao* Company, under the watchful eye of brew master R. Schuster. He had crafted a German style Pilsener beer using traditional German techniques and mineral water from the Laoshan spring, refreshing the palates of holidaymakers attracted to the climate, the racecourse and the polo ground. Serving its first stein in November 1904, it was to face many vicissitudes in the years to come but has survived to this day.

The only Chinese nationals tolerated in the European quarter were servants, and they were strictly segregated in 'coolie houses' out of sight of their masters and mistresses. As in the treaty ports, most others were confined to their own areas, here known as the *Taidoongzhen* and *Taixizhen* zones, which had been allocated to them. They were small and crowded with something of the air of the ghetto about them, though neatly laid out in a strict grid pattern presided over by a police station situated in the centre. As a compromise, a zone in which all races could mix, trade and work was set aside and called *Dabaodao*, and in the early days the wealthier Chinese had to be content with this. Consequently, Putnam Weale found it very busy 'because the Chinese are permitted to live and do their business here'.[93] There was little open fraternisation between the sexes, intermarriage was frowned upon and mixed-race children were excluded from German schools. Even the better-off Chinese were barred from the Tsingtau Klub and other social amenities, although they were allowed to use the beaches. However, there were separate toilets and changing facilities, and in death, strict segregation was applied, with different cemeteries for each community.

A Place of Dingy Dilapidation

The Chinese were subject to German law, exercised by the Commissary for Chinese Affairs, overseen by a district officer or *Bezirksamtmann* who was responsible for all inhabitants. A mixture of German and Chinese law was applied depending upon the circumstances, both sets imposed on the Chinese but only German law on foreigners. In cases in which a German litigant faced a Chinese one they were tried by the German Imperial Court only, and in appropriate cases a Chinese found guilty of serious offences could be flogged, fined, sentenced to hard labour, the notorious cangue, or decapitated. There were unsurprisingly, separate prisons for European and Chinese malefactors.

However, despite initially excluding the Chinese from daily life, it soon became clear that the success of the settlement lay in inclusivity. As an early step, local born Chinese were granted leasehold citizenship, which entitled them to residency and freedom from extradition to Chinese territory. Furthermore, whereas in most German colonies and protectorates the natives were referred to as *Untertanen*, subservient or subject, like the German residents they were known as *burghers*. Wealthier Chinese were soon allowed to vote in elections to a mixed European-Chinese council of advisers to the governor, and in 1902 a Chinese Committee of twelve members was formed. These measures were largely welcomed by the European business community, and prompted one bank director in November 1904 to applaud how Chinese citizens were now enjoying 'civil rights' and were fully involved 'in the affairs of the colony'.[54] The opening of a Chinese Chamber of Commerce in 1909 further entrenched their active participation, and they were later allowed to play tennis at the Tsingtau Klub. Following the revolutions of 1911/1912 the flight of Qing loyalists into the territory resulted in most of the remaining social barriers coming down and the existing restrictions on settlement in the European quarter were finally lifted.

The new landlords sought to win their wards over with acts of altruism, and in 1905 the Weimar Mission created the first mixed schools. Presided over by German and Chinese tutors, these institutions provided a Sino-German curriculum, with Chinese lessons taught for the first five years, and German for the last two. Philanthropist Paul Rohrbach helped to found a school for Chinese girls in 1908-1909, leading von Tirpitz to express his belief that 'the more reasonable among [the Chinese] came more and more to the conclusion that the occupation of Tsingtao was a blessing for them'.[95] Putnam Weale was less convinced. He came away with the impression that the Chinese 'have already realised that if Tsingtao finally becomes a success it will not be they who will reap the benefit, but the beer drinking foreigner with the Imperial moustaches'.[96] No one would gain if the concession could not pay for itself, and few were more optimistic on this score than von Tirpitz. Among other projects, he had promoted the construction of

> ... an inner harbour, itself protected against heavy seas... Quays and docks were then built which we could have extended at our pleasure. Tsingtao began to be an important harbour for the import of the petroleum from the Sunda Islands which was urgently needed in China. A splendid impetus was provided by the Shantung coal, a much-coveted commodity in Eastern Asia. Iron works were to be erected, with steel mills and crushing mills facilitat[ing] the settlement of industrial undertakings. No iron works in Eastern Asia or Western America had such prospects; the iron and steel market would have passed into our hands.[97]

Following its freeport status in 1898, two syndicates were formed to exploit this potential, the Shandong Railway Company and the Shandong Mining Company. Nonetheless, unlike most concessions ceded to foreigners, Putnam Weale believed that Qingdao was located in 'probably the poorest corner of Shantung. There are no rich Chinese cities near which will enrich it with their barter ... the soil only succeeds in poorly feeding a vast population, and what this population possesses in surplus cash for the purchase of commodities, and the amounts of raw stuffs it can offer for export, will not for many decades make the German colony self-sufficient.'[98] Indeed, little serious interest was shown by big companies such as the steel giant Krupp, who refused three separate invitations to become involved in developing the concession. As a consequence, Putnam Weale could only find 'a number of local enterprises such as silk filature, saw mills, brick and tile factories and machine shops ... little money is being made except by such undertakings as are directly concerned with the upbuilding of the place', rendering it overly reliant 'on direct or indirect government expenditure... If all government works suddenly ceased and the garrison were reduced to its normal level of 1,200 men, the condition of the colonists would soon be a parlous one.'[99] Consequently, despite the £4,000,000 pumped into von Tirpitz's pet projects in 1898 and £700,000 in 1905,[100] Putnam Weale remained convinced that the colony could never be self-supporting.[101]

As we shall see, Germany's tenure was to prove too short in any case, for von Tirpitz's plans to be vindicated. At the outbreak of the First World War it was to fall into Japanese hands, and their residency would last only until 1922. So for the time being, Putnam Weale's prognosis for this little corner of the German Empire was not very encouraging, and he left having found it 'not very gay ... [but] better than Dalny',[102] the Russian concession 250 miles away to the north. Nestling on the Liaodong Peninsula overlooking Talianwan Bay, like Qingdao it was to enjoy mixed fortunes.

Located 4,000 miles from Moscow it certainly lived up to its new name, being 'far away' from the seat of Imperial power. When it came into Russian hands it was another small fishing village, in the words of correspondent George Lynch little more than 'a barren treeless tract of desolation',[103] but the Russians almost immediately set about its transformation. It was laid out originally by architect K. G. Skolimovskii who designed its streets to radiate from a hub like the spokes of a giant wheel, so that Inzhernerny Prospect, Timmovskaya Street, Belyayevskaya Street and Ugolny Prospect converged on Nikolaevskaya Square in the centre. The architecture was a combination of neo-Russian and classic Chinese, and some public buildings such as the Russian Library, built in 1900, was an exotic combination of Victorian, Bavarian and Swiss styles. All in all, they reminded Lynch 'of a respectable London or Glasgow suburb ... solidly built of brick, faced with cut stone [and] of slightly varied design ... the roads are well macadamised and the footpaths edged with cut limestone'.[104]

Russian Orthodox, Catholic and Protestant churches, a museum, bank, police station, schools for girls and boys, a hospital, parks and gardens combined to provide its occupants with all the creature comforts, and in anticipation of future urban sprawl roads panned out towards as yet vacant plots. To render this environment more attractive they had 'set about clothing the hills, and thousands upon thousands of young trees can be seen, which they have already planted down their sides'.[105] For the more adventurous there were also some recreational facilities. Talianwan was 'an ideal bay for yachting, and the journey [there] and back just makes a delightful trip'.[106]

The Russians made a start on the port in 1898, lauded as one of the finest ice-free deep harbours in the Pacific, with capacity for ships drawing upwards of thirty feet of water at low tide. By 1902, $6,000,000 had been invested in the construction of five large piers, railway tracks and warehouses with elevators, all powered by gas and electricity and supplied with mains water. They deepened the harbour, built moorings, breakwaters and shipyards and in 1903 opened a rail link to Harbin. They had employed upwards of 20,000 labourers on these projects, but it was estimated that there remained scope for a further $20,000,000 to be spent. To attract investment, promotional campaigns were launched, with a prospectus published in 1902 extolling the commercial potential. An optimistic headline in the 2 April edition of the *Sphere* magazine referred to it as 'the mushroom port of Dalny', asking rhetorically if it was set to be 'The New York of the East'.

Yet despite Lynch referring to it as 'one of the marvels of the modern age',[107] it was to prove something of a white elephant. Traders preferred to do business with nearby Port Arthur, and even the governor chose the latter as the site for his palace. This inevitably had a knock-on effect for the development of the city itself, and the planned expansion into the suburbs failed to materialise. In 1903, the highly anticipated sale of lots that were expected to realise 15,000,000 roubles could in fact only raise some 500,000[108] and when, to everyone's horror, the supposedly ice-free harbour actually froze, its reputation was further undermined. Then the disastrous Russo-Japanese War brought their tenure to an end anyway, but, as the New Hampshire *Nashuah Telegraph* reported, the former occupants were determined not to leave anything of use behind. A correspondent visited the town and found that the departing Russians had implemented a scorched earth policy: 'Wharves, piers, warehouses and public buildings have been all blown up.'[109]

A Place of Dingy Dilapidation

With its new name of Dairen, the Japanese nonetheless set to work. They transformed the port, extending the breakwater to 14,121 feet enclosing an area of 800 acres and added two new piers. By 1922, the total length of the wharves was two-and-a-half miles, allowing steamers totalling 85,000 tons to be docked at the same time. There were seventy-three warehouses with room for 400,000 tons of cargo, forty-three miles of railway track within the wharf compounds, and cargo working capacity of 37,000 tons per ten-hour day. By 1933 it was China's second port after Shanghai, the city both the Russians and the Japanese had sought to emulate. From handling just 1,357 vessels totalling 1,829,921 tons in 1908,[110] it grew to 14,056,392 by 1929. Total trade worth just over £1,000,000 in 1918[111] would surpass £50,000,000 by 1929, 66 per cent of all the business passing through Manchuria.[112]

Their predecessors' failure to attract sufficient investment to the city had also left large swathes of open plots to be exploited. On these, trees were planted and shops and houses erected in the Japanese style, juxtaposing with their Russian and Chinese counterparts. Czarist Nikolaevskaya Square was renamed Dai hiroba, or simply 'Large Square', and Shinto temples followed, along with a new police station completed in 1908. The Tianfu Tea Garden opened for business in 1911 and the Yamoto Hotel welcomed its first guests in 1914. These were followed in 1917 by the Post Office, and in 1919 and 1920 respectively two branches of the Industrial and Commercial Bank of China were opened. More schools, hospitals and a City Hall were built and imported trams began plying their trade along the streets. Visitor W. H. Holmes found it to be, under its new owners 'a fine town. Its streets are broad, well paved and clean. Trees and gardens are plentiful [with] plenty of bright, clean and attractive shops, well stocked with all the products of Japanese, American and European factories.'[113] He also unearthed a seedier side: 'Enterprising Japanese cabaret and brothel keepers keep a few White Russian girls, as well as geishas, so that all tastes may be catered for.'[114] He also found that although illegal, 'the Japanese dealer has no scruples about engaging in [another] highly profitable trade... they import more morphine than is consumed in any area of the world'.[115]

Instrumental in the successful development of the port and city was the South Manchuria Railway, effectively the parent company for numerous commercial and industrial concerns. It not only managed the Yamato chain of hotels but supplied the electricity, gas and trams of Dairen. Its tentacles reached as far as Mukden, Antung and Changchun, where in 1930 it would invest £71,000,000 in various enterprises.[116] In 1917, the Company began constructing a steel works at Anshan alongside the railway to exploit the nearby vast iron ore deposits, and the first blast furnace, with a capacity of 200 tons a day, was completed in 1918, swiftly followed by a second in 1920. They also diversified into other areas, the Manchuria Cotton Spinning Company in Liaoyang being established in 1923 with 31,360 spindles, the Naikoi Cotton Company opening in Jinzhou in 1924 with 24,000 spindles, and a year later the Fukushima Spinning Company in Dairen with 18,000 spindles.[117] The company also built an oil distillation plant at Fushun costing £1,000,000, with an annual output of 75,000 tons of fuel oil, 18,000 tons of ammonium nitrate and 15,000 tons of paraffin, reducing Japan's reliance on imports from other countries from ninety to forty per cent.[118] Food production was another imperative, and 4,721,000 tons of soya bean, or forty-one per cent of its total needs, was being exported from there to Japan by the 1930s.[119]

The exploitation of China's resources had thus opened the door to endless opportunities for foreigners to prosper, but the vast majority of ordinary Chinese saw few material benefits. Apart from some intrepid merchants, traders and entrepreneurs, the majority lacked agency and faced the prospect of unremitting toil in menial, low-paid jobs as labourers, hired hands and servants. They found themselves serving the foreigners who were making huge profits at their country's expense.

8

The Very Scum of the Population

Notwithstanding its silk, porcelain, tea, spices and raw materials, another of the empire's most abundant assets was its infinite supply of manpower. Driven by war, poverty and unemployment, the Chinese workforce could easily satisfy the needs of domestic and foreign employers, and with a reputation for hardiness and endurance undertake work far too arduous for Europeans to tackle. The arrival of the Portuguese provided early outlets for their strengths, and they found the residents of Guangdong indispensable as dockhands and general labourers, loading and unloading ships and hauling cargo to and from the wharves. Demand for these services increased with the arrival of the Dutch, Spanish, English, and French, especially after the treaty ports were opened. They would also prove indispensable as logistical support in the frequent conflicts with the Qings.

One example was the grandly named Canton Chinese Commissariat Corps, formed in 1860 in preparation for the renewal of the war against Beijing. Recruited mainly in Hong Kong, it was not long before its members acquired a notorious reputation. Referred to more pejoratively as the Canton Coolie Corps, their ranks, according to expedition member Robert Swinhoe, consisted of the 'very scum of the population',[1] who only signed up for the opportunities to rob and pillage. He went so far as to claim that 'after the departure of the expedition [from Hong Kong], robbery had become a thing almost unknown on the island'.[2] Where a town or village was encountered, they were among the first to rob the unfortunate inhabitants, although Europeans were far from blameless in this regard, but Swinhoe said the 'Canton coolies'[3] were the worst. It was therefore fortunate that they were not representative of the average worker. Author and traveller Trumbell White later found those he encountered to be 'of a phlegmatic and impassive temperament [possessing] great powers of physical endurance'.[4] He claimed to have witnessed 'labourers more than seventy years of age working daily at their trades' and some still going strong at the age of ninety or more.[5] It was inevitable therefore, that despite it being illegal to leave the empire, many followed the land and maritime Silk Roads to seek employment opportunities farther afield. These pioneers later earned for themselves the epithet *Huaqiao*, or Chinese living and working abroad.

In the eighteenth century, western Borneo offered those with the stamina and endurance employment in its gold and tin mines. For the more entrepreneurial there was also the chance to branch out and move into senior positions. One particularly enterprising individual was Low Lan Pak from Guangdong, who in 1777 founded *Lanfang*, a mining company which became a pseudo-statelet with himself as president the Lanfang Republic. To protect his business interests and his employees from Dutch encroachment, he allied himself with local sultans and declared himself to be a tributary of the Qings, sending the customary gifts to cement the arrangement. This remarkable setup succeeded in resisting the Dutch until 1884, when it was finally overwhelmed and many of its citizens fled to Sumatra and Singapore. Strangely, it was not until 1912 and the complete overthrow of the dynasty that the Dutch absorbed it into their East Indian possessions completely.

Such achievements were beyond the reach of the vast majority, and they would find themselves consigned to the humbler positions in life. Some found work on merchant ships, transporting their country's goods back to Europe and, when the Royal Navy found itself short-handed during its frequent wars with France, they were often used to fill the void. Such was the demand that in 1799 the EIC established accommodation exclusively for Chinese seamen in Shadwell in the East End of London, creating one of nation's earliest Sino-British communities.

Later, more organised arrangements were devised to lure likely candidates from their homes, through what was to become known as the notorious indenture system, essentially a form of people smuggling. This was an agreement by which they would sign up to contracts committing them to work for a defined number of years in return for guaranteed rates of pay and working conditions. These documents would find them sent to places as diverse as British Malaya, Singapore, Peru, Cuba, Canada, the United States, the West Indies and South Africa. But when demand outstripped supply, 'crimps', men who worked on behalf of the agents in the treaty ports to recruit the labour, looked further afield. They were none too particular about how they secured workers. Some exploited the flotsam produced by the frequent uprisings against the Qings, or combatants captured in conflicts such as the Punti-Hakka clan wars. This was fought in Guangdong between 1855-1867, causing widespread devastation and upwards of 1,000,000 deaths. Thus, the human collateral that emerged fed the insatiable demands of the crimps. When these tactics failed, they would often hike into the countryside to scam poverty-stricken villagers with various ruses. Astute elders sometimes seized the opportunity to rid themselves of the sick, disadvantaged or simply undesirable by 'volunteering' them to a life of which they could barely conceive. Campaigner Watt Stewart explained how these 'ignorant rustics ... are made to believe that a year in foreign countries equals six in China, and that a dollar in those countries is worth as much as two in this'.[6] When these options failed to meet the quotas, even darker forms of skulduggery were employed. 'Villagers or fishermen were forcibly kidnapped upon the coast ... individuals tempted by prowling agents to gamble [in Macao], on losing surrender their persons in payment according to the peculiar Chinese notions of liability in this respect.'[7]

Australian human rights activist Persia Campbell described how in some instances, 'coolies were deliberately drugged ... hustled under false pretences of debt or delinquency and carried off a prisoner never to be heard of [again]'.[8] This kind of chicanery was perpetrated against boys as young as eleven, and when that did not work men were sometimes simply abducted straight off the streets, held captive and forced to sign a contract under duress. This became known as Shanghaiing, and such was the notoriety of the crimps and agents, reported Tianjin's US consul Eli T. Sheppard, that every foreigner 'in the estimation of the Chinese... was little better than a kidnapper'.[9] Fear of abduction soon led to a 'Shanghaier' being seen around every corner, and they also attracted the wrath of officialdom. In April 1859, the Governor of Guangdong Province issued a decree directing that 'the villains that inflict this misery'[10] be summarily executed. But as late as September 1888 a coolie broker was beheaded in Swatow after being convicted of attempting to procure workers under false pretences.[11] It was worth the risk, with crimps earning an average of eight to ten dollars per head, and their agents six times that figure.

For those who had agreed to sign up more or less voluntarily, the prospect of travel was made more palatable by being told that they would only be going a relatively short distance, when in reality they might be destined for work as far away as the Americas. Nonetheless if the penny should drop and they changed their minds, there was little hope of redemption from authorities who were frequently in collusion. Having reached the port of embarkation, explained agent Franciso Abello, port officials made only a cursory check to ensure that they had signed up of their own free will:

> They would address a group of coolies through an interpreter, who often only knew one of eleven dialects ... asking them if they were willing to embark. Silence on their part was taken for consent.[12]

On those occasions when 'these men of the fields understand the deception of which they have been the victims and want to go back they are immediately made to suffer the most cruel punishments of the whip etc'.[13] They were then forced into squalid holding cells or barracoons and, as one victim recounted, 'the gates were closed... and as all exit was prevented we perceived how we had been betrayed'.[14] The extent of Macao's complicity can be gauged by the fact that between 1 January and 19 October 1872 alone, fifteen Peruvian, ten French, nine Spanish, three Dutch and one Austrian boatload of labourers had been acquired by crimps for transportation to various destinations.[15] One American resident reflected the official mood: 'The government feels keenly the wrong and injustice of having a portion of its territory taken possession of by a foreign government and made a depot for smuggling operations, and a slave mart for the forcible and fraudulent sale of its own subjects.'[16] Such was the opprobrium heaped on the territory that in 1874 the governor finally announced that the colony would no longer be involved in the trade.[17]

Earlier, in 1855, the British had made some efforts to try and curtail the practice, or as some cynics remarked the competition, by the passage of the Chinese Passengers Act. This made any British ship carrying Chinese to the Straits Settlements liable to inspection to ensure that they were actually volunteers, but it was no guarantee that any action would be taken as a consequence. Persia Campbell cited an inspector who judged that out of 208 ready to sail from Hong Kong, 'not more than eighty-one were voluntary ... he did not detain the ship, nor did he disembark the doubtful cases'.[18] From 1859 a tighter process was attempted, whereby British and Chinese officials operating out of an emigration house would check that the worker was acting of his own volition. With proper contracts drawn up, signed and witnessed by bureaucrats everything should have been above board. The British consulate in Hong Kong and the Chinese authorities also cooperated in intercepting suspect vessels, with the River Police boarding and seizing any smuggling illicit workers. The 1866 Coolie Convention was drafted by Prince Kung and the Yongli Yamen in an attempt to further protect the worker's rights, but the British declined to ratify the treaty.

Despite these efforts the crimps continued undeterred. A senior police officer in Penang, Superintendent Plunket admitted that 'there are a large number of men who have no occupation [other than] going about the country getting coolies to go to Deli, Sirdang and other places in Sumatra'.[19] In February 1877, a number of Chinese in Singapore had their contracts 'sold' to the agent of a Dutch mine owner on the island, and when they refused to go, were threatened with arrest and deportation.[20] Concerned by the increasing lawlessness of those involved, a further series of ordinances were enacted by the Governor of the Straits Settlements. The Chinese Immigration Ordinance of March 1877 instituted a Chinese Protectorate Office to ensure migrants understood the contracts they had signed, and it granted powers for ships to be boarded and inspected by officials. Depots were also provided with more humane accommodation for workers on arrival in the territory. A Crimping Ordinance was passed to license and regulate agents. But it would not be until 1911 that Colonial Secretary Lord Harcourt could announce the termination of indentured labour in British Malaysia entirely, and then it would not be fully implemented until 1914, once existing contracts had expired.[21]

Females were also much in demand. These were generally provided in the shape of the *mui tsai*, some of whom were needed, according to Straits Settlements official and lawyer Jonas Vaughn 'to prevent if for no other reason, the fearful crimes that prevail among the Chinese in the consequence of paucity of females'.[22] Elsewhere, they became a very valuable 'commodity' in their own right, and in the Dutch East Indies the small Chinese community had among its number some highly valued *mui tsai*. As late as 1901, Java newspaper *Het Bataviaasch Niewsblad* reported how some commanded sums as high as 1,900 Guilders, and even twenty-two years later the *Voorwarts* would relate how one father received 30,000 Guilders, a house and 14,000 Guilders'-worth of jewellery for his daughter.[23] The practice would endure far longer than indentures, it was so entrenched in tradition, and even the League of Nations Anti-Slavery Convention of 1926 could not secure its complete eradication. Life for workers who found themselves relatively close to home was bad enough, but the ordeals endured by those transported to the Americas almost beggared belief.

By the 1840s Cuban plantations were providing over 21 per cent of the world's sugar, some 161,000 tons a year, but they were experiencing a serious manpower problem. The annual supply of African slaves to work on them had plummeted from 10,000 in 1844 to just 1,000 in 1847, leaving the owners with a large shortfall.[24] Similarly, Peru needed to boost its workforce if it was to grow the economy, but the *Mestizo* population had their own farms and smallholdings to tend and the country's 17,000 black slaves would be freed by the end of the decade. Neither group relished doing backbreaking work on plantations or in dangerous mines for paltry wages. This realisation spurred both governments to despatch agents to China, and with 500 workers obtained there for 30,000 to 50,000 pesos expected to realise 100-120,000 pesos at their destination,[25] they, too, harboured few qualms about how they met their quotas. Altogether some 80 per cent of the 125,000 shipped to Cuba between 1847 and 1874 testified that they had been subjected to various ruses before confinement in barracoons, there to await passage on specially adapted *lorchas*. These were ships with Chinese decks and rigging and larger capacity European hulls, otherwise known as 'devil ships', owned and operated by British, American, Danish, Swiss, and Norwegian companies. The interior of one was described by an American in 1857:

> Down the whole width of both lower decks were built tier on tier of berths – or rather shelves, for they were without sides or dividing partitions ... over every hatchway save one were set iron gratings to prevent too free access from below.[25]

Not only were they packed in like sardines, it was dark, stank and they had insufficient food, brackish water for drinking, and little air. Sanitation was almost non-existent, in fact almost impossible in such conditions. Writer Alexander Laing described it as 'a Dantean dream', the ship having 'become the lid of Hades, and the damned were below'.[27] Those en route to Cuba had to endure these conditions for up to 150 days, perhaps more depending upon the prevailing winds, and those to Callao in Peru for the duration of the 11,400-mile crossing. Evidently, a decree issued by the Peruvian authorities in October 1864 had done little to improve their lot. It had directed that vessels carry no more than one passenger for each registered ton of goods, that food had to be 'healthy and in quantity', that their clothing be appropriate and their bedspace 'spacious, clean and sufficiently ventilated'. A qualified doctor was also supposed to sail with each ship to check on their welfare.[28] However, with the rules widely open to interpretation, port authorities prone to bribery, and with few resources to enforce them anyway, there was little incentive to follow them. Consequently, as many as 16,400 of the 141,439 who set off for Cuba between 1847 and 1874 are calculated to have perished in transit, and a comparable proportion of the estimated 95,000 who went to Peru suffered the same fate.[29]

Men would frequently take matters into their own hands, and some ships had barely left port when the coolies struck. In February 1866, the French-owned *Hong Kong* bound for Havana was taken over within a few miles of the coast, and the majority of the 300 labourers on board ransacked the vessel before escaping back to shore. Less fortunate were those aboard the Italian vessel *Napoleon Canavaro*, who after an altercation with the captain were all locked below. They then started a fire, which prompted the crew to escape in their lifeboats, leaving the hatches locked and the doomed Chinese to their fate.[30] In 1871, the Lima newspaper *El Comercio* reported that 'there is not a boat that arrives in Callao with Chinese immigrants on board, on which there has not been one or more uprisings, or threats of uprisings at least, during the voyage ... boats with more than 300 coolies aboard had been scuttled, burned or in other manners destroyed, or taken possession of ... with great loss of life'.[31] Conditions only really improved when it was accepted that if more of the human cargo reached its destination alive the greater the profit would be, and by the 1870s death rates had plateaued at around 6.6 per cent.[32] Their ordeal of course did not end when their journey was over.

On 3 June 1847, the *Oquendo* docked in Havana, Cuba with 212 so-called *colonos asiaticos*, from which they were led to 'men markets', where their contract was re-sold to the highest bidder for anything between $70 and $170.[33] They were then stripped and examined for any obvious signs of disease or other incapacity, an exercise described by one as 'shameless and before unheard of by us'.[34] Some went to tobacco and coffee estates, farms and market gardens but around 80 per cent to the dreaded sugar plantations.[35] There they were housed in squalid accommodation little better than on the ships. One witness in Matanzas, on the northern shore of the island described 'large stone houses forming a long parallelogram with one entrance ... the rooms rarely have windows'.[36] They were cramped, dirty, disease-ridden and practically uninhabitable.

In any case, they were not expected to spend much time in these hovels, because eighteen- to twenty-one-hour working days were the norm, in direct contravention of government decrees. These, enacted in 1849, 1854 and 1860, confirmed their entitlement to four pesos a month, a maximum twelve-hour working day with Sundays off, and three days to celebrate Chinese New Year. Instead, having been advanced between eight to twelve pesos for their passage and a clean set of clothes, they first had to pay that off before they could hope to see any wages. Even then, instead of cash they were invariably paid in vouchers which were redeemable only in plantation shops, and because their rations were so poor they frequently had to use them up buying extras at greatly inflated prices. If they tried to shop elsewhere for a better deal, one worker explained, 'it is said that we are running away'. Hounds tracked them down, and they were ' compelled to work with chained feet'.[37]

This breached another rule whereby only reasonable punishments were supposed to be administered, ranging from 'one to ten days imprisonment or deductions from wages for the same period' for minor transgressions,[38] with flogging, leg chains or the stocks reserved for serious crimes such as insurrection.[39] With brutality common currency in both disciplining labourers and squeezing more work out of them, sickness and exhaustion were inevitable, but this was cynically interpreted as malingering, to be cured by more flogging rather than medical care. Such was the scale of the cruelty that within the first twenty years 53,502 out of 114,081 men sent to Cuba were believed to have perished from overwork or abuse.[40] Yet the persecution was not over, even after their contract expired. If after two months they had not either extended their contract or left the island, they were confined to a depot and obliged to undertake unpaid work. Those who sought to avoid this further exploitation joined other absconders as *cimarron*, or lawless runaways, often finding a place with one of the rebel groups fighting to overthrow the government. Some proved such an asset to the rebels that in 1870 the Captain General of the island appealed to Madrid for an end to their employment altogether.[41]

When this state of affairs reached Beijing in November 1873, the Zongli Yamen appointed a commission to investigate. An appeal was made for corroboration of the claims, which elicited over a thousand depositions and eighty-five petitions supported by 1,665 signatures.[42] Behind each was a desperate individual telling harrowing stories of institutionalised mistreatment. One wrote that it felt as though he was 'sinking in a strange place and living in a hell on earth',[43] and another begged 'earnestly to be taken care of by the embassies of other countries so that we can escape from this disaster. Please save our lives'.[44] This shocking litany of wrongdoing so horrified the Chinese Government that in 1874 it forbade further exportation of labourers to the island, although those whose contracts had not yet expired had to wait until they had completed their indentures.

Nonetheless, there was no doubt that their blood and sweat had made a huge contribution to the island's economy, as sugar production reached 768,672 tonnes between 1847 and 1874, and fell into sharp decline thereafter.[45]

Their compatriots, 100,000 of whom were destined for Callao in Peru in two tranches between 1849-1874, had essentially the same experience. A cursory inspection followed by an auction, after which most went to the north-central province of Libertad, where the lucky ones were employed as house servants, cooks, bakers, mill hands, gardeners and handymen, the less fortunate in the equally notorious sugar plantations. Again, the usual ruses were employed to short-change them. They were supposed to be paid four pesos a month, of which one peso was deducted towards the advance given in China but any period of illness was added to the contract. Entitlement to food, clothing, accommodation and medical care was rarely forthcoming and the indentured was confined to his plantation or other place of work. He was worked like a dog. One correspondent in Lima reported:

> He is roused before daylight, and turns out with his fellow prisoners to answer the muster roll. Should he be lax in attending, two or three blows are sure to fall to his lot. He is driven to the field or sugar house and immediately set to work... At dusk he is driven back to his pen ... at night-time they are all locked up together in the *galpones*, as their prisons are termed. The lash is unsparingly used as the punishment for the smallest peccadillo, and it is most cruelly applied by the halfblooded Spanish negroes who evidently enjoy their brutal task.[46]

US Ambassador General Alvin Hovey, who as a Union General during the American Civil War had witnessed more than his fair share of cruelty and bloodshed, was equally appalled. 'The overseers and major domos beat the Chinese for the most insignificant faults, often without any cause whatsoever.'[47] Another correspondent pitied these poor creatures for whom 'the day dawns with labour; labour pursues him through its weary hours, a labour which will bring no good fruit to him, and the shadows of night provide him with nothing but dreams of the tormenting routine which awaits him tomorrow'.[48]

Again, attempts to improve their treatment were routinely frustrated by corrupt officials, devious plantation owners and the victimisation of the Chinese who were too frightened to complain. So instead, when the misery became unbearable, mutinies broke out on the plantations. The labourers would escape and invariably find their way into neighbouring towns and villages to rob, pillage and rape, causing federal troops to be despatched to round them up. Having suppressed the banditry and exacted brutal revenge, the men were returned to their prisons only for the cycle of violence to begin again. Uprisings of his nature became such a feature of life for ordinary Peruvians that many bought weapons for the protection of their families, turning 'every farmhouse [into] a little armoury',[49] in anticipation of the next bloody insurrection.

An even worse fate awaited those sent to work on the notorious Chincha Islands, thirteen miles off the southwest coast. Three tiny granite specks bordered by steep cliffs, the largest only 0.8 miles long and 0.6 miles wide, their vast guano deposits, rich in potassium, nitrate and phosphate, were highly prized as fertiliser. Contributing hundreds of thousands of pesos to the economy annually, the industry had been thriving since the 1840s, but for the damned souls expected to clear from four to five tons of a day, it was an existence almost without parallel. Visiting British mining engineer A. J. Duffield considered that 'no hell has ever been conceived ... that can be equalled in the fierceness of its heat, the horror of its stink, and the damnation of those compelled to labour there, to a deposit of Peruvian guano when being shovelled into ships'.[50] In 1870, a visiting US consul recorded the brutal treatment endured by the workers first-hand:

> One fourth of their number become sick ... while they retain strength to stand up are compelled to work on their knees, picking

the small stones out of the guano and when their hands become sore from the constant use of the wheelbarrow, it is strapped upon their shoulders, and in that way they are compelled to fulfil their daily task.[51]

Another witness added that 'besides being worked almost to death, they have neither sufficient food nor passably wholesome water',[52] driving many to try and throw themselves off the cliffs to escape their nightmare. At last, towards the end of 1873, reports of conditions in the plantations and guano beds had reached China, when coincidentally, a mission headed by Captain Garcia y Garcia arrived seeking a trade agreement. Prince Kung did not mince his words. He subjected his visitors to a tirade in which he insisted: 'Until they return all the coolies to their own country, and agree not to hire any more, no treaty can be made with them.'[53] Garcia strongly objected, and claimed that not all the Chinese in Peru would wish to return in any case, but Kung was aware of the various decrees that had been enacted and ignored and insisted that this was the only solution to their plight.

Months of negotiations followed, during which time Li Hongzhang asked a friend who was living in the United States to see the conditions for himself. His report confirmed Li's worst fears, so he demanded that all be released, and those who wished to do so, be returned to China at the expense of the Peruvian Government. Furthermore, any future migrants would have to be afforded the same rights as American, British or German expats. Garcia had to agree and the trade agreement was eventually signed and ratified, but the strict conditions attached to it did not suit the planters and the guano peddlers. The last ship containing contract labour from China docked at Callao on 2 July 1874, although as was the practice, existing contracts had to expire and the trade did not end entirely until 1882.

Back in the West Indies, a successful slave revolt on the French island of Haiti in 1804 so rattled the British that they feared copycat uprisings in their own slave-based economies. As a consequence, the decision was taken to experiment with Chinese labour instead. They would have to be indentured and sign contracts, but this was offset by the belief that being more pliant than their volatile African

The Very Scum of the Population

counterparts they were less likely to stage an insurrection. In 1806, the first 200 arrived in Trinidad, but it would be some years before the idea caught on, and British Guiana would not operate the system until 1853, long after slavery was abolished throughout the British Empire. Furthermore, having learnt of the consequences of the Cuban and Peruvian systems, they decided to use their own agents rather than the Chinese crimps. Nonetheless, this approach proved to be no panacea.

According to Henry Kirke, who spent twenty-five years in the colony and served as Sherriff of Demerara, the early incomers were 'the offscourings of Canton – gaolbirds, sturdy beggars, loafers and vagabonds [and] showed no inclination for sustained toil in the fields ... nearly all of them deserted after a few months'.[54] His assessment was shared by Wesleyan missionary Reverend H. Bronkhurst who found them to be 'ignorant, degraded people, filthy in their habits'.[55] Kirke later discovered that many of those who absconded had instead taken to 'peddling, rum smuggling, illicit distillation, keeping gambling houses, brothels, burglary, robbery, and petty larceny'.[56] As with those bound for Havana and Callao, mutinies were not unknown en route. One ship, the *Prince of Ganges* with 300 labourers on board had barely got up steam when the Captain and purser were thrown overboard, and the crew forced to take them to Hainan Island.[57]

Fortunately for the good people of Georgetown, the vast majority of the 14,500 or so who followed displayed far better characters. Kirke found these to be 'most worthy, law abiding people ... industrious, truthful and honest'.[58] Furthermore, when their indentures expired many remained to pursue a variety of productive occupations, Bronkhurst noting that 'we have in the colony Chinese carpenters, cabinet makers, builders of houses etc',[59] many of whom 'are the only people in the colony who keep barbers shops, and the latter have plenty to do, shaving heads and cleaning ears'.[60] Others went on to own high-end businesses, including 'the shops or stores of Messrs Wo Lee and Co. and others in Lombard Street, well fitted up and stocked with Chinese commodities new and rare, and largely patronised by ladies and gentlemen'.[61]

Nonetheless, his claim that 'in British Guiana, the Chinese and all other nations [enjoy] equal privileges and are free subjects'[62] did not stand up to scrutiny when the colony was visited by Sir George William DesVoeux, who had served as Administrator on the island of St Lucia. His observations, and the reports that found their way to him, prompted a lengthy missive condemning the abuse meted out by some plantation owners and their overseers. In 1871, a Royal Commission was appointed to look into his claims, among which was of one 'immigrant [who] had been dreadfully beaten by an Indian watchman while in the act of stealing', suffering as a consequence, 'fractures of limbs, two compound and three simple, both legs and both arms being broken'.[63] DesVoeux added that they only risked such beatings because they were 'obliged to steal or they could not have lived',[64] having been denied the pay, conditions and other benefits to which they were entitled. Moreover, as in other countries, when ill they were 'not allowed to stay in hospital but were considered well'. Those 'who by their physical condition showed that they were unfit to work'[65] were forced to return to their labours. If they then failed to perform their tasks, they were subject to the perverse logic that 'an immigrant is liable to be punished for neglect of work if he is not on the hospital books'.[66] DesVoeux's testimony went some way to so discrediting the system here, so that it endured for only a few more years and the last transport, containing 388 Chinese labourers, arrived in 1875.[67]

The plantation owners of neighbouring Dutch Guiana also toyed with the idea of employing Chinese, and in 1853 the colonial authorities on Java in the Dutch East Indies procured for them eighteen labourers. This process proved rather expensive, so in 1858 it was decided to recruit them directly from Macao, but when they arrived in Paramaribo they discovered that they, too, had been duped. The plantation owners wanted them to replace slave labour, but they did not want to shoulder the cost of employing so-called free labour. Instead, the workers' contracts were unilaterally amended to give the whites greater say over their terms and conditions, and they enforced the new regulations in the face of angry demonstrations. Only around 2,500 would in any case make the long journey and like their compatriots in British Guiana, some remained at the end of the contracts and went into business. They also intermarried with local women.

The Very Scum of the Population

Many were lured abroad not by the prospect of working for someone else, but by the stories of gold discoveries in places such as California in the United States. Between 1852 and 1875, 200,000 would migrate to seek their fortunes, and there were 30,000 in San Francisco alone by 1876.[68] When the gold ran out, they found themselves competing for work in agriculture, industry and fisheries, draining swamplands and building canals, and inevitably this caused friction among whites who viewed them as cheap interlopers. This was countered by men such as university professor George Payne, who explained that on the contrary, '[they] are not cheap labourers, they demand the current wages and refuse to work for less'.[69] Instead he insisted that 'the Chinese [can] compete with profit under the hardest circumstances when the whites would not be able to earn a livelihood and [this] provokes the fear and envy of the whites'.[70] In fact, if anything they were simply extremely canny:

> His thrift and his laborious patience ... organised more thoroughly and minutely into unions ... have an adaptability and a keenness which enable them to distribute themselves quickly to the districts and the occupations where competition is least and wages highest ... among the fifty or sixty thousand remaining in California, the most of whom were originally labourers, the majority are now the owners of small independent businesses or employed in small independent undertakings.[71]

Publications such as the *Royal Gazette* of 1 January 1870 agreed. In California alone, it stated, 'there are 100,000, and they are said to be extremely industrious ... there are in San Francisco some three or four hundred Chinese stores',[72] and at harvest time 'they dotted the fields from one end of the state to the other' gathering strawberries and digging potatoes. The planters of the Southern States also wanted them to replace freed slaves. The *Ville de St Lo* sailed from Hong Kong to New Orleans in February 1870 with 200 labourers to work in the Arkansas Valley, defying in the process a resolution of Congress passed in January 1867.[73]

Yet the undertaking for which they would become synonymous was that great infrastructure project which drew some

20,000 volunteers between 1865 and 1869. This was the 1,911 mile Central Pacific section of the transcontinental railroad linking Sacramento to the Missouri River, an endeavour to which they would contribute as much as 90 per cent of the workforce. Author Edwin Sabin described the somewhat curious impression they made at first, as they 'trooped in from Sacramento and San Francisco in their basket hats, their blue blouses and flapping pantaloons ... to face heat and cold, storm and toil and American curses'.[74] They soon showed that appearances could be deceptive, as they went to work blasting and digging cuts, carving out tunnels through solid granite at high altitudes, dumping spoil to create fills, constructing trestles across deep canyons and building retaining walls. Others drilled holes for blasting suspended perilously from baskets, but whatever task they undertook, they earned a reputation for efficiency and acumen. Once shown what to do and how, 'the Chinaman became an efficient toiler', wrote Sabin[75] and, added George Payne, proved to be 'the ideal industrial machine, the perfect human ox. He will transform less food into more work [being] patient, docile, industrious, and above all "honest" in the business sense that they keep their contracts'.[76] Furthermore, they 'drank not... gambled only among themselves, they toiled but they did not spin; they offered no inducements to whiskey pedlars and monte men'.[77] So, when their Irish colleagues went on strike, the Chinese were sent for, and they did so well filling their shoes that the employers issued a call for 5,000 more. Sabin observed that 'unenthusiastic Celts' were brusquely displaced by 'Mongolians';[78] but the 'Celts' ultimately turned the tables, and many 'Mongolians' found themselves working under Irish foremen who subjected them to typically abusive treatment.

Another reason that they were favoured was because on average they were paid around two-thirds what their Irish received. But by the spring of 1867, by which time there were 14,000 toiling on the Central Pacific section, they had decided enough was enough. Demanding parity with other workers, they went on strike for $40 a month, a ten-hour day and shorter shifts. Many had already absconded to work in nearby mines where the rewards for equally hard work were greater, and their loss was being felt by the railway bosses. Nonetheless, fearing the consequences of backing down they refused to concede to their demands outright. They eventually went back to work. However, such was their value to the project, no disciplinary action was taken and slowly their pay and conditions did improve.

It was in large part due to Chinese muscle that the Central Pacific and Union Pacific Railroads finally met at Promontory Point in Utah on 10 May 1869, becoming the Transcontinental Railroad. After it was finished and most men had left, President of the Central Pacific Leland Stanford conceded that it would have been 'impossible to complete the western portion of this great national highway within the time required by the Acts of Congress' without them.[79]

It has been estimated that up to 2,000 workers forfeited their lives, plummeting from bridges and viaducts, crushed under landslides and tunnel collapses, and from attacks by Native Americans. In the process they had cut the journey time across the United States from months to a week, and the cost of doing so by 85 per cent, from about $1,000 to $150. Apart from the accolades of Stanford, they received scant reward for their sacrifices. Instead, the passing of the 1882 Chinese Exclusion Act suspended further immigration for ten years and denied them the same rights to naturalisation as European migrants. It was extended again over the years until by 1924 migration from China, apart from students, diplomats and other exceptions, was almost zero. It was only in 1943, with Nationalist China's recognition as an ally against Germany and Japan, that the rules were relaxed.

Canada hosted the earliest Chinese visitors in 1788, when they accompanied British merchants to Nootka Sound in what was to become British Columbia. The traders planned to catch sea otter pelts to sell in Guangzhou, but the Spanish had already laid claim to the area and drove them out, leaving the Chinese marooned. They and their descendants managed nonetheless to make a living and remained there largely alone for another sixty years until they were joined by compatriots drawn to Barkerville in the Fraser Valley after gold was discovered. When it ran out, several thousand decamped to Vancouver Island where they joined the 5,000 to 6,000 shipped from Hong Kong in 1881 to work on Canada's Pacific Railroad. Between then and 1884 a total of 15,701 arrived from the US, or directly from China to serve as labourers,[80] of whom around 600 would perish in the same harsh conditions their fellow countrymen further south had endured.

Similarly, once they had served their purpose they found themselves unwanted, and pressure mounted for a Royal Commission to investigate claims that they were now having a negative impact on society. Waiting for the railway to be completed first, the Commission was appointed in 1884, hearing evidence at various meetings across the Province. Witnesses eagerly accused them of dishonesty, dirtiness, lawlessness, a predilection for gambling and drugs and vouched for their general unsuitability for assimilation. Although the Commission found most of these claims either unfounded or that they merely proved that the Chinese community was no worse than other migrants, the pressure was there for some action to be taken, particularly from trade unionists who feared competition for jobs.

Consequently, from 1885 Chinese migrants had to pay a $50 'head tax', and those who managed to be admitted into the country at all were subjected to various restrictive covenants. These prevented them from buying land or from practising certain professions such as law and accountancy, and most particularly there were strict rules on where they were permitted to live. As a result they were hemmed into the smallest and least salubrious corner of Victoria on the southern end of Vancouver Island, where their community turned into a squalid, cramped ghetto. Their predicament was graphically described by sympathisers such as Persia Campbell who reported air 'polluted by the disgusting offal with which they are surrounded ... the vile accumulations are apt to spread fever and sickness in the neighbourhood. There is no question that the Chinese quarters are the filthiest and most disgusting places in Victoria, overcrowded hotbeds of disease and vice'.[81]

Rather than accept such evidence as proof of the deprivation and squalor to which the Chinese community was subjected, it served instead as grist to the mill for those seeking to marginalise the newcomers even further. In 1900, the head tax was raised to $100, and when that failed to have the desired effect a second Royal Commission was appointed in 1902. It reached a completely different assessment to that arrived at by its predecessor, and in its estimation the Chinese were now deemed to be

> ... a people that will not assimilate, or become an integral part of our race and nation. With their habits of overcrowding and an utter disregard for all sanitary laws, they are a continual menace to health ... they are obnoxious to a free community and dangerous to the state.[82]

This scathing assessment was followed by an increase in the head tax to $500 in 1903, which cut immigration from 4,719 to eight almost overnight, and a law passed on Dominion Day 1923 suspended immigration altogether, discriminatory measures which would not be rescinded until after the Second World War. Canadians, moreover, were not alone in viewing with morbid fear the prospect of thousands of Chinaman coming to live among them. Many in the Antipodes, too, had developed an equally irrational loathing.

Records show that one Mak Sai Ying, otherwise known as John Pong Shying, arrived in Port Jackson, New South Wales, aboard the *Laurel* in 1818. He appears to have been accepted readily enough by the locals, working as a carpenter, buying land in Paramatta and becoming a successful licensee in 1829. He also married twice and had four sons, but as far as it can be determined, he remained one of only a handful of migrants in the colony until at least 1849. Then came men who had answered the call for labour to work on the land, but as they became more of a presence, they were met with increasing suspicion. *The People's Advocate* of 10 March 1849 noted that they had become 'not a mere matter of experience but a regular and systematic trade'.[83] but when news of gold discoveries in Victoria reached Guangdong in 1853, their profile increased dramatically. Some 2,000 reached the gold fields by 1854, and the reaction from whites was predictably hostile. Clashes with other prospectors and opposition by Chartists and trade unionists who met them with cries of 'No coolies, no coolies!'[84] led to demands for action. An Act followed in 1855 allowing only one Chinese to every ton of shipping, along with a levy of £10 upon entry. Although many simply landed in neighbouring South Australia instead and crossed over, the South Australian Government caught on to the ruse and passed a similar Act in 1857.[85]

Nevertheless, by then there were already 26,370 Chinese in Victoria out of a mining population of 82,428,[86] and further clashes with white gold miners prompted the imposition of a bi-monthly licence fee of £1.00 on every Chinese national who was not natural born or a British subject.[87] By 1859 the population had grown to 42,000, mainly confined to reworking played out claims or those not thought worthwhile by whites. A further levy of £40 and an annual fee of £4.00 saw their numbers fall to 20,000 by 1863,[88] but many would have been making their way home in any case, as the claims proved uneconomic to work and the heyday of the gold rush was over.

New South Wales also drew prospectors, partly to avoid the Victoria taxes and by 1861 they numbered 12,988, but again they were driven out after the colony passed the same legislation. Gold discoveries in Queensland prompted the Gold Fields Act of 1873, which specified how large a claim could be, how many prospectors were permitted, how claims should be marked out and the annual fee to be charged. Although a translated version of the rules was produced for the benefit of the 7,000 Chinese prospectors, very few could read or understand its contents, so they ran the risk of breaching the regulations by default and giving the authorities a pretext for invalidating their claims.

Nor was the discrimination confined to the gold fields. When the Australian Steamship Navigation Company decided to employ Chinese on its service to the East in 1878, trade unionists again intervened, and a thirteen-week strike was called until the company backed down. The Queensland Government then added a clause to future mail contracts disqualifying Asiatics or Polynesian seamen from being employed at all. Nonetheless, racists continued to stoke people's fears and suspicions. An Anti-Chinese League was formed in Sydney, which demanded among other things that they be denied the same naturalisation rights as Europeans, and in Victoria moves were taken to deny them the vote. This atmosphere of near hysteria belied the fact that by 1881 out of a total population of 2,252,617, only 38,397 were now Chinese anyway,[89] and many of these were just passing through. Irrespective of the facts, oppressive steps continued to be imposed by the colonies to marginalise them, and their powers to do so increased drastically following federation in 1901. The government of the new Commonwealth of Australia was now free to pass whatever wide-ranging legislation it wished to maintain its so-called 'White Australia' policy. This would remain in place for another forty or more years.

New Zealand's experience was similar to its larger neighbour, with prospectors drawn to Otago on the southern end of South Island after gold was discovered in 1861. Many came from Australia and California and then made the perilous journey across terrain pitted with deep valleys and criss-crossed by treacherous rivers before arriving at the equally inhospitable mining settlement of Arrowtown on the Arrow River. From around 200 in 1866, their numbers grew to over 4,000 by 1871,[90] mining worked out claims abandoned by Europeans. Almost from the outset they were marginalised, excluded from the main town and relegated to the banks of Bush Creek on its outskirts. Here they constructed crude, elementary shelters which generally consisted of tiny huts, many no bigger than the average garden shed. The only materials they had to hand was the local shist, a type of metamorphic rock, which was nonetheless highly adaptable and could be used to make walls and floors to topped off with a corrugated iron roof. In these tiny buildings they had to try and survive the bitter winters, and because of the segregation imposed upon them by the Europeans, became a self-contained community. Many died here in poverty, but then they were restricted to their own section of the cemetery, or buried outside its walls.

One of their few contacts with the outside was Ah Lum's store, which served from 1883 as a shop and a bank, and its owner as interpreter. Their very existence irked the European miners, who formed a committee to follow up on claims that they were smoking opium, gambling and engaging in other iniquitous activities. These lies were soon debunked by an investigation which found that on the contrary they were almost entirely 'industrious, frugal and orderly',[91] keeping to themselves and not bothering anyone. Yet once again, the bigots were not prepared to let the facts get in the way of their prejudices, and white supremacists persisted in their efforts to restrict and if possible exclude them from New Zealand society entirely. In July 1881, a £10 poll tax was imposed on Chinese migrants, and only one person was permitted entry for every ten tons of cargo. In 1896 the tax was hiked to £100 and the tonnage to migrant ratio raised to 200 tons. From 1888 legislation similar to the measures taken in Australia and Canada was also passed, so that there were just 2,570 left in the country by 1907, and 2,147 in 1916.[92] This legislation was only relaxed during the Second World War, but it was not until the 1970s that attitudes really changed, and subsequent immigration laws made the Chinese more welcome.

In South Africa, the discovery of gold and diamonds in the Transvaal in the 1870s acted as a magnet for prospectors from all over the globe, but the Chinese contingent soon found itself discriminated against and refused licences. Instead, many turned to commerce and opened businesses, but as their numbers grew the white-dominated governments took steps to stem the flow. The Transvaal Immigration Restriction Act of 1902 and the Cape Chinese Exclusion Act of 1904 were passed, sitting alongside other discriminatory by-laws and ordinances aiming to limit where they could live and what professions they could followTheir fortunes changed when the owners who monopolised the mining industries faced a growing labour shortage. They were competing for workers with other developing sectors such as the railways, which was short of 56,000 labourers, and agriculture where another 80,000 people were needed to work on vineyards and farms.[93]

Although in theory there were more than enough potential native workers to go round, they proved singularly reluctant to take up employment in the mines. Transvaal's Labour Commissioner Sir Godfrey Lagden calculated in 1903 that one native in every eight to ten of the whole population was capable of working in the mines, but the actual number was just one in twenty-five.[94] One of the reasons behind this was not hard to find, as during the Boer War the British army had paid top dollar to native farmers for their cattle. This sudden prosperity offered little incentive to risk life and limb in dirty and dangerous mines,[95] notorious for wretched conditions that took the lives of seventy in every 1,000 workers.[96] So comparatively high salaries had to be offered to try and lure them in, but eventually this meant that between 50 to 60 per cent of production costs were absorbed by the wage bill.[97] The answer somehow lay in recruiting more men, but offsetting the necessarily larger workforce by forcing down pay. Although there were also workers from the Indian sub-continent who might be enlisted, too few were willing to volunteer. So, reluctantly and in the face of stiff opposition, the Transvaal Labour Importation Ordinance finally authorised the employment of Chinese labour, but strictly limited to the Witwatersrand mines. The authorities then engaged in the necessary negotiations and signed an agreement with the Chinese government in May 1904.

Recruitment was the responsibility of the Labour Importation Agency of the Chamber of Mines, which used Hong Kong to sign all contracts and from where the labourers were to be shipped. By June 1904, the first batch was ready in what became known as the 'Experiment', and between 1904 and the end of the scheme approximately 100,000 would be transported to southern Africa. Having had their fingers burnt so many times before, Chinese subjects who were engaged in this exercise were supposed to be properly looked after. A Superintendent was appointed by the Lieutenant-Governor of Transvaal, and below him inspectors, physicians and clerks would inspect the mines to ensure adequate sanitation and medical care was provided and any complaints acted upon. In return, they were to ensure that employers secured a 'satisfactory amount of labour from them'.[98] To this end they were confined to compounds on mine property, with each company employing up to 3,000 men, overseen by the mine manager. A sub manager ran the compound, assisted by European Chinese speakers and they were divided into gangs of twenty or thirty under an overseer called a 'headman'.

Despite such safeguards, the usual unscrupulous agents succeeded in getting in on the act, never slow to exploit an opportunity to make a quick buck. Interested only in their commission, they recruited whoever was willing to go so long as he was capable of getting through his medical examination and sign his contract. Few checks were made about the character of the applicant, their suitability or aptitude for the work involved. Furthermore, desperate for money and to escape the grinding poverty of their lives, those volunteering to go probably asked few questions either. It was hardly surprising therefore, when the High Commissioner Lord Selbourne admitted on 18 September 1905: 'While I believe the Chinese were told that they were coming to work on a mine, I also believe that many of them did not understand what work on a mine entailed'.[99] Consequently, a total of 2,142 had to be returned to Hong Kong, of whom 354 were criminals, 375 too unfit for the work required[100] and 1,416 unsuitable for other reasons.[101] For all that, the 55,000 that passed muster seemed to impress their employers, and commentator George Payne found that they demonstrated an 'efficiency equal to that of the whites and double that of the natives'.[102] Subsequently, the mining workforce grew from 100,098 in 1898 to 177,812 in 1905, allowing the number of mines to increase from 164 to 298. As a result of their brawn, the combined output of all the mines rose from $84,775,000 to $115,720,000,[103] but the honeymoon did not last.

A Report of the Foreign Labour Department for the Transvaal for 1905-1906 revealed that only 'three women and five children have accompanied the labourers in the past year, whilst one woman and two children have returned to China, leaving a total number of four women and twenty-six children on the Rand'.[104] The consequences of this deficit for thousands of lonely, homesick men was soon felt. Combined with the working conditions, being cooped up in their compounds with little to do but gamble and smoke opium, this lack of women further undermined morale and discipline. Reports of male prostitution leaked out which, it was claimed, 'prevails in most if not in all of the compounds',[105] inflaming a general air of insubordination and declining productivity. There were also growing tensions between Chinese and African workers and fighting became more commonplace between the two groups. The Chinese gamblers code of honour, which dictated that men settle what they owed or face the consequences, became another issue. Threatened with violence or worse if they failed to pay up, many were left with no option but to abscond to escape retribution. This alone became such a problem for the authorities that 400 men from the South African Constabulary had to be deployed to hunt them down and return them to their mines. Those that eluded the law remained at large looking for food, shelter or some means of paying off their debts, prompting rumours of bloodthirsty bandits prowling the veld and threatening Afrikaners in their isolated homesteads. In May 1906 Transvaal Premier Louis Botha reported that they had become so concerned for their families that they 'seldom venture from their farms in order not to leave their women and children defenceless'.[106]

In aggregate, these infractions translated into 13,532 out of 49,000 Chinese on the payroll during 1905-06 being convicted of criminal offences or of breaking their contracts. This contrasted with just 3,824 out of the 85,000 natives employed in the mines.[107] At his wit's end to restore discipline, Governor Lord Milner sanctioned illegal flogging,[108] and when this revelation reached London there was outrage. Bernard Seymour, Second Baron Coleridge, described to his peers how transgressors could find themselves summarily 'tied up by their pigtails to poles so their heels are off the ground, and then lashed with canes'.[109] This came hard on the heels of the Secretary of State for the Colonies Alfred Lyttelton's previous undertakings to the House of Lords that no such punishments had been sanctioned. He was subsequently forced to admit that they had indeed been resorted to, but only 'as a disciplinary measure with the permission of the Transvaal authorities'.[110] This cut little ice with the critics of the scheme, and the general situation in the mines forced a complete re-evaluation.

By the beginning of 1906, the trial, which many by now had openly condemned as 'Chinese slavery',[111] had been completely discredited, and in Lord Coleridge's opinion 'we have now had very nearly a year's working of an experiment which is undoubtedly a novel experiment, and, as some of us think, a disastrous experiment'.[112] Many in government concurred, and on 31 March Lord Milner informed parliament: 'My ministers are resolved that the employment of Chinese labourers on the mines of the Witwatersrand shall cease at the earliest possible moment.'[113] The necessary Act received Royal Assent in August 1907, and in the words of George Payne, with 'the experiment with Chinese labour in South Africa a failure, the labourers were returned, and the whole matter was permanently closed'.[114]

Such controversies had of course long dogged the employment of Chinese labourers, and in 1899 Emperor Guangxu belatedly issued an Imperial Edict in which he decreed: 'In our anxiety for the welfare of our subjects, and especially those sojourning in foreign countries, we herewith command our ambassadors and consuls as far as in their power, to extend help and protection to the Chinese in their districts.'[115] One of these was his Ambassador in London, Lew Ta-Jen, who lodged a formal complaint against the 'exceptional and exceptionable laws which some of the colonial legislatures of Australia and the Dominions have ... enacted against Chinese subjects'.[116] But constitutionally there was little the Government in London could now do, and the laws and discrimination would remain in place for years to come. In fact, as the new century began and the Great War approached, European bigotry showed no sign of abating. The *North China Daily News* summed up the prevailing school of thought in 1913 when it described the average Chinese as belonging to 'an order of which the average European comprehends little, and that, as a human being ... sooner or later he dies the death of a neglected dog'.[117]

Thus, the average Chinese was still viewed as little more than cheap and expendable labour, sentiments the Chinese government itself did little to disabuse when in early 1915 finance minister Liang Shiyi offered its services to the Allied War effort. This was to come in the form of *Yigong daibing*, or non-combatants rather than combat troops, who could serve as labourers and auxiliaries. They would work behind the frontline, undertaking a variety of tasks such as digging trenches, working in supply dumps or laying railway lines. The offer was promptly accepted by the French as they were already suffering horrendous casualties and badly needed to replace men for the front-line, but the British were more reticent. It took them another year to realise the merits of the proposal and, as British Prime Minister David Lloyd George later recorded in his memoirs, his right-hand man Sir Eric Geddes 'sent an officer to China to recruit 15,000 Chinese labourers for work in France, out of whom 6,000 were required to work on the railways and 1,000 for inland water transport, the others being employed at various tasks on the roads, railheads dumps etc'.[118]

Britain would recruit a total of 94,146 men for the new 'Chinese Labour Corps' and these came primarily from northern China. They were first sent to Weihaiwei, and from there shipped to Noyelles-sur-Mer in France. Upon reaching their destination, they were examined by a medical officer who checked for cases of tuberculosis, venereal disease, beri beri and trachoma, with those deemed fit registered and marched to their camps. Here they were segregated according to whether they were skilled or unskilled. They were a mixed bag, many being recruited from prison after being promised remission of sentence. They had their fingerprints taken to stop them trying to draw another man's pay. Private Norman Miller of the 4th Bedfordshire Regiment remembered them as 'damned good, hardworking and faithful [but] terrible thieves'.[119] They would earn every centime of their one or two francs a day, working for ten hours up to seven days a week. Lloyd George was also impressed, describing them as 'immensely powerful fellows it was no uncommon spectacle to see one of them pick up a balk of timber or a bundle of corrugated iron sheets weighing three or four hundredweight, and walk off with it as calmly as if it weighed only as many stone'.[120]

They needed to be robust as the work was relentless, and even when sick, there was little respite. Sergeant John Ward of the 12th Battalion Kings Royal Rifle Corps was attached to a Trachoma Company, 'a convalescent camp for Chinese who had been sick or wounded and they nearly all suffered from weeping red eyes. But that didn't prevent them from working and we used to send them out in gangs on different jobs every morning ... until they had fully recovered'.[121] Others were members of pioneer and labour battalions following behind the advancing troops, clearing unexploded ordnance and recovering lost equipment and weapons.

Stationed mainly round Montreuil and along the coast between Calais and Le Havre, their contracts specified that they should not be exposed to danger, but this clause was routinely broken. Lloyd George noted rather whimsically:

> At times ... these Chinese coolies came under aerial bombardment or long-range shelling. That did not greatly perturb them; they were far less nervous under fire than the British West Indian Auxiliaries... If they suffered any fatal casualties, they would all break off work to attend the funeral, and neither threats nor cajolery had the least effect on them, nor would bombing or shelling by the enemy scatter their cortege, until the obsequies had been duly completed.[122]

The number of Chinese who died from shelling, the Spanish flu, or maltreatment is unknown. European records put the number as unconvincingly low as 2,000. There are 838 Chinese gravestones at the cemetery of Noyelles-sur-Mer alone, for example. More worked for the British in the Middle East, primarily at the docks in the Iraqi port of Basra on the Shatt-al-Arab. Here 6,000 were employed building vessels for the war against the Ottomans, of whom at least 227 lost their lives. There was little safety even when in transit, and when German submarine *U-65* sank the French merchant ship SS *Athos* on 17 February 1917, 543 of the 900 Chinese workers aboard died. Those who sustained wounds and other injuries would have been overlooked, had the Chinese government not created the Bureau of Overseas Chinese Workers. Through this they were able to put pressure on the British and French to pay compensation to those who had been maimed in their service.

When the fighting finally came to an end in 1918 large numbers remained behind, faced with the gargantuan task of cleaning up years of devastation from the battlefields. They would eventually help in the removal of thousands of tons of the detritus that had been produced and help recover the remains of countless unburied dead. Those that did venture home however, found it still under the sway of foreign powers, men whose appetite for their exploitation remained unsated.

9

China Belongs to the Chinese

Little sympathy had been elicited among the foreign powers for the country's ongoing internal problems, rather they continued to capitalise on them to further their own ends. In 1913 Germany took advantage of the power vacuum to secure the rights to build two new railway lines in Shandong, one from Qingdao southwest to join with the Tianjin-Pukou Railway, and another to extend the Shandong Railway to join with the Beijing-Hankou Railway.[1] Britain meanwhile, ever mindful lest the security of its Indian Empire be threatened by the turmoil next door, sought to further consolidate its northern flank. In July 1913-14, the McMahon Line was agreed with Tibet, which ceded the territory later referred to as Arunachal Pradesh to India and demarcated the frontier to its advantage. These developments caused much disquiet in Beijing, despite having put its initial signature to the agreement. With the benefit of hindsight, it reneged on it, claiming the Chinese signatory had not been authorised to approve such an undertaking, but Delhi persuaded Lhasa to proceed with the treaty anyway without Beijing's consent.

The Japanese were also watching events with interest. In 1913, Foreign Minister Kato Takaoki told Lord Grey frankly that they would move to safeguard their interests in the country at the right 'psychological moment', and that came soon enough when war broke out in August 1914. With Qingdao far from reinforcement and resupply, it was now seriously compromised, and Tokyo proceeded to make good on Takaoki's promise. An ultimatum was presented to the German governor on 15 August instructing him to 'withdraw immediately from Japanese and Chinese waters [and] to deliver on a date not later than September 15, to the Imperial Japanese authorities without condition or compensation, the entire leased territory of Kiaochau'. Failure to comply would invite 'such action as it may deem necessary to meet the situation'.[2] As von Tirpitz freely admitted, 'even with great expenditure of capital we could not have built a fortress to resist the attack of a Japanese army',[3] but the garrison of 4,000 still had to be seen to be fulfilling its duty 'to the utmost'.[4] The ultimatum was rejected and the Japanese declared war on 23 August, landing a force of 20,000 supported by 1,500 British soldiers. They besieged the port with 140 artillery pieces and naval vessels engaging the Germans from offshore. The defenders managed to hold out until 7 November.

Tokyo then assured the Chinese that once matters were normalised, the port would be returned to them, an undertaking which soon rang hollow when they presented them with the notorious Twenty-One Demands in January 1915. Euphemistically referred to as 'outstanding questions' for which they required 'satisfactory' responses, in reality they constituted further far-reaching infringements of Chinese sovereignty. They claimed that because the removal of the Germans from Shandong involved 'immense sacrifices in blood and money,[5] this justified special consideration of Japan's interests in the region. Furthermore, if, after digesting their contents Beijing demurred, they threatened 'vigorous methods'[6] to secure their compliance. When the public became aware of them there was almost universal outrage, widespread demonstrations and boycotts of everything Japanese, but Yuan Shikai's options by this time were extremely limited. He now headed a government fighting for its survival in the face of opposition from groups seeking his removal, in response to which he was trying to reinvent himself as head of a new imperial dynasty. He had few resources to resist the Japanese.

Despite practically unanimous opposition he reluctantly acceded to the demands, and on 25 May 1915 the Sino-Japanese Agreement was signed. Under its terms, 'the Chinese Government agrees to give full assent to all matters upon which the Japanese Government may hereafter agree with the German Government relating to the disposition of all rights, interests and concessions which Germany, by virtue of treaties or otherwise it possesses in relation to the Province of Shantung'.[7] Japan's presence and special rights in Manchuria were to be reaffirmed and the government undertook not to grant any more leases to Europeans. Those held on Port Arthur, Dairen, the South Manchuria Railway and the Antung-Mukden Railway were extended to ninety-nine years, whilst Japanese subjects were to be permitted to enter, travel, and reside in South Manchuria for trade, commerce and agriculture without restriction. More towns were opened to trade in Eastern Inner Mongolia and only Japanese capital was to be used to build railways in either territory.

Nine mining districts in Manchuria were also to be made available to Japanese enterprise and Japan was to have first refusal if foreign advisers or instructors were recruited.[8] They also demanded that only Japanese nationals be employed in the political, financial and military fields of government and that Japanese police be stationed in some cities. Half of China's war material also had to be purchased from Japan. In 1916, beleaguered Yuan's sudden death provided Tokyo with a further opportunity. The Japanese Governor-General of Korea sent an emissary to Beijing with instructions to cultivate the loyalty of pro-Japanese warlords. They hoped that these alliances would entrench their influence and create two weaker power blocks, North and South, neither powerful enough to resist it effectively.

They also sought to block any attempt by the Allies to involve China in the war militarily, which they believed would compromise their divide-and rule agenda, warning of the potentially 'great changes to civilisation'[9] if millions of Chinese soldiers were mobilised. Although, as we have seen, the Chinese never contemplated military involvement, Britain, France and even Russia did not want to risk antagonising Tokyo. This was because at the war's outset they had hoped to secure Japanese help in the European theatre. Most significantly, the British Admiralty desperately needed the assistance of Japanese surface ships for escort duties in the Mediterranean, where it was sorely stretched against a coalition of German and Austro-Hungarian naval assets. Although the prospect of ground troops was a nonstarter, the new government of Tarauchi Masatake showed itself in 1917 to be amenable to supplying warships, but at a price. As a quid pro quo, it demanded that the

British Government recognise Japanese rights to Shandong, and to undertake to support its claim at the end of the war.

Consequently, in a secret 'Understanding' signed on 16 February 1917 London agreed to 'support the claims of Japan in regard to the disposal of Germany's rights in Shantung and possessions in the islands north of the equator'.[10] The French Government were also keen for help in the Mediterranean but were likewise eager to tease from Japan their agreement to China entering the conflict. They put their signature to an almost identical document on 19 February:

> The Imperial Japanese Government proposes to demand at the time of the peace negotiations the surrender of the territorial and special interests Germany possessed before the war in Shantung [and] the Imperial Japanese Government confidently hopes it may count on [France's] full support on this question [provided] that Japan gives its support to obtain from China the breaking of its diplomatic relations with Germany.[11]

The Japanese could hardly believe their luck. An elated Minister for Foreign Affairs Viscount Motono Ichiro wrote to the British Ambassador expressing his joy at this 'fresh proof of the close ties that unites the ... Allied Powers'.[12]

Irrespective of Japan's contribution to the war effort, the shameless tactic of secret protocols irked many critics when they came to light. American journalist Thomas F. Millard railed at such duplicity 'at a time when the United States was on the verge of entering the war, was trying to induce China to adopt similar measures and sever diplomatic relations with Germany, and was assuring the Chinese Government that China's territorial integrity and rights would be secured thereby'.[13] He saved the strongest denunciation for the Japanese, whom he accused of using methods 'which can be termed blackmail without stretching the usual definition of the word, to obtain concessions from her allies in war while giving comparatively little military help' in return.[14] He may have been unaware, however, that true to their word a Japanese fleet of seventeen warships had been despatched to the Mediterranean in early May 1917. Here they did sterling work, escorting twenty-one British warships and 700 troopships. They also saved the lives of around 7,000 victims of German submarines who might otherwise have died, including 3,000 in one operation alone. Whether it ought to have been China that paid the price would be something he would have found highly debatable.

Even after China formally declared war on the Central Powers on 14 August 1917 the scheming continued and contrary to Millard's assertions, the United States was not completely untarnished either. The Lansing-Ishii Agreement of 2 November 1917 confirmed that whilst neither party intended to 'infringe in any way the independence or territorial integrity of China',[15] the 'Government of the US recognises that Japan has special interests ... particularly in the part to which her possessions are contiguous'.[16] Although the State Department later rowed back on the inferences to be drawn from such statements, they did not bode well when the subject of Shandong arose at the Versailles Peace Conference.

Despite the chaos following the death of Yuan Shikai, the machinations of Japan and the country's descent into warlordism, the Chinese succeeded in cobbling together a delegation representing its various and largely conflicting interests. It was at least largely of one voice in wanting to wipe the slate clean, ending extraterritoriality, annulling the Twenty-One Demands and repatriating the concessions in Shandong. But they faced an uphill struggle, and from the outset their case was not helped by the fact that some delegates were overtly xenophobic, particularly foreign minister Lu Zhengxiang, who had been overheard referring to Europeans as 'long-nosed hairy barbarians'.[17] Self-evidently, he would need to keep such personal views under his hat if he hoped to achieve his objectives and sway the conference. To this end, his entourage, which fortunately also included the more affable and circumspect Ambassador to the United States Wellington Koo, embarked on a charm offensive. They proceeded to lobby, wine and dine fellow delegates, give speeches, participate in debates, entertain experts and even donate to the Belgian and French relief appeals, hoping to build up a fund of goodwill.

There was certainly some sympathy for the Chinese position. British delegate to the conference Harold Nicolson pointed out that 'the demands of Japan were a flagrant violation of the principles of President Wilson',[18] namely his much lauded Fourteen Points. French delegate Jean Jules Jusserand agreed: 'All the powers who entered the agreement for the negotiation of peace after the armistice of 11 November practically accepted the basis of peace as laid down by the American Government ... any prior engagement such as the secret treaties ... ought not to be held any longer in force.'[19] There were other concerns, which transcended natural justice and simple morality. US Ambassador to China Paul S. Reinsch feared that 'should Japan be given a freer hand [in China] forces will be set in action which make a huge armed conflict absolutely inevitable within one generation'.[20] US Secretary of State Robert Lansing concurred, fearing another 'Prussia' had been unleashed,[21] and Britain's own Ambassador in Tokyo, Charles Eliot, condemned the Japanese as 'opportunistic [and] selfish'.[22] British Foreign Secretary Lord Curzon was less sympathetic to China's position. He characteristically dismissed its delegates as representatives of 'a great, helpless, hopeless and inert mass ... utterly deficient in cohesion or strength, engaged in perpetual conflict between the north and south'.[23] Nationalist Japanese commentator Naomi Tamura, for one, seethed with indignation at Chinese backtracking, accusing them of having acted in bad faith all along. He noted how 'the attitude of the Chinese peace delegation toward Japan completely changed', and the Fourteen Points were now being 'cunningly juggled by them'[24] for their own ends. He lay the blame for Beijing's current predicament entirely at its own doorstep: 'Had China been strong enough to check the tide of European invasion, the world now might have been different. The simple truth is that Japan was obliged to take a defensive attitude to preserve her own existence as a nation.'[25]

They only had to point to the audit trail of undertakings which China, France, Britain and the Americans had made. They drew the conference's attention to the concessions contained in the Twenty-One Demands, the secret protocols and the text of the Lansing-Ishii document. They stuck to the line that the Chinese had made agreements with them, which, now peace had returned, they were trying to renege upon. One Japanese official claimed that a Chinese diplomat in Tokyo had originally 'gladly agreed'[26] to all of Japan's demands. Finally, if the cold facts of treaties, verbal assurances and realpolitik failed to sway the Conference, the Japanese had another trick up their sleeve. The concept of a League of Nations was

President Woodrow Wilson's pet project, but it faced many hurdles as its various clauses were debated by the Conference. One of these was the heated issue of racial equality, sponsored by Japan but highly contentious in a world still dominated by White Anglo-Saxons. Thomas Millard, however, believed it was simply a shrewd ploy, concocted to do some arm twisting over Shandong, that the Japanese had consciously opened this can of worms 'to enable Japan to pose as having a grievance which should be redressed or compensated [for] by the Conference'.[27] In the final analysis, wrote Millard, Wilson was 'fearful of a disruption of the Conference, and ... in order to secure Japan's adherence to the League of Nations he had thought it necessary to accept a solution that was insisted on by Japan'.[28]

So, finding himself virtually held to ransom, on 21 April 1919 Wilson met with premiers Georges Clemenceau and David Lloyd George to adjudicate. The decision was really a foregone conclusion, and after little debate the appropriate Clauses 156, 157 and 158 officially signed all German interests in Shandong over to Japan. In return, demands for the racial equality clauses were conveniently kicked into touch. This shady arrangement was met with almost universal opprobrium, Lansing condemned it as 'selfish materialism tinctured with cynical disregard of manifest rights',[29] whilst historian G. Zay Wood asserted: 'It may safely be said that there is no single instance in modern history which has stood out so conspicuously as a case of imperialism and international immorality as this so-called Shantung Question.'[30] Professor Edward T. Williams of the University of California and Chief Advisor on Far Eastern Affairs to the American Commission at Paris shared their sentiments. He told the Senate Committee on Foreign Relations:

> The railways and mines in Shantung ... ought to have gone automatically to China ... they were taken by Germany from China by an act of piracy; the fact that some other power had driven the Germans out of Shantung does not seem to constitute a title to this property, which naturally should revert to the rightful sovereign of the territory.[31]

Wilson clumsily sought to assuage the Chinese, disingenuously assuring them that once the organisation was up and running, they could 'secure justice from the League'.[32] This was particularly unlikely, because as Millard pointed out, 'the same major powers that comprise the decision in the Shantung question'[33] would also dominate the League Council. Naturally, Chinese students living in Paris were furious when they heard and took to the streets in protest. They were immediately joined by their compatriots back home, where a groundswell of opposition had already been building up. This came to a head on 4 May when 3,000 students congregated in Tiananmen Square in Beijing to voice their opposition. Despite the best efforts of the police and their own professors to stop them, they set out en masse for the foreign legations, some carrying placards demanding 'Give us back Qingdao', 'Refuse to sign the peace treaty', and 'China belongs to the Chinese'.[34] Others handed out leaflets which warned:

> This is the last chance for China in her life and death struggle. Today we swear two solemn oaths with all our countrymen: 1.) China's territory may be conquered but it cannot be given away: 2.) The Chinese people may be massacred, but they will not surrender our country. Our country is about to be annihilated! Up Brethren![35]

Accompanied by cries of 'On to the foreign ministry! On to the homes of Chinese traitors!' the crowd only made it part of the way before it was scattered under the blows of police batons. Thirty-two were thrown into jail. The extent of the violence alarmed Wellington Koo. He feared that unless he rejected the decision out of hand, he would be signing his own death sentence.[36] Lu shared such concerns, and on 6 May issued a press release in which he expressed his country's 'deep disappointment at the settlement proposed by the Council of Three... I have registered a formal protest', and referred the matter back to Beijing.[37] On 26 May he further advised the Council that 'the Chinese delegation have received messages from the Parliament, the provincial legislatures, the chambers of commerce, educational and agricultural associations and other important organisations both in China and abroad, urging the Chinese delegates not to sign the Treaty of Peace with Germany'.[38]

Having received no response and desperate not to leave empty-handed, they proposed a compromise on 28 June. They would sign the Treaty on condition that it included caveats: 'The undersigned plenipotentiaries of the Republic of China, considering as unjust Articles 156, 157 and 158 hereby declare in the name and on behalf of their Government, that their signing of the Treaty is not to be understood as precluding China from demanding at a suitable moment the reconsideration of the Shantung question.'[39] When the Council refused to entertain this option, they finally accepted the inevitable and informed the Council that 'after failing in all their earnest attempts at conciliation, and after seeing every honourable compromise rejected ... they refrained from signing the Treaty altogether'.[40] They left Versailles with nothing to show for their efforts after all, except for some astronomical equipment seized by the Germans in 1900. The only other achievement was the annulment of Germany and Austria-Hungary's share of the Boxer Indemnity, worth the equivalent of US$88,000,000 over the repayment term,[41] but this was little compensation. Although the government decided to join the League in January 1920, they stuck to their guns and on 21 May 1921 negotiated a separate peace with Germany.

One other crumb of comfort came from the new Soviet regime in Russia. Keen to identify itself as another victim of Imperialism and distance itself from its Czarist past, it threw its hat in the ring. On 25 July 1919, the magnanimously worded Karakhan Declaration assured Beijing that 'the government of the workers and the peasants has declared null and void all secret treaties concluded with Japan, China and the ex-Allies',[42] including the Boxer Protocol and all treaties signed with Japan between 1907 and 1916. Furthermore, they promised to return 'to the Chinese people without demanding any kind of compensation, the Chinese Eastern Railway'.[43] Pointedly however, the communiqué made no mention of either the 1858 Treaty of Aigun, or the 1881 Treaty of St Petersburg. In May 1924, the status of the Chinese Eastern Railway as a joint enterprise was also confirmed, although the ambiguity of the wording allowed the Soviets to create bogus appointments, and as a consequence maintain de facto control.

In the meantime, President Wilson's role in the debacle had brought him under fire, so in an effort to draw a line under the matter he agreed to be grilled by the Senate Committee on Foreign Relations. In doing so, he instead revealed his surprising naivety as to Japan's motives. Convened on 19 August 1919 under the chairmanship of Henry Cabot Lodge, a fiery Republican and fervent opponent of the Treaty of Versailles, it was not a comfortable experience. Republican William Borah asked him bluntly 'when the first knowledge came to this government with reference to the secret treaties between Japan, Great Britain and France concerning the German possession in Shantung'. The President claimed it was after he reached Paris.[44] Republican Porter J. McCumber pressed him on whether 'in those conversations it was fully understood that Japan was to return Shantung as soon as possible'.[45] Wilson confirmed this was so, and McCumber then asked if any definite date had been agreed. To this Wilson replied, 'No sir. No. We relied on Japan's good faith in fulfilling that promise.'[46] He nonetheless insisted that the compromise 'was the best that could be got in view of the definite engagements of Great Britain and France and the necessity of a unanimous decision [in signing off the League of Nations Covenant]'.[47] Unconvinced by his arguments, the Committee recommended withholding assent to the three Articles entirely. In the event, the Treaty was never ratified by the United States anyway and it refused become a member of the League of Nations. In effect, Wilson had sold China down the river for nothing, leaving it bitter and divided and its various factions still fighting among themselves.

One of these was led by Sun Yat-sen, who had returned to the country in 1916 and established a base in Guangzhou from where he hoped to reassert his authority. In 1924, still confined to the city, he sent out feelers to the newly founded Chinese Communist Party (CCP) which had been established in Shanghai in July 1921. He believed that they could crush the warlords together and reunite the country if they formed a United Front. Although the CCP agreed to cooperate, it would prove to be a short-lived experiment because Sun Yat-sen succumbed to cancer in 1925, and fervent anti-Communist Chiang-Kai-Shek stepped into his shoes. Once he manoeuvred himself into the post of Generalissimo, Chiang proceeded with his plan to eliminate the Communists altogether. In April 1927 he initiated the 'White Terror', which would kill tens of thousands of suspected opponents and drive as many again into the countryside. They sought refuge in Jiangxi Province, where they garnered the support of the locals by promising land reform and the eradication of the landlords. Many peasants were also recruited into the nascent People's Liberation Army (PLA) and began training for a showdown with the Republicans.

In July 1926, Chiang embarked upon the Northern Expedition, gradually overwhelming the warlords and establishing Nanjing as his capital in 1928. He then captured Beijing, renaming it Peiping, or 'Northern Peace' and gained international legitimacy when his regime was recognised by the US and Germany. By the end of 1928, ten more countries, with the notable exception of Japan, had signed treaties with the new government. On 30 October 1928, a new Nationalist constitution was promulgated, with Chiang formally confirmed as President. Henceforth, he and the KMT would be accepted as the sole legitimate power in the country, a de jure status that would endure for another fifty years. But in reality, he was to preside over a fractious, war-torn nation as he sought to overcome two distinct threats to his rule.

First, the Communists of course. In 1931, the Chinese Soviet Republic was formally established in Jiangxi under the redoubtable Mao Zedong. He proved true to his word and began implementing the promised reforms, which involved the slaughter of the landlords and peasant landowners and the redistribution of their land among the people. They were not out of the woods yet, as Chiang launched repeated attacks against their stronghold, threatening to overrun the Soviet and destroy the PLA. Finally, in October 1934 with his position under imminent threat of liquidation, Mao decided to seek a safer and more defensible base in northern China. In what was later mythologised as the 'Long March', he and his followers endured an arduous trek of over 6,000 miles to Shaanxi Province, arriving in October 1935. They were pursued all the way by the KMT, and by the time they reached their objective had lost between 150,000 and 170,000 men, women and children to battle, sickness and desertion.

Whilst Chiang was confronting the PLA, a second, and arguably more serious immediate threat had been maturing across the Yellow Sea. Here Japan was experiencing its own internal political struggles, and whoever emerged the victor was destined to decide China's fate into the next century.

10

We Do Not Want to Become Like the Koreans

Immediately following the First World War, leading lights such as moderate Minister for Foreign Affairs Viscount Uchida were at the helm. His government sought to reassure his neighbour of Japan's friendly intentions, particularly over the running sore that was Shandong. On 2 August 1919, he announced that Japan was 'quite willing to restore to China the whole territory in question and to enter upon negotiations with the government at Peking as to the arrangements necessary to give effect to that pledge, as soon as possible after the Treaty of Versailles shall have been ratified by Japan'.[1] He assured them Japan only ever sought to retain 'the economic privileges granted to Germany... upon an arrangement being arrived at, Japanese troops will be withdrawn'.[2] As a further conciliatory gesture he proposed that the railway could become a joint enterprise, and Qingdao a 'general foreign settlement, instead of an exclusive Japanese one'.[3] As an added guarantee of Tokyo's good intentions, it put its signature to the Nine Power Treaty of February 1922. In this document, underwritten by the US, UK, France, Portugal, Belgium, Italy, China and the Netherlands, they undertook to honour 'equal opportunity for the commerce and industry of all nations throughout the territory of China'.[4] Uchida's successor as Foreign Minister, Kijuro Shidehara, was keen to build on these gestures, and sought to promote a 'Friendship Policy' so that the two countries could become 'good neighbours'[5] through economic cooperation, tariff reform and more equal trade.

We Do Not Want to Become Like the Koreans

Hot on the heels of such diplomacy, far darker forces were also at play. A growing clique of extreme right-wing nationalists had embraced a so-called 'Positive Policy', which saw aggression against China as the means of solving the country's economic difficulties. Its proponents included Ikki Kita, often identified as the founder of Japanese fascism, and many Kwantung Army officers such as Lt-Col Kingoro Hashimoto, who later founded *Sakurakai*, or the Cherry Blossom Society, and Colonel Daisaku Kumoto. Their views had the ear of Prime Minister General Tanaka Giichi, leader of the Rikken Seiyukai party, and they all felt emboldened by US Secretary of State William Hughes admission that the US 'would never go to war over any aggression on the part of Japan in China'.[6] In addition to the country's deteriorating economy, they had become animated by the KMT's progress north, which they saw as a direct threat to their interests in Manchuria. In particular, their fears centred around the fate of their client warlord, Zhang Zuolin, who had declared independence from Beijing in May 1922 and faced being unseated by Chiang. Consequently, a cabal of Kwantung Army officers led by Hashimoto and Kumoto, began to secretly prepare contingency plans to block his progress, all without the prior knowledge or approval of liberal politicians back home.

The plot thickened when rumours leaked out that Zhang was making overtures to the US and Britain, offering them similar trade and investment opportunities to those enjoyed by his Japanese sponsors. This development convinced Kumoto and his Kwantung gang that Zhang had to be removed and replaced with his more pliable opponent, General Yang Yuting. Consequently, on 4 June 1928 Zhang was mortally wounded when explosives were detonated under a bridge over which his train passed. But Kumoto had jumped the gun, moving before fellow officers could mobilise and install Yuting in power. Instead, Chiang intervened and appointed Zhang's son Zhang Xueliang, who promptly had Yang Yuting executed. Not only had the fumbled plot failed, but the botched coup angered the advocates of the 'Friendship Policy' in Tokyo and most significantly the youthful Emperor Hirohito himself. He demanded that Giichi take immediate action against the plotters, and when he failed to impose his authority, he was dismissed. Seeking to distance itself from the actions of the Kwantung Army, the government signed the Kellogg Pact on 27 August 1928. This treaty, signed by fourteen other states including the US, Great Britain and France, optimistically sought to outlaw war entirely. It would not be long before such a high-minded aspiration faced its first significant hurdle.

After the fall of the Giichi administration, a more liberal government under Prime Minister Hamaguchi Osachi and his Rikken Minseito party was formed. He also favoured economic and social reform over military solutions for the country's problems and looked to the armed forces to make cuts. Consequently, in April 1930 Japan joined the UK, US, Italy and France in agreeing to the London Naval Treaty. This was an attempt to curtail military expenditure by limiting the respective sizes of the participants' navies, but such pacifist policies was anathema to right-wingers and particularly the militarists of the Cherry Blossom Society. In response to the treaty and hoping to incite rebellion, Osachi survived an assassination attempt in November 1930, although he was hospitalised and died nine months later. The political situation then slid further into turmoil and as matters deteriorated the country was racked by more attempted coups and assassinations. Many of these were orchestrated by right-wing elements in government and the Kwantung Army conspirators, whose commanders were continuing with their plotting. In particular, unsettling events in Manchuria between July and December 1929 raised fears over the Soviet Union's plans for the region. It had responded to Chinese attempts to eject the Russian representatives of the CER, after Moscow loaded it with officials to give them a controlling interest. Military intervention subsequently forced a climbdown, but also gave the Russians possession of Heixiazi, or Bolshoy Ussuriysky Island. This not only gave them complete control of the Amur and Ussuri waterways, but placed considerable military assets in the region which could potentially threaten Japanese interests.

Among those pondering the implications of these developments were Colonels Seishiro Itakagi and Kanji Ishiwara, who had devised their own scheme to secure control of Manchuria. This was to be better coordinated than the previous fiasco and involve contriving an 'incident' near Mukden, which would provide a pretext for hostilities. At approximately 10:20 p.m. on 18 September 1931, explosives were detonated on a stretch of railway where troops loyal to Zhang Xueliang were stationed. They then claimed that the explosion was a prelude to an attack on their citizens, and citing self-defence the Kwantung Army immediately swung into action, setting the Chinese to flight and occupying Mukden. Although he was initially kept in the dark about the plot, the commander-in-chief of the army was soon on board, and he gave orders for Mukden to be reinforced. His men then fanned out from the city and conducted further operations to secure control of the province.

On 21 September the Chinese Government lodged formal protests with the League of Nations, invoking Article 11 of the Covenant. This called for immediate steps to be taken 'to prevent the further development of a situation endangering the peace of nations'.[7] But it did nothing to deter the invaders, who insisted that they were acting in self-defence and in order to restore order in a region which had become lawless and ungovernable. They continued to invest the province, and by November 1931 were in control of most of the major towns in Liaoning, Jilin and Heilongjiang.

On 10 December 1931, in response to China's plea the Council of the League appointed Britain's Lord Lytton, former governor of Bengal and for a short time Viceroy of India, to head a commission of enquiry consisting of representatives from Italy, France, the United States and Germany. Their remit was to examine the claims of the two parties, gather evidence and publish their recommendations. But by the time they were able to begin work on the ground, the Kwangtung Army's already firm grip had tightened. Its officers did everything in their power to manipulate the evidence and influence the commission's perceptions. Access to sites was tightly controlled and contact with witnesses hostile to the Japanese obstructed wherever possible. They also exploited the media to broadcast anti-Chinese propaganda and published salacious claims of atrocities. Few were fooled, and in addition to violating the Covenant of the League Japan was arraigned for breaching the Nine Power Treaty and the Kellogg-Briand Pact, in addition to various other undertakings made over the years. US Secretary of State Henry Stimson responded with his 'Doctrine' of 7 January 1932, whereby the US refused to recognise any change to a nation's territorial status achieved by force of arms. 'The American Government ... cannot admit the legality of any situation de facto, nor does it intend to recognise any treaty... which may impair the treaty rights of the US or its citizens in China.'[8] The British were also alarmed at the prospect of losing their privileges and in a communiqué of 9 January confirmed that 'His Britannic Majesty's Government stand by the policy of the open door for international trade in Manchuria'.[9]

Back in Tokyo, the ruling Rikken Minseito party, now led by Prime Minister Wakatsuki Rejiro following the death of Osachi, had also condemned the invasion, in response to which right-wing elements in his party staged a palace coup. He was ousted and replaced by a coalition under Seiyukai party leader Inukai Tsuyoshi, but more significant was the appointment of firebrand General Sadao Araki as War Minister. These measures also chimed with the mood of the public dissatisfied with efforts to improve the economy, and they would soon demonstrate which horse they backed at the ballot box. The ongoing election campaign was mired in corruption, intimidation, violence and even murder. The poll, held on 20 February, gave the Seiyukai party 301 out of 499 seats in parliament. *Times* leader writer Wickham Steed condemned this worrying turn of events, but also blamed the outcome on 'the failure of the governments represented on the League Council to give timely support, by firmness in word and deed, to [moderate] civilian influences in Japan'.[10] The result was also a boost for the rebellious officers in Manchuria, who were already exploiting the turmoil to stage their next mutinous act. Along with Manchurian puppets and Chinese collaborators, they had concocted a sham convention in Mukden between 16 and 18 February seeking to legitimise their actions. From this emerged an entirely bogus declaration of independence, its authors claiming that they were fulfilling

> ... the aspirations of thirty million people, who have for years been trampled under the undemocratic rule of self-seeking militarists, who wish to be governed on the principle of racial self-determination, and to live independent of the Republic of China.[11]

This was followed on 1 March by a 'Proclamation of the Establishment of Manchukuo', and eight days later the new 'government' was inaugurated with Henry Pu Yi, the last Manchu Emperor as 'Chief Executive', ruling from his capital at Chungchun. The new state was, its creators claimed, 'a constitutional democracy [existing] by the will of the people',[12] adding that 'the Manchukuo Government commences its career as a state fully recognising the rights of man to liberty of person and private property'.[13] Nonetheless, they felt it necessary to point out that 'it is not yet possible for the State Council to promulgate an election law or to plan for an election [until] peace has been restored'.[14] So long as, as one astute commentator observed, 'real power is in the hands of the Japanese militarists, and not in those of the puppet Chinese',[15] this was unlikely to materialise any time soon.

The declaration simply added to the bad blood already spreading across China, producing widespread KMT-inspired anti-Japanese demonstrations, boycotts and violence. They became so serious in Shanghai that Tokyo despatched warships and 12,000 troops to protect its 20,000 expats. Japanese aircraft also bombed the city, killing hundreds and causing widespread damage before a ceasefire was agreed on 3 March. A neutral zone was established for non-combatants and foreign nationals, but fighting then resumed amid accusations of war crimes, and particularly of wholesale rape, which provoked worldwide condemnation. The League Council flatly refused to recognise the new entity, a decision widely supported by world opinion. Tom Johnston, the editor of Glasgow's socialist newspaper *Forward*, told the audience at a public meeting: 'It is madness and suicide not to back the League and the Covenant against mad-dog militarism in Japan or anywhere else.'[16] Little more could be done before the findings of the Lytton Report were made public, although expectations were not high. The *Observer* of 11 September 1932 anticipated little more than a 'clever essay in diplomatic finesse',[17] but when it was published on 1 October, it was anything but.

In a withering critique of the situation in the country as a whole, its authors began by condemning the existing KMT regime. They blamed it for 'introducing .. into the Nationalists of China an additional and abnormal tinge of bitterness against all foreign influences',[18] most significantly the million or so Japanese and Koreans. They were charged with sponsoring and orchestrating large-scale discrimination, and encouraging the boycotting of Japanese goods, harassment and worse. It also identified two other serious problems, the prevalence of 'banditry' and Communism,[19] which affected the Japanese 'more than any other Power [because] two-thirds of foreign residents are Japanese'.[20] This situation in turn was blamed on the fact that 'China has two completely separate governments' and was badly in need of 'effective internal reconstruction', but this could not be achieved without 'friendly relations with all countries',[21] including Japan. However, having chided the KMT, the report had an even more scornful critique in store for the Japanese.

The report claimed that 'although at present the central government's authority is still weak in a number of provinces, the central authority is not, at least openly, repudiated',[22] contradicting one of the main planks upon which the invasion had been justified. Its actions therefore 'cannot be regarded as measures of legitimate self-defence',[23] because the Chinese 'had no plan of attacking the Japanese troops, or of endangering the lives and property of Japanese nationals'.[24] It also debunked

> ... the Japanese claim [of] having moved in to restore order... The independence movement, which had not been heard of in Manchuria before September 1931, was only made possible by the presence of Japanese troops ... and the activities of Japanese officials, both civil and military. For this reason the present regime cannot be considered to have been called into existence by a genuine and spontaneous independence movement.[25]

Claims that Manchukuo was an independent entity were also undermined by the fact that 'Japanese advisers are attached to all important departments [and are] the heads of the various Boards [which] exercise the greatest measure of actual power'.[26]

The Commission found little appetite at all amongst the population for the new state. It learnt that Chinese officials served the new administration 'under duress',[27] out of fear of reprisals, and overall 'we found the Chinese majority either hostile or indifferent'.[28] Of the 1,550 letters received by the Commission, all except two 'were bitterly hostile'[29] to the regime, substantiating the claim of one witness: 'We do not want to become like the Koreans.'[30] It came to the conclusion that because 'the vision of a China unified, strong, and hostile, a nation of four hundred millions, dominant in Manchuria and in Eastern Asia, is disturbing to many Japanese',[31] the invasion and setting up of the new state was entirely self-serving.

Despite such a damning indictment, Lytton's recommendations turned out to be little more than a mild rebuke. The report only proposed a series of timid measures which appeared designed more to appease them than provide redress for China. Believing that 'there can be no ... rapprochement so long as the political relations between them are so unsatisfactory as to call forth the use of military force by one and the economic force of boycott by the other',[32] it called on Japan to abandon its military and political ambitions in the province, and for the two parties to agree to a Sino-Japanese treaty allowing for 'the free participation of Japan in the economic development of Manchuria, which would not carry with it a right to control the country either economically or politically'.[33] The Report also made a number of other moderate proposals, and they fell far short of what the Japanese had been demanding, in particular international recognition of the new state. In response, on 7 October Manchukuo's pseudo foreign minister Hsieh Chieh-Shih wired the US State Department expressing his outrage at the findings. He insisted that the report simply proved that the commissioners 'had been considerably influenced by malicious anti-Manchukuo propaganda so ingeniously conducted by old north-eastern militarists... The refusal to take due cognizance of independence of Manchukuo absolutely fails to reflect actual conditions here ... publication itself of such a report will naturally stimulate activities of lawless elements rampant within our state.'[34]

The findings of the report also alarmed senior British politicians, who felt trapped between a political rock and an economic hard place. Whilst Foreign Secretary John Simon was wary Japan would resign from the League and thus deny Britain 'the opportunities of contact with and influence over her',[35] he also realised that China had to be kept on side. Consequently, whilst 'we must explain [to Japan] that the course we take is pro League and not anti-Japan, we have to remember the serious consequences to our trade of our antagonising China ... we must strive to be fair to both sides. But we must not involve ourselves in trouble with Japan.'³⁶ Simon's worst fears were realised and the *News Chronicle* of 21 November reported Japan's 'flat refusal' of the report,³⁷ submitting the statutory two year's notice of its intention to leave the League.

Undeterred by the country's new status as an international pariah, the Ministry of Colonial Affairs proceeded to expand its long-cherished policy of turning the territory into a second Japan. Plans that had been ongoing since the Russo-Japanese War were revised and expanded upon, so that 10 per cent of the population would be Japanese within twenty years. This would transform the demographics of the country, and also relieve the economic pressures being felt in the homeland. So once the puppet Manchukuo government was in place, it gave Tokyo the green light to go to work. An elaborate campaign was launched to encourage the mass migration of settlers, including incentives of 1000 yen and ten hectares of land, payment for which did not have to commence for five years. Around 270,000 members of the 'Manchurian-Mongolian Pioneer Corps' would take up the offer, and from 1938 the Pioneer Youth Corps of Manchuria and Mongolia recruited around 86,000 boys aged between fourteen and twenty to clear the land in preparation for the newcomers. Like moths to a flame, lured by the promise of land and prosperity, they were unaware of the terrible fate that ultimately awaited them.

The Kwantung Army had yet to pacify their prospective new home, and there were estimated to be at least 40,000 to 50,000 rebels still holding out. There was also the question of the thousands of ordinary men, women and children who lived on the land earmarked for the interlopers, but discriminating between them would be too time-consuming. Instead, a policy of wholesale terror was to be employed, one advocated at the highest levels. President of the Privy Council Hiranuma Kiichiro said that either the Chinese submitted or 'we have no other alternative but to exterminate them'.³⁸ General Kuniaki Koiso explained that the 'racial struggle between the Japanese and Chinese is to be expected ... we must never hesitate to wield military power in case of necessity'.³⁹

This task would be fulfilled by soldiers that been ruthlessly inculcated in the warrior code of Bushido. Through this ethos martial skills were ingrained in men through brutal training until they lost all individuality and became desensitised to suffering, both their own and their enemy's. Nowhere was this credo exercised with more gusto than in China, where any feelings of humanity were expunged by relentless brainwashing. Every Chinese was seen as *Chancorro*, or as one veteran later admitted, 'below human, like bugs or animals [who] didn't belong to the human race'.[40] To remove any lingering doubts, units arriving in theatre were met by special welcoming committees. These consisted of local farmers, suspected bandits or any other random victims abducted for the purpose who would be lashed to trees and used for bayonet practice. One perpetrator later conceded, 'Once I did it, it became easy. I didn't think about the man I killed.'[41] No act of bestiality became too egregious, as entire towns and villages were put to the torch and their occupants slaughtered by bayonet, bullet or machine gun. Men, women and children whose lives were estimated as being of no value died in their thousands, women and girls often after being raped by gangs of soldiers. Should the conventional methods of extermination prove too slow, the invaders also had recourse to the perversion of modern science to achieve their ends.

In 1935, the first of two secret bacteriological warfare units were formed under the command of Lieutenant-General Ishii Shiro. One was code-named 'Water Supply and Prophylaxis Administration of the Kwantung Army' and the other the 'Hippo-Epizootic Administration of the Kwantung Army'. Later they would be renamed respectively Detachments 731 under Shiro and 100 under Major-General Wakematsu of the Veterinary Service. Detachment 731 had a staff of 3,000 bacteriologists and support personnel, numerous laboratories and ancillary buildings twenty kilometres from Harbin, concealed behind a special Forbidden Zone. It also had its own aircraft and proving ground for aircrew to practice dropping plague-infected 'Ishii aerial bombs' on civilians.[42] To achieve this, as much as 300 kilograms of plague bacteria agents a month would be produced from 4,500 incubators,[43] infecting 3,000,000 rats capable of producing billions of plague-infected fleas.[44] Far greater quantities of cholera and typhoid material were produced. Experiments were performed on humans to test their efficacy, and to this end between 500 to 600 people were consigned to Detachment 731 annually, of whom hundreds died and thousands more were crippled as a result of the trials which were carried out on them.[45] Many thousands more were exploited in other experiments, such as freezing, exposure, the effects of high-altitude and more, being expendable guinea pigs who could then be disposed of. Once the trials proved successful, various means were employed to distribute the organisms, one officer explaining that he had been assigned to Detachment 100 charged with 'carrying out sabotage measures ... infecting pastures, cattle and water sources with epidemic germs'.[46] Cholera, typhoid and paratyphoid bacteria were also dropped into wells and reservoirs; plague-infected fleas and anthrax bacteria were spread through rice fields,[47] and Ishii even ordered that innocuous looking biscuits be infected with typhoid and left in people's homes to be eaten by unsuspecting children.[48]

Whilst Manchuria was being debased by such barbarism, Japan's generals had been absorbed by plans to extend their conquests even further. The vast expanse of greater China lay before them and the success of their operations in Manchuria convinced them that its neighbour was ready to be plucked like a ripe apple. Consequently, on 7 July 1937 another false flag incident was carried out at the Marco Polo Bridge near Beijing. Using the same sophistry that sought to justify invading its neighbour, propagandists claimed:

> Our nation tried to persuade China to cease its lawlessness and to stem the disturbance; however, [it] not only continued, but also increased its unjust activities. Thus Japan dispatched an army to punish China for its violence, and the war expanded from northern China to central and southern China ... the goal of the war was to awaken China and to establish a new order in East Asia.[49]

Beijing fell on 28 July and Tianjin the following day, the League condemning the invasion as a further breach of the Nine Power Treaty and Kellogg Pact, and calling for a meeting of its signatories. The Japanese not surprisingly declined to participate, War Minister Sadao Araki sneering that it was like 'telling a man not to get involved with a woman when she is already pregnant by him'.[50] Instead, on 13 August a second front was opened at Shanghai, where 950 factories and workshops were destroyed and 1,000 damaged by indiscriminate bombing. Murder, rape and pillage were then pursued without respite as its residents fled in terror, or tried to hide from their persecutors. Suzhou to the west followed on 20 November, and Hangchow 10 miles to the south on 24 December, progress marked by a trail of death and destruction. One correspondent vividly described 'cities bombed and pillaged; towns and villages reduced to shambles; farms deserted',[51] and in Guangzhou, bombed on 23 September he encountered corpses 'as thick as flies on flypaper, with limbs and mutilated bodies piled in the utmost confusion'.[52] Meanwhile forces had marched up the Yangtse River to attack the capital Nanjing, compelling Chiang to move his capital to Chongqing, 600 miles further upriver. The aerial bombing of Nanjing had already commenced in November preparatory to the city being occupied, and those who could do so made good their escape. Some took advantage of American gunboats which were taking Europeans away, and an international incident was narrowly avoided when the *Panay* was sunk by Japanese aircraft. Most people however, had no choice but to await their fate, among whom were many westerners, but as none were as yet from nations at war with Japan, they believed they would be able to stick it out.

On 13 December 1937, the Japanese stormed the city, immediately embarking on a killing spree that put most of its earlier war crimes in the shade. Doctor Robert Wilson was one of three Americans working at the University Hospital at the time: 'I could go on for pages telling cases of rape, and brutality almost beyond belief.'[53] What he did describe would go down in history as the 'Rape of Nanking', in which at least 12,000 people were killed and 20,000 women and children raped in the first three days alone. A post-war analysis placed the total number murdered during the course of the Japanese occupation of the city at 295,525, of whom two-thirds were men, around a quarter women, and two per cent, or approximately 6,000, young children and infants.[54] Thousands of homes and businesses were looted and whole streets set on fire, creating infernos which destroyed a third of the city. Even hardened Nazis were said to have been shocked by the 'bestial' atrocities that they saw committed.⁵⁵ Seeking to obscure the truth of their behaviour, the January edition of the Chinese language *Sin Shun Pao* was published by the Japanese in Shanghai. Its shameless propaganda saw headlines claiming 'Japanese troops Gently Soothe the Refugees', and 'Harmonious Atmosphere of Nanking Develops'.⁵⁶ It asserted that 'before the Japanese troops entered the city, they suffered from the oppression of the anti-Japanese armies of the Chinese', and that the occupiers had in fact 'stretched forth merciful hands in order to examine and to heal'.⁵⁷

By the end of 1937, Japan had occupied most of northern China, and in 1938 would renew its offensive in three directions, by which time foreign correspondents had been sending regular accounts of their cruel rampage. One described how 'the whole thirty-nine-mile route between Shanghai and Sungkiang is like a desert, with rice crops ungathered and left rotting in the fields'⁵⁸ as villagers fled in terror. Among reports of civilians being shot, bayonetted, and machine-gunned at the whim of the invaders were even more horrifying accounts. In one village a 'large number of civilians were reported to have been burned to death with kerosene or gasoline'⁵⁹ as revenge by soldiers for a military reverse. The absence of any contrition was underlined by a piece in the American-owned and run English language Tokyo daily, the *Japan Advertiser*. It ran a story describing how two officers had engaged in a competition to see who could decapitate one hundred victims first. It referred casually to this 'friendly contest ... in individual sword combat', which they carried out just for fun.⁶⁰ Many soldiers were so blasé about their actions that they would include accounts in their letters home, prompting nervous senior officers to order that the practice be actively discouraged.

Such news could not help but have a negative effect on public opinion abroad. One Gallup poll taken in the US in August 1937 had shown only 43 per cent support for China, but this had leapt to 74 per cent when re-taken in May 1939.⁶¹

As the fighting dragged on and opinion in the US hardened, increasingly harsh sanctions were being imposed. By 1941, with essential supplies of oil, rubber, steel and other vital commodities running out, the military commanders concluded that unless the scope of the war was broadened, all could be lost. Their only option was to seize the resources they needed from the European colonies to the south, and at the same time cut China off from its sources of supply. On 7 December 1941, simultaneous attacks were launched on the United States at Pearl Harbor and the Philippines, Great Britain in Malaya, Singapore and Hong Kong, and the Dutch East Indies. At the same time, their nationals were no longer bystanders, and thousands of European missionaries, businessmen and their families became enemy aliens. Those treaty ports that had not fallen so far would succumb to the onslaught, and tens of thousands found themselves interned for the duration of the war in often pitiful conditions.

Meanwhile, Thailand succumbed on 9 December and three days later troops marched into Burma, capturing Lashio, the southern terminus of the Burma Road, on 29 April 1942. When a major attack was launched along the Yunnan-Burma border at the town of Baoshin the Japanese supplemented conventional bombs with weapons from their bacteriological arsenal. Aircraft dropped 'maggot bombs' containing a sticky, waxy yellowish substance to which were stuck live flies struggling to extricate themselves. The cholera they contained spread like wildfire, and with no medicines available anything between 10,000 and 60,000 deaths resulted.[62] By 16 May, Burma had been overrun and the Chinese divisions decimated, one column retreating with US General Joseph Stillwell westward to Ledo on the Indian border and another to China to help in the battle for Yunnan.

Another series of offensives was launched in May 1943, establishing a north-south corridor connecting Guangzhou, Hankow and Beijing, whilst another seemed for a time to threaten Chongqing, but by the end of the month the operation had stalled. To the west, Allied forces including US-trained Chinese divisions under Stillwell attacked from India across northern Burma and drove toward Yunnan. There was a simultaneous drive down the Burma Road from Kunming and on 28 January they linked up seventy-five miles north of Lashio, which fell on 7 March. The Communists also embarked on large-scale operations, establishing themselves further south. Faced by US, British Commonwealth, and both KMT and PLA forces, it seemed that at last the Allies were gaining the upper hand, particularly now that the overstretched Japanese had been compelled to transfer troops to other fronts in the Pacific theatre. All the while Japan's armed forces continued with their almost unbroken fifteen-year reign of terror. This had also been extended to every territory which they occupied and which contained Chinese nationals, such as Malaya, Singapore, Hong Kong, and Burma. Here they were singled out for special treatment, often at the hands of the notorious Kempeitai military police and murdered through the most brutal means.

A total of nearly 16,000,000 Chinese civilians, and 3,000,000 military deaths had been the direct consequence of Japanese aggression, alongside the displacement of perhaps another 95,000,000 people. In addition, the cost of the material and physical destruction totalled as much as US$380bn as vast swathes of the country were wantonly devastated and rendered uninhabitable by the deployment of bacteriological weapons. No one was spared, man woman or child, and as commentator W. H. Holmes observed, they left behind them such as legacy that 'the hatred of the Japanese is bitter, deep and wide'.[63] He also sagely predicted that 'it'll come back to them a hundredfold someday',[64] but he could never have imagined the form it would take. It would in any case mainly be the women and children of Japan who paid the price when atomic bombs were dropped on Hiroshima and Nagasaki on 6 and 9 August 1945. Although many war criminals such as General Tojo were tried after the war and executed, and thus the worst excesses committed by the Imperial Japanese army exposed, many remained convinced that too many had escaped justice. These included Emperor Hirohito himself, whose own role remains somewhat ambiguous, given his objections to the war in Manchuria. He was spared and his throne preserved, largely in the interests of securing a swift surrender.

Victory did not remove the deep misgivings that had emerged regarding the KMT's contribution to the war effort. Its performance rarely matched the huge demands Chiang had made of his Allies, and the deficit widened as the war progressed. He was more preoccupied with fighting Mao, and in January 1943 the Joint Intelligence Committee reported that 'the value of China as a member of the United Nations is out of all proportion to her material contribution'.[65] But US President Roosevelt had become beguiled by Chiang, whom he regarded as the 'undisputed leader' of his people,[66] convinced that alongside the US and Great Britain he could help police the post-war world.[67] This was a prospect British Prime Minister Winston Churchill dismissed as 'an absolute farce',[68] although his judgment was probably coloured by Chiang's support for Indian independence. However, it was the US voice that carried the most weight, and Nationalist China signed the UN Charter on 26 June 1945 as one of the 'Big Five', whilst the Communists were left out in the cold.

11

A Mutually Beneficial Relationship

Despite his many shortcomings, Chiang had secured what the peacemakers at Versailles had failed to achieve a quarter of a century before. The Cairo Conference, held in November 1943 had recognised the independence of Korea, and directed that all the territory Japan had annexed since 1914, including Manchuria and Formosa, was to be returned. These demands were reiterated in the text of the Potsdam Declaration of July 1945 and by 1946 the extra-territorial agreements made with the European powers in the treaty ports and elsewhere had been annulled, a move the *New York Times* hailed as 'the dawn of a new epoch in the Far East'.[1] There were two notable exceptions. Despite Nationalist demands, Britain was determined to regain Hong Kong, counter to Roosevelt's naïve hope that they would return the colony 'as a gesture of goodwill'.[2] On 1 September 1945, a small British contingent re-entered the colony and ran up the Union Flag. Likewise, the Portuguese managed to retain control of Macau, despite demands for its return.

Once the initial glow of victory had passed, the two antagonists returned to settle old scores. Although both Chiang and Mao espoused a desire to work together to build a society based on democracy and equality, this would prove a chimera. Representing polar opposite views, negotiations soon broke down and even the best efforts of US envoy General George Marshall to broker an agreement ended in failure. Inevitably, fighting resumed and from 1946 spread to most of central and eastern China. Although the Nationalists made early headway and captured the Communist capital of Yan'an, morale was already deteriorating within the ranks. Corruption and graft had been endemic throughout the KMT almost from its inception, with funds intended for food and supplies siphoned off into the pockets of officers and politicians. The ordinary people were being antagonised and alienated by the taxes extorted from them to pay for the conflict. As Mao's army bounced back and went on the offensive, Chiang's stock plummeted further, and by the end of 1943 the Communists had completed the conquest of Manchuria. The KMT started to dissolve as one defeat followed another, and hundreds of thousands of men deserted or defected to Mao.

Fighting an increasingly unpopular war, Chiang faced strikes and protests which were mercilessly suppressed, whilst wherever territory was liberated the hated landlords were dispossessed, their property distributed among the peasants and their debts cancelled. In January 1949 Chiang lost Shandong and Beijing, and was defeated at the decisive battle of Huai-Hai near Xuzhou. Nanjing followed in April and in the autumn Xinjiang Province was invaded. After peace talks again broke down the Nationalists disintegrated completely. On 10 October, Mao declared the People's Republic of China and on 8 December most of the remaining Nationalists fled to Formosa. By the end of 1949 the Communists had mopped up most of the remaining pockets of resistance and controlled virtually all of the mainland. In 1950 Hainan fell, whilst he promised that his country was set to join 'the large family of peace-loving and freedom-loving nations of the world'.[3]

Inevitably, blame for the 'loss' of China and the privileges that had been accrued there fell most heavily on the US State Department. The US had accounted for between 48 and 57 per cent of Chinese imports,[4] and with the Communist victory this business virtually evaporated. Secretary of State Dean Acheson attempted to vindicate his department's role in the debacle with the publication of the 'China White Paper', which sought to explain the context in which Chiang had been defeated. He cut little ice with conservative opinion growing increasingly wary of the impending Cold War. The fact that the democracies now faced a Communist China as well as the Soviet Union was causing considerable anxiety, with much of the vitriol being directed at Mao.

Senator Henry Cabot Lodge Jr accused him of planning to 'uproot all Western activities and interests'[5] in the country, and he insisted that it was therefore incumbent upon the free world to seek his removal. To this end he promoted a policy of 'positive hostility' in the form of embargoes which he believed would lead to the 'eventual collapse'[6] of the regime. Washington had already laid out its stall when the Truman Doctrine committed the US to offering its 'support for democracies against authoritarian threats' everywhere.[7] Although Chiang could by no stretch of the imagination be called democratic, Beijing could read the runes and moved closer to Moscow for mutual support. Stalin was already supplying the PLA with arms, transport and other supplies and this was stepped up as the perceived threat developed. If the West was left in any doubt, Mao gave his defiant 'lean to one side' speech on 30 June 1949 as a gesture of solidarity, and in which he affirmed that henceforth China would be bound ever closer to the Soviet Union. This was formalised by the Treaty of Friendship, Alliance and Mutual Assistance signed on 14 February 1950, which simultaneously nullified any undertakings given to the Nationalists. Yet despite Stalin's help, the sanctions urged by Cabot Lodge were beginning to bite. By 1951, Hong Kong's export trade to China would plunge from $235,000,000 in January to $141,000,000 by June, and its exports to Macao, of which 90 per cent were re-exported to China, fell from $28,000,000 in January to $21,000,000 by September.[8] As the lines were drawn, it became inevitable that some sort of clash would occur somewhere.

The now ostensibly liberated Korean Peninsula had been of growing concern ever since the Red Army entered Pyongyang in August 1945. Here they had installed puppet dictator Kim il-Sung as leader north of the 38th Parallel, supplying him with advisers, weapons and other equipment. Although Moscow was the key player, the State Department saw the hand of Beijing behind these developments, so it countered by sponsoring right-wing nationalist Syngman Ree as leader south of the Parallel. It had been the United Nations' intention that the two zones unify following all-Korean elections, but as tensions increased, futile negotiations reached an impasse. Subsequently, Syngman Ree announced the creation of the Republic of Korea on 15 August 1948, claiming jurisdiction over the entire peninsula. The North promptly responded by declaring the establishment of the Democratic People's Republic of Korea, likewise claiming sovereignty over the whole country, and received Soviet recognition in October.

As reports emerged from the South that repression against suspected Communists was causing growing unrest, Kim felt emboldened to strike and reunite the peninsula by force. Moscow was broadly in favour, but Mao was more reticent, his priority being the consolidation of his victory over Chiang. There were still pockets of resistance to mop up, and he was keen to release men from the PLA to help reconstruct the devastated country. However, in the interests of solidarity he transferred 14,000 Koreans serving in the army to Kim and agreed to station troops closer to the border as show of strength. Once everything was set, Kim's forces poured across the Parallel on 25 June 1950, taking Ree and the US completely off guard. Despite Mao having been lukewarm at best, he took much of the blame for the invasion. Former president Herbert Hoover not only advocated that the US send the Seventh Fleet to the Taiwan Strait to prevent any aggression against the island, but also to assist a Nationalist assault on the mainland. Respected General Omar Bradley balked at such precipitous action, warning an all-out war with China would be 'the wrong war, at the wrong time, in the wrong place against the wrong enemy'.[9]

President Truman shared the General's analysis and refused to widen the war, instead warning Beijing that 'the occupation of Formosa by Communist forces would be a direct threat to the security of the Pacific area and to US forces performing their lawful and necessary functions in that area'.[10] He did, however, move the Seventh Fleet into the Strait as a safeguard, and intensify sanctions.

In the meantime, the United Nations Security Council authorised the despatch of a force to defend the South, under the supreme command of General Douglas MacArthur. Although the invaders had captured almost all the peninsula, he orchestrated a series of master strokes which drove them back to their starting point. Then Bradley's worst fears were realised when Truman authorised their pursuit across the Parallel, despite Chinese insistence that they would not 'sit back with folded arms and let the Americans come to the border'.[11] When, in defiance of the warning, UN troops crossed on 7 October, they made good on their threat. A million 'volunteers' struck back on 25 October 1950, with orders to 'resist the attacks of US imperialism'.[12] Although they initially threw the UN forces into headlong retreat, the coalition managed to recover and hold a defensive line. A three-year stalemate ensued, during which thousands perished in fruitless fighting as face-saving negotiations dragged on. Finally, with both sides exhausted and unable to gain the initiative, a ceasefire was agreed at Panmunjom on 27 July 1953. A war which had killed at least 5,000,000 Koreans, 30,000 Americans, 110,000 Chinese and 1,300 Commonwealth troops resulted in insignificant territorial gains for both sides and the creation of a demilitarised zone. South Korea and the US signed a Mutual Defense Pact which committed the latter to come to the former's defence if attacked, and this was underwritten by the formation of the Southeast Asia Treaty Organisation.

Despite achieving a technical draw, the war had done little to enhance Beijing's standing in the world. The US used its influence to prevent its membership of such bodies as the UN, the International Telecommunications Union, the Red Cross, the World Health Organisation and the International Monetary Fund. More promising signs came from its participation in the Asian-African Conference at Bandung in Indonesia in April 1955. This provided access to newly emerging states with whom, along with India, it sought to forge a non-aligned movement. Mao ingratiated himself further by offering loans and assistance to help develop their economies, and he supported the many independence movements now struggling against colonialism. These achievements, however, were offset by a deterioration in relations with the Soviet Union following the death of Joseph Stalin in 1953. In 1955, his successor Nikita Khrushchev undertook a complete re-evaluation of his reputation and legacy. However, Mao did not share Khrushchev's condemnation of his predecessor, nor his new policy of 'détente' and 'peaceful co-existence' with the West. His refusal to comply with Moscow's new strategy contributed to an increasing estrangement, culminating in 1960 with Moscow ending all economic and technical support.

Instead, the PRC charted its own course, one in which neither détente nor peaceful co-existence were to play much of a role.

A Mutually Beneficial Relationship

In March 1959, ten years after promising to join the 'peace- and freedom-loving nations of the world', Mao ordered his troops into Tibet. The Dalai Lama was forced to flee, along with 100,000 refugees, whilst an estimated 90,000 more died as Beijing consolidated its rule. The economic reforms which were imposed created a famine in which another 340,000 people are said to have perished between 1960 and 1962. When it was overrun by the Cultural Revolution, thousands of Buddhist temples, religious texts and other symbols of Tibetan culture were destroyed in an attempt to eradicate its identity. Brushing aside worldwide condemnation, Mao sought to cloak his actions under a veneer of legitimacy by creating it an autonomous region of China in 1965.

Further afield, Beijing had been stepping up support for the Viet Minh in their war against France in Indo China, supplying them with arms and providing training facilities. France's ultimate defeat at Dien Bien Phu in 1954 forced them to quit the country, and the Geneva Conference of April-May led to the recognition of Communist North and a more US-leaning South Vietnam. It was meant, as in the case of the two Koreas, to be the precursor to reunification, but again the respective parties failed to reach an agreement. After conflict broke out and US troops were drawn in on the side of the South, Presidential aide Arthur Schlesinger Jr asserted in 1965 that 'the Viet Cong [had become] the instruments of Chinese expansionism in the Far East',[13] a belief which informed much of US policy under President Johnson. Fearing the collapse of the South, with its unpopular government and unreliable military, Washington became bogged down fighting the Viet Cong, which Johnson sought to defeat by massive bombing of the North, the use of napalm and the deployment of the toxic defoliant Agent Orange. Such measures prompted critics such as Albert Gore, Senator for Tennessee to call him 'a desperate man, who was likely to get us into a war with China',[14] sentiments shared by Assistant Secretary of State McGeorge Bundy. He feared that Johnson's tactics would invite 'a massive Chinese counter intervention with ground forces',[15] but as desperate as Johnson was, he did not repeat the folly that crossing the Yalu had proven to be for President Truman. Instead, the war dragged on without any end in sight, and he became increasingly disillusioned and shattered by the responsibilities of his office. He refused renomination for the 1968 presidential election, which saw Republican Richard Nixon assume office, publicly declaring his determination to end the conflict. Consequently, US troop withdrawals began in June 1969 and billions were squandered re-equipping and training the South Vietnamese Army in a futile attempt to transform it into an efficient fighting force. The bombing of the North was also intensified, despite claims to the contrary, particularly in March 1970 and November 1972 as Washington sought to bring Hanoi to the negotiating table. Sponsored, supported and supplied by China, the North stood firm.

Beijing's growing presence on the world stage was also forcing a serious reconsideration among many governments of its pariah status. After an atomic bomb was successfully detonated in 1964, followed by a hydrogen device in 1967, the policy of excluding Beijing from the counsels of the UN whilst the small island state of Nationalist China retained its seat appeared increasingly ludicrous. Indeed, despite maintaining its stance in public, secret Sino-American Ambassadorial talks had begun as early as the 1950s in an attempt to ease tensions, whilst Beijing's estrangement from Moscow made a rapprochement and admission to the UN more palatable. American public opinion, however, fed a regular diet of anti-Communist propaganda, remained largely in favour of the Nationalists, with some commentators advocating that if Beijing was accepted the US should resign. A compromise proposal that would allow both Chinas to be members never gained any traction, but as the organisation's more sympathetic African and Asian states joined, Beijing's enlightened anti-imperialism made the Nationalists appear all the more reactionary and unpalatable.

The pendulum continued to swing in Beijing's favour until on 25 October 1971 the UN General Assembly finally arrived at an epiphany and voted to recognise the People's Republic and expel the Nationalists. In 1972, the US lifted its embargo and President Nixon embarked upon an official visit to Beijing, leading in 1979 to a Joint Sino-US Communiqué on the establishment of diplomatic relations. US recognition of the PRC as the legal government of China was accompanied by the termination of the Sino-American Mutual Defence Treaty with Taiwan, a move which was far from universally popular. Although the US only had 753 troops on the island by that time, the dissolution of the Military Assistance Advisory Group was of huge symbolic significance. Many hawks fiercely opposed the change of policy, with Senator Barry Goldwater condemning the decision as a 'betrayal'.[16]

Admission to the UN and rapprochement with the US was no magic bullet. Friction over Taiwan and the war in Vietnam were still ongoing, and the potential for them to escalate remained, but when in 1973 the North's Prime Minister Pham van Dong urged a final offensive to conquer the South, he was warned off. Mao reminded him that he still did not have 'a broom long enough to reach Taiwan, and you do not have a broom long enough to reach Saigon'.[17]

Instead, in January 1973 a ceasefire was agreed and talks resumed, whilst the last US troops departed leaving only a few advisers. The subsequent negotiations nonetheless proved futile and intermittent hostilities persisted until they broke down completely in April 1974. Now, with the broom long enough, the North invaded, sweeping the South Vietnamese forces aside and capturing Saigon on 30 April 1975. The victors formally announced the founding of the unified Socialist Republic of Vietnam, once more within the ambit of Beijing and laying to rest the humiliations suffered under France since the 1880s.

The honeymoon period did not last, and relations began to cool with Vietnam's growing closeness to the Soviet Union. In 1978 it joined the Russian-sponsored Council for Mutual Economic Cooperation, COMECON, and the two countries signed a Treaty of Mutual Friendship and Cooperation. When in the same year the Vietnamese attacked the PRC-backed Khmer Rouge in Cambodia, Beijing finally snapped. Fighting along the border cost tens of thousands of lives before China withdrew its troops, though it insisted that it was they who had taught Vietnam a lesson.

Mao's death in 1976 had in the meantime prompted a re-evaluation of priorities. Henceforth, support for revolutionary movements abroad and foreign aid was to be given less emphasis than domestic economic and political issues. High on the agenda were those last two bastions of European privilege on its soil, boils which his successor Deng Xiaoping was determined to lance.

In 1979 he asserted that 'the thoughts of our compatriots in ... Xianggung (Hong Kong) and Aomen (Macao) turn in longing to their motherland and their sense of patriotism has grown stronger',[18] meaning their repatriation was only a matter of time. In the event, the return of Macao would prove straightforward enough, mainly because after the Portuguese revolution of 1975 the new left-wing regime was avowedly anti-imperialist, and it immediately gave independence to all of its overseas territories. They offered to return Macao in the same vein, demilitarising the territory and slowly winding down their presence until by 1985, 80 per cent of Macao was run by locals.

Formal handover negotiations commenced that year, when a Basic Law and joint declaration was followed by the creation of the Preparatory Committee for the Establishment of the Macao Special Administrative Region. This agreed the process for the formation of a 200-member Nomination Committee which would elect the territory's first government following the handover. At midnight on 19/20 December 1999, nearly 500 years after it was first settled, Governor Vasco Joaquim Rocha Viera presided over the seamless return of his country's last overseas possession. To this day, it continues to thrive as the 'Las Vegas of the East', a gambling and tourist mecca hosting 10,000,000 Chinese visitors a year, 60 per cent of all tourists. Pursuing a pastime which has been a favourite of Chinese people for millennia, it manages to generate billions of dollars in revenue annually for the territory. Certainly, its repatriation and subsequent fortunes have proved far less of a gamble than that of its neighbour.

By the 1970s, Hong Kong was Britain's last really significant overseas possession, but it had also become indispensable to the economy of the mainland. Thirty-five per cent of exports now passed through the colony and its finance houses provided vital capital for Beijing's own economic development. Some in Whitehall found it difficult to come to terms with parting with the territory. A few diehards argued that in the strict legal sense only the lease on the New Territories ran out in 1997, the island was held in perpetuity. This was true, but the colony without the New Territories was unsustainable, which is why they were leased in the first place. In any case and as Deng had made clear, China would never countenance such a compromise. In 1984 British MP Edwina Curry had to admit that the future of the entire territory clearly now lay with China,[19] and that negotiations would be undertaken on that basis. However, there were also millions of British subjects in the colony to whom, the *New Statesman* insisted, Britain had a 'moral duty'.[20] Therefore, and under some pressure, Britain granted full citizenship to around a quarter of a million people, of whom by 1989 180,000 had found new homes in Canada, Australia, the US and Singapore. That still left several million facing an uncertain future following the handover.

After lengthy and sometimes fractious negotiations, the Joint Sino-British Declaration and the Basic Law were agreed, which lay the groundwork for the complete recovery of the territory by 1 July 1997. Deng had tried to reassure sceptics that the One Country, Two Systems model Beijing had devised would make Hong Kong a Special Administrative Region, and he undertook to honour its existing rights and privileges until at least 2047. Chris Patton, the last governor of Hong Kong, nevertheless angered the Chinese by attempting to push through reforms prior to the handover which he apparently hoped they would be forced to accept as a fait accompli. Instead, he was labelled an opportunist, and a 'political harlot',[21] and it was made clear that any such measures would simply be swept aside when they took over. It was under something of a cloud therefore, that the world witnessed the last rites of empire played out. The old colonial flag was lowered and that of the new regime raised as Prince Charles and a tearful Chris Patten watched the final British garrison, in full tropical regalia, march into history.

Despite widely held reservations, Beijing appeared to have been true to its word, as the territory continued to flourish following its repatriation. By the 2020s, financial services, trading, logistics and professional services had created a GDP of US$346bn and per capita income of US$46,323. But as much as Beijing left its money-making institutions pretty much to their own devices, it proved less hands off with regards its system of government. In 2003, anti-sedition laws were only narrowly averted following widespread opposition, and in 2012 demonstrations and strikes forced Beijing-centric changes to school curriculums to be abandoned. In 2014, an attempt to impose shortlists for candidates to elections also failed, but Beijing's apparatchiks, like the Imperial mandarins of old, bided their time and kept their powder dry.

Gradually, the administrative organs of the territory were infiltrated with placemen and the Legislative Council became barely recognisable by any measure of democratic accountability. Only thirty-five of its seventy members are elected directly and the other half selected by a committee approved by Beijing. The territory has seen no direct and open elections for the office of Chief Executive, and despite being enshrined in the Basic Law there is no firm date for them to take place. Protests result in arbitrary arrests, whilst politicians who voice their support have been expelled from the council chamber. Groups such as the Umbrella Movement have taken to the streets waving the former colonial flag as one means by which to express their disgust at repeated breaches of the Handover Agreement.

Upon the death of Queen Elizabeth II in September 2022, Hong Kongers marched once again. Referred to as *Si tau por*, or 'boss lady' in Cantonese, the sense of loss at the passing of the monarch was much in evidence. Partly because the authorities could not easily intervene under the circumstances, it was also exploited as a moment in which to express their antipathy towards Beijing. People made for the British Consulate in large numbers, laying flowers and displaying the Union Flag, making it clear that British rule remains, in the minds of many, far more palatable than that of Beijing. But there is little the international community, let alone the UK on its own, can do to prevent China from slowly absorbing the territory into the mainland, and international indignation is largely shrugged off by a regime impervious to criticism. The protests of the so-called 'Five Eyes' grouping of the UK, US, Canada Australia and New Zealand are met with silence or rebuffed with icy responses. To one such protest, a Foreign Ministry spokesman remarked that 'regardless of whether they have five eyes or ten, if they dare to harm China's national interest, they should be wary of those eyes being poked blind'. To amplify their contempt, Vice President Han Zheng, believed to have been the man behind Hong Kong's plight, was sent to represent the country at the coronation of King Charles III.

Elsewhere, China's attempts at revanchism have proved equally contentious, challenging the legitimacy of borders imposed by Russia during the nineteenth century. Prompted in part by deteriorating relations between the two states, they frequently led to tense stand-offs, resulting in an undeclared war from March to September 1969 near Zhenbao Island on the Ussuri River. Numerous clashes caused hundreds of casualties on both sides, only ending in an inconclusive ceasefire which left the dispute unresolved. The mood slowly began to improve in the 1980s, culminating in a visit by President Mikhail Gorbachev in 1989 clearing the way for meaningful dialogue. The 1991 Sino-Soviet Border Agreement followed, and in 2001 the twenty year Sino-Russian Treaty of Good-Neighbourliness and Friendly Cooperation was signed by Jiang Zemin and Vladimir Putin. This far-ranging document included a commitment by both nations to pursue entirely peaceful resolutions to any future disagreements, and in 2004 Russia agreed to a series of concessions, including the transfer of Yinlong Island and half of Heixiazi.

Putin's invasion of Ukraine led in June 2022 to Xi Jinping vowing to support Moscow's sovereignty and security. In turn, Putin backs Beijing in its stance on Taiwan and its territorial disputes in the South China Sea. However, such gestures have not entirely erased memories of historic bad blood. At Blagoveshchensk in Manchuria, monuments still recall the massacres that took place on the Amur River in 1900. One, a bronze statue surmounted by an orthodox cross, honours the perpetrators, whilst in a Chinese museum across the river a painting depicts the events from the victim's perspective.

Russia is far from being the only country with which Beijing has territorial disputes, and it has resorted to various devices in pursuit of its objectives. In January 2021 the Land Borders Law was passed, containing a raft of measures designed to 'resolutely defend territorial sovereignty and land border security'.[22] This statute is now applied to disputes such as that with India over Arunachal Pradesh, or South Tibet, as it calls the territory. Ceded to British India by the Tibetan government in 1913, it has never been recognised by Beijing and first led to clashes between the two countries in 1962. In January 2022, China was reported to have invoked the Land Borders Law to rename fifteen villages in the disputed territory, sparking further confrontations which in May of that year resulted in another twenty deaths. In 1974, fighting broke out with Vietnam over the Paracel (Xisha) Islands and in 1988 over the Johnson South Reef in the Union Banks Region of the Spratly (Nansha) Islands, sovereignty of which would deliver its possessor extensive oil and gas exploration rights in the surrounding seas. In February 1992, China sought to impose its will unilaterally when it framed the Law on the Territorial Sea and Contiguous Zone and defined the Spratly and Paracel Islands as Chinese territory. The problem is further complicated by the fact that Malaysia, Brunei the Philippines and Taiwan also claim the Spratlys, along with other reefs and otherwise insignificant pinpricks of land.

Following United Nations adjudication on the matter, it published its Convention on the Law of the Sea in 2016. Beijing was censured for its assertions of 'historic rights', its denial of fishing access to other states and its illegal construction of artificial islands, upon which it is suspected of building military bases. Furthermore, the UN found it to be in violation of international navigation-related regulations and of damaging the environment. Naturally, Beijing rejects these findings, and continues to defy the international community in other areas. In 2021, the Maritime Traffic Safety Law required foreign-flagged vessels entering its 'territorial waters', meaning the Spratlys, Paracels and Taiwan, to meet certain safety and environmental standards. Under its provisions, warships, nuclear powered submarines and vessels carrying radioactive, toxic or hazardous materials have to give advance notice. These measures have naturally provoked more anger in Washington and London, amid accusations that it further breaches freedom of navigation laws.

These tensions prompted 91 per cent of Filipinos and 83 per cent of Vietnamese polled to express their belief that armed conflict at some point is a distinct possibility,[23] and influenced Canberra's decision to sign the AUKUS Treaty with the UK and the US, the primary aim of which is to help Australia build its own fleet of conventionally armed nuclear-powered submarines. Early in 2023, a review of Australian defence policy led to an announcement that its military intended to adopt 'precision strike' missiles as a contingency against fallout from a war over Taiwan. In January 2022, the Reciprocal Access Agreement between Japan and Australia was signed, designed to ease restrictions on the movement of weapons and supplies for joint training and disaster relief operations. In May 2022, a similar arrangement was agreed between the UK and Japan and in early 2023 it was reported that the US was to re-establish a military presence in the Philippines, with joint military exercises planned. But although some critics have condemned such measures as counterproductive and even provocative, Beijing's neighbours feel they have every reason to prepare for the worst-case scenario.

Taiwan, of course, has been in Beijing's crosshairs since 1949, nearly sparking all-out war during the Korean conflict and again in 1954-1955, when the PLA shelled Nationalist-occupied Jinmen (Quemoy) in the Taiwan Strait. In response, the US Congress passed the Formosa Resolution of 29 January 1955 which empowered the President to defend Taiwan, if necessary with nuclear weapons, and although Mao was forced to back down he then pressed ahead with his own nuclear weapons programme. A second crisis flared up in 1958 when the PLA again shelled the islands, prompting the despatch of the US Seventh Fleet and additional military aircraft. The number of American troops on the island was also increased to 20,000. This crisis, too, ended in stalemate. Nonetheless, the sabre rattling has persisted intermittently ever since, with successive Chinese leaders re-asserting claims of sovereignty.

Taiwanese politicians such as former President Lee Ten-hui continue to distance the island from Beijing. He even spoke fondly of his experiences under Japanese rule and claimed that the island benefited from its occupation. In 2014 he expressed doubts over such highly sensitive topics as the Nanking Massacre and backed Japan in the dispute over the Diaoyu or Senkaku Islands in the East China Sea. In 2015, he even dared to express his opinion that Japan had historic claims to the island at least as legitimate as Beijing's. The question of sovereignty is further complicated by the passage of time. Polls carried out in 2022 suggested that 70 per cent of islanders now identify exclusively as Taiwanese and do not consider themselves as Chinese at all. This is a huge increase on the 50 per cent who made that distinction ten years before, whilst half of respondents went so far as to support de jure, rather than simply de facto, independence.

In the face of growing seditious sentiments, an Anti-Secession Law was passed in 2005, and there are repeated intrusions into

Taiwanese airspace and military exercises carried out close to its shores. In addition to more flyovers, an embargo was imposed in June 2022 affecting farmed Taiwanese Grouper fish, worth as much as US$2,000 each, of which the mainland accounted for 80 per cent of exports. The loss of this lucrative market was of much more symbolic than economic significance compared with the island's dominance of the vast microchip market.

Having developed into a technology powerhouse, some 65 per cent of the world's electronic equipment, from mobile phones to tablets, depend entirely upon the computer chips produced here. The Taiwan Semiconductor Manufacturing Company, valued in 2021 at US$100bn, enjoys a monopoly over half the world's market, and as China accounts for only 5 per cent, the consequences should it control Taiwanese production are self-evident. Clearly, America has an enormous vested interest in Taiwan's assets remaining beyond Beijing's reach, raising threat levels and drawing Taipei closer to the protective arm of Washington. The US State Department's website has quietly removed a line which had previously confirmed that it did not support Taiwanese independence, and in August 2022, Speaker of the House of Representatives Nancy Pelosi visited the island in a show of solidarity. This alleged provocation was followed in early 2023 by a meeting between Taiwanese President Tsai Ling-wen and US House Speaker Kevin McCarthy in California.

It is certain that should China ever make good on its threats, there would be no contest without American assistance. The island can field at best 100,000 troops. The Chinese army is the largest in the word by some margin, with over two million active military personnel; 860 tanks could be fielded against 6,300, and 300 fighter aircraft against 1,600. An invasion fleet could be protected by aircraft carriers, thirty-two destroyers, forty-eight frigates and seventy-one submarines, and of course Beijing can deploy its vast arsenal of rockets, both conventional and nuclear. With a defence budget of US$293 billion compared to the United States' US$801 billion, it nevertheless eclipses Taiwan's US$19 billion. On 23 May 2024, China mobilised land forces and sent warships and jets into the waters off Taiwan as 'punishment' for President Lai describing the island as a 'sovereign and independent' country in his inaugural speech. The PLA statement added that their reaction should also act as a 'stern warning against the interference and provocation of external forces'. With some 75 per cent of islanders expressing their determination to resist an invasion, any such undertaking could nonetheless prove a costly venture. As President Putin discovered to his cost following the invasion of Ukraine in February 2022, wars expected to be over in days or weeks can drag on interminably in the face of determined resistance, and at the time of writing that in Ukraine shows no sign of resolution.

Early post-war relations with arch enemy Japan appeared surprisingly promising following an admission by Mao that they should not all be condemned for the acts perpetrated by the Imperial Japanese Army. Although his conciliatory attitude was readily reciprocated, it proved an all too brief clinch once it became clear that Japan was now a willing protégé of the United States. Under its strong influence, Japanese militarism was expunged and its political system entirely reformed, turning the country into a democratic constitutional monarchy. As such, Tokyo followed Washington's lead in foreign policy and recognised Nationalist China in 1952, signed a defence treaty with the US, and supported the UN coalition in Korea. Only a mutual distrust of the Soviet Union provided any shared interest, and over the years the two countries quietly discussed normalising their relations, crystallised in September 1972 with the signing of the Joint Declaration. Diplomatic relations were restored, Japan recognised the 'One China' approach, and the two parties agreed that they would work towards these ends by 'taking history as a mirror and facing up to the future'. In 1974, regular commercial flights commenced between Beijing and Tokyo, and cultural exchanges became possible, with opera companies, art troupes and youth visits taking the lead. A Treaty of Peace and Friendship was concluded in 1978 and a bilateral Long Term Trade Agreement negotiated, by which Chinese coal was exchanged for science and technology. In 1979 Japan commenced Official Development Assistance (ODA) to fund infrastructure projects such as power stations, ports and transport networks. Although China had agreed to drop demands for reparations, some cynics interpreted the programme as an attempt to atone for Japan's actions in the Second World War without officially conceding culpability.

Improved relations also provided an opportunity for more stranded Japanese still living in China to return home. These were referred to as the *Zanryu Koji*, or 'stranded children' who had been adopted into Chinese families and *Zanryu Fujin* or 'war wives', who had been married off to farmers. Around 1,500,000 Japanese and Koreans had been left behind in Manchuria in 1945, of whom 245,000 are believed to have perished at the hands of the Russians and vengeful Chinese. Many others had committed suicide, and approximately 500,000 were shipped off on the orders of Stalin for forced labour in Russia. During the brief window open between 1946 and 1948, around 1,235,000 were repatriated, and a further 30,000-35,000 returned from 1953 to 1958. In 1959 the Japanese tried to draw a line under the matter, when around 30,000 more were officially declared dead and removed from family registers. It was also decided that only those under the age of thirteen at the end of the war would be deemed as stranded, and those over that age classified as having remained of their own free will.

Nor was the government over-keen to facilitate the return of the relatively few that were left. Women could not take their Chinese children to Japan with them, and initially only one visit every ten years was allowed with a maximum of two visits in a lifetime. Those wishing to return permanently also had to have a Japanese sponsor financed by the individuals concerned. However, these punitive rules were constantly challenged and the authorities were gradually shamed into backing down. By 1989, supporters rather than sponsors were considered sufficient, and in 1993 one visit every five years was permitted. Finally, in 1995 the government agreed to fund annual visits itself. By the time the repatriations were concluded, up to 100,000 had made the journey, once extended families were taken into account, but that was not the end of the matter. Refused citizenship, unable to find jobs, having no language skills and with little knowledge of their new surroundings, many felt as stranded in Japan as they had in China. They also had to live on meagre allowances equivalent to only US$178-268 a month, a tenth of that needed to live decently. In 2003, several hundred plaintiffs sued the government, asserting that at the end of the war they had been effectively abandoned and left to fend for themselves. They demanded the equivalent of US$300,000 each as compensation for their experiences, but they faced long, drawn-out legal battles to get justice.

Another, arguably even more tragic legacy of the war was the stain of officially sanctioned so-called *Ianfu*, literally translated as 'Comforting, consoling women'. Following the largescale rapes in Shanghai in 1932 so-called 'comfort stations' were created by the military as organised brothels. This was allegedly endorsed by Emperor Hirohito himself, and when the numbers of Japanese prostitutes proved insufficient, Chinese women and girls were among the tens of thousands procured through deceit, abduction or kidnap to work in them. They were worked long shifts, sustaining terrible injuries and contracting venereal disease in the process. Death was the inevitable consequence for perhaps 90 per cent of the victims, either as a direct result of their abuse or through suicide after they could not bear such an existence any longer. Memories of such treatment understandably did not fade, and relations took a hit in the early 1980s when revisionist Japanese school textbooks sought to downplay the role of the armed forces in all the countries and territories it occupied between 1931 and 1945.

In 1989, Tokyo imposed sanctions and suspended financial aid following the Tiananmen Square massacre. However, in October 1992 the Emperor used the occasion of an official visit to attempt to heal their historic differences. In a landmark speech of massive understatement, he admitted: 'In the long history of relationships between our two countries, there was an unfortunate period in which my country inflicted great suffering on the people of China. About this I feel great sadness.'[24] The following year Prime Minister Morihiro Hosokawa made a more unequivocal acknowledgement of Japan's aggression and offered a formal apology. Then in 1998, Jiang Zemin took the opportunity of a visit to Japan to castigate the country once again over wartime atrocities and took great offence when Prime Minister Junichiro Koizumi visited the Yasukuni Shrine in Tokyo, insisting that such actions were against the spirit of the 1972 Joint Statement. The Shinto shrine lists more than 2 million men who died in the service of Japan – including a thousand convicted war criminals.

The two countries continue to experience a roller-coaster relationship. Top-level diplomatic contacts resumed after 2001 and in 2005 another joint statement was issued, which seemed to show that they had finally buried the hatchet. It confirmed that henceforth their interests would be best served within a 'mutually beneficial relationship based on common strategic interests', including politics, economics, finance, security, culture and personal exchanges. In April 2007, Premier Wen Jiabao paid a visit in which Japan's post-war record of peacefulness was now praised, and he expressed his country's appreciation for the repeated apologies for its wartime actions, a gesture which opened the way for Koizumi's successor, Shinzo Abe, to reciprocate with a visit to China. During President Hu Jintao's visit to Japan in 2008 the two nations discussed cooperating in the exploitation of the gas fields in the East China Sea.

Then relations soured again, when in January 2008 Chinese-made gyoza dumplings were laced with insecticide, poisoning eighty Japanese consumers. Although the factory where they were produced was immediately closed and all exports to Japan suspended, panic ensued in which imported Chinese food was dumped wholesale, and the Japanese media added to the ill-feeling with its inflammatory reporting.

A largely sympathetic reaction to the earthquake which shattered Sichuan Province in May 2008 saw Japan among the first countries to offer emergency rescue teams, but in September 2010 a Chinese fishing boat collided with two Japanese Coast Guard vessels near the Senkaku Islands and its crew was arrested. Tempers calmed following their release, and when the earthquake and tsunami hit Japan in March 2011, Hu Jintao offered his country's help. Then on 13 September 2012, the Japanese parliament took the contentious step of nationalising the Senkaku islands, reopening wounds and prompting massive anti-Japanese demonstrations across China. These coincided with the 18 September anniversary of the Mukden Incident, the commemoration of which resurrected more bad memories. China has asserted the islands' return was covered by the decisions of the Cairo Conference of 1943 and the Potsdam Declaration of 1945. Japan insists that they were uninhabited when they were annexed, and therefore were not acquired as the result of aggression but in accordance with international law prevailing at the time.

In 2015, the State Archives Administration of China released never before seen handwritten confessions by Japanese war criminals outlining their actions during the Second World War, which of course reignited emotions. They corroborated both contemporary and post-war accounts, further discrediting the attempts by successive Japanese governments to downplay the extent of the crimes perpetrated by the army. Once passions eased, the atmosphere improved once more, and in May 2018 Premier Li Kequiang paid an official visit to Japan. In October of that year Prime Minister Abe returned the gesture and made the first such visit to China in seven years. In 2019, President Xi Jinping attended the G20 summit in Japan, and a state visit was also scheduled, but in late 2022 further tensions prompted Tokyo to announce a massive increase in defence spending. This fraught relationship is often reflected in opinion polls. One undertaken in 2016 suggested that only 11 per cent of Japanese admitted to having a positive opinion of China. Fifty per cent of Japanese believed they have apologised enough for the atrocities committed in China, but only 10 per cent of Chinese agreed; 80 per cent of Japanese and 59 per cent of Chinese believed another war was a real possibility.[25] It is in part for this reason that the United States still maintains a formidable military presence in the country, amounting to some 54,000 personnel, with a further 45,000 stationed in Hawaii.

Following the confrontations of the 1970s, more cordial relations have been established with Vietnam. Despite their ongoing territorial disputes, gradual progress followed the collapse of the Soviet Union in 1991, with both supporting the post-1991 Cambodian regime and their respective efforts to join the World Trade Organisation. In 1991, the 'Sixteen Word Guideline' was signed, opening the way for deeper bilateral relations, and a 'Joint Statement for Comprehensive Cooperation' followed in 2000. That year the two countries also resolved outstanding disputes over their land border and maritime rights in the Gulf of Tonkin. In 2002, Jiang Zemin visited and the two states signed further trade, territorial and mutual cooperation agreements, followed in 2008 by a Comprehensive Strategic Cooperative Partnership. As a consequence, the total value of trade between them reached US$517bn by 2019, with Vietnamese crude oil, coal, coffee and food being exported and

Chinese pharmaceuticals, machinery, petroleum fertilizers and other commodities received in exchange.

Progress however, has been compromised through the latter's closer ties with the United States and Japan. Hanoi keeps its military options open by maintaining formidable armed forces which it updates with US and Japanese weaponry, causing ruffled feathers in Beijing. Another bone of contention has been the Comprehensive Strategic Cooperative Partnership which Washington has been suspected of trying to emulate. In recent years Hanoi has hosted high-level visits from senior American diplomats and such luminaries as Vice-President Kamala Harris in August 2021. Consequently, in order to assuage its concerns, Prime Minister Pham Minh Chinh has repeatedly assured the Chinese that his country would never adopt a hostile attitude towards it, and to this end maintains a strict neutrality. It firmly espouses its policy of having no military alliances, no affiliation with one country to the detriment of another, no hosting of foreign military bases, and no force or threatening to use force in international relations.

In 1992 China and South Korea established 'friendly and cooperative relations', following which progress was made in a number of areas including foreign policy, security, the economy and culture. Prior to the 2022 elections, sitting President Moon Jae-in also confirmed his commitment to the 'three nos'. These were no new Terminal High Altitude Missile Defence Batteries (THAAD), no trilateral US-Japan-South Korea missile defence systems and no trilateral US-Japan-South Korea security alliance. His successor Yoon Suk-yeol, however, had no such reservations, and early on indicated a drastic policy shift. He advocated a tougher stance towards North Korea following its provocative missile tests, including the adoption of THAAD and a 'comprehensive strategic alliance' with the US and Japan. Historic disputes with the latter regarding its exploitation of 'comfort women' and the treatment of Korean labourers during the Second World War remain a sticking point. The US has been trying to act as honest broker between the two governments, but as yet there is little sign that these issues will be resolved and that consequently, any trilateral defence arrangement can be fully implemented. Beijing meanwhile remains as suspicious about Seoul's closer ties with Washington and Tokyo as it would be about Hanoi's, seeing THAAD in particular as unnecessary overkill and a threat to its own strategic interests. It also shares the North's disquiet about the 25,000 US troops permanently stationed in the country, and the regular US-South Korean military exercises are a constant cause for resentment. Nonetheless, Xi Jinping did make a ground-breaking gesture when he called Yoon to congratulate him on his election, which was the first time that a Chinese leader has done so.

Matters are naturally further complicated by the fractious relationship between North and South, which has been in limbo since the ceasefire in 1953. The peninsula has been in an almost constant state of tension due in large part to the recalcitrance of the North, and its frequent forays into low-scale aggression and attempts to undermine Seoul. Despite signing a formula for reunification in 1972 and concluding a Pact of Reconciliation in 1991, neither measure has gained traction. Progress appeared to be made when in 1994 the North agreed to drop its nuclear research in exchange for two US reactors capable of generating electricity, and in 2000 both appeared at the Olympic Games under one banner, although they competed separately. Later, negotiations resulted in long-awaited family reunions being facilitated, and a joint free trade facility at Kaesong was opened in 2003. This held out the prospect for improving the economy of the North and making it more interdependent with the South.

Behind the scenes, however, the North was betraying its earlier undertakings and admitted in 2005 that it had still been pursuing nuclear research, carrying out its first tests in 2006. Nonetheless, in 2007 trains were allowed to cross the border both ways, and a summit was held between President Roh Moo-Hyun and Kim Jong Il in Pyongyang. The South's more conciliatory approach took a different turn when Roh was succeeded that year by Lee Myung-Bak, who felt a firmer stance was needed in the face of the North's posturing, but in 2009 Pyongyang closed the land border and all non-military links were suspended. It then announced that all existing agreements were cancelled and the trade facility at Kaesong was closing.

A serious incident took place in March 2010 when a South Korean warship exploded and sank near the maritime border.

North Korea was blamed, and the South put on alert, in response to which Pyongyang used military exercises as an excuse to bombard the South, prompting Seoul to reply in kind. When Kim Jong Il died in 2011 he was succeeded by his son Kim Jong-Un, who accelerated the nuclear programme but then agreed to a suspension in return for food aid. In 2016, Pyongyang claimed that it had successfully tested a hydrogen bomb, although there was little seismic evidence to support this assertion. When an ICBM was launched in July 2017, the decision was taken to consider the adoption of THAAD.

The 2018 Olympics again held out the prospect for a rapprochement, and high-level meetings and a summit followed, after which both promised to work together towards the 'complete denuclearisation' of the peninsula. Then a disastrous summit scheduled for 2019 between US President Trump and Kim led to further recriminations and another impasse. Since then the North has continued with ever more menacing missile tests, heightening tensions and threatening any chance of reconciliation. Their proximity to Japan was also a factor in that country announcing increases in defence spending, which of course has only caused disquiet in China. And so the spiral of distrust and recrimination continues well into 2023, reaching such a pitch that the South Korean Nuclear Policy Forum advocated for the first time that the country consider developing its own independent nuclear deterrent. In April 2023, Washington received an undertaking that Seoul would refrain from pursuing this strategy, in return for which the US would station its own nuclear armed submarines in South Korean territorial waters on an ad hoc basis. The two governments would consult closely on any nuclear-related issues which might affect the peninsula.

Whilst the bickering interspersed with occasional sabre-rattling continues, the living standards of the two Koreas continue to diverge. South Korea's market-led economy now boasts a GDP of US$1.626 trillion compared to the North's US$32.1 billion, leaving the North's population of 25,600,000 far poorer than most of the 51,000,000 living a largely affluent consumer lifestyle in the South. With an average GDP of US$1,800, 2 per cent that of the South, reports describe a heavily repressed and censored society, with no access to Google or Facebook or the internet itself, relying instead on inferior domestic equivalents. Life south of the border is in stark contrast, one of typical consumer-led capitalism. Consequently, life expectancy is also favourable, eighty-three years compared to only seventy-two in the North. For decades however, the threat of another invasion did have a stultifying effect on democracy in the South. Nonetheless, as demographics have changed, especially from the 2000s onward, younger people are demanding more democratic accountability. Despite this a centralised presidential system continues to exercise widespread patronage, with the power to implement changes many interpret as self-interested and nepotistic. It is nonetheless free from the overtly brutal repression such movements would invite in Pyongyang.

Like North Korea, China interprets any manifestation of opposition whatsoever as counter-revolutionary treachery, and deals with it accordingly. In the mid-1980s student-led demands for greater democracy combined with disquiet over economic problems grew into hundreds of protests across the country, which in May 1989 threatened to overshadow the state visit of Russian leader Mikael Gorbachev. A serious clampdown was imposed but the protests continued, culminating on 15 April with thousands congregating in Beijing's Tiananmen Square. Here, where the first stirrings of the Fourth of May and other Chinese freedom movements found their feet at the end of the First World War, a showdown was inevitable. Martial law was declared and when the protesters still refused to disperse, units of the PLA moved in during the early hours of 4 June. Upwards of 2,000 unarmed students were allegedly massacred, and thousands more injured as tanks and live rounds were used against them. Roundups of suspects followed, but despite every attempt to suppress and censor reporting, international condemnation, sanctions and UN resolutions followed. In response, sympathetic Chinese journalists were sacked and foreign ones expelled, whilst any discussion of the affair was prohibited.

Beijing is equally uncompromising when faced by manifestations of unorthodox but largely innocuous doctrines that do not chime with government dogma. In the early 1990s, religious leader Li Hongzhi founded the *Falun Gong* or 'Wheel of Law' movement in Changchun in Jilin Province. Innocently enough it would have seemed, it preached the laudable virtues of truth, benevolence and forbearance through meditation and exercise. Nonetheless, its promise to bring salvation to the faithful brought it under the full glare of diligent authorities, who soon marked it out as a dangerous cult. Its members experienced increasing police harassment and in April 1999 a prominent Tianjin newspaper printed criticism of the movement, which in response protested outside its offices. The police then intervened and broke the meeting up, provoking outrage and a huge demonstration of 10,000 people in the Zhongnanhai Gardens in Beijing. Unimpressed, the government accused them of being charlatans who peddled feudal superstitions and outlawed them completely. Chinese Christians, too, remain as marginalised today as they had been prior to the pogroms of 1870 and 1900, and to hold Christ above Communism or even national religions is considered tantamount to heresy. The extent to which Xi Jinping saw it as a threat was elucidated at the Ninth National Congress of the Communist Party of China on 18 October 2017. Here he promised to

> ... fully implement the party's basic policy on religious affairs, uphold the principle that religions in China must be Chinese in orientation and provide active guidance to religions so that they can adapt themselves to socialist society.[26]

Communist Party officials are expected to eschew any religious beliefs as a matter of course, and applicants who dare to express affiliations are rejected automatically. All religious groups have to be registered and sanctioned by the state, and some have been instructed to install CCTV where services are held, display the national flag and include patriotic songs in their services. Landlords are pressured not to lease space to worshippers, or to evict those who have been rented accommodation. Failure to comply invites an array of punitive sanctions. As a result, many clergy and their flocks practise their faith clandestinely, and despite such persecution there are still estimated to be at least 44,000,000 Christians throughout the country, most of whom have no alternative but to worship in secret to evade government scrutiny and interference.

Even toeing the line and conforming to the state's edicts brings few benefits, with the internet, Twitter and other social media monitored, censored and filled with pro-government propaganda. Tiananmen Square demonstrated what the fate of anyone 'guilty' of dissent can be, and even those engaging in mild criticism are at the very least chastised. In such an atmosphere of intolerance, the TV, radio, newspapers and magazines cannot disseminate what they find, only that which is ordained by the long arm of the state. Consequently, whilst gay, lesbian and women's rights are poorly defended, mention or criticism of this is barely possible. Criticism of the government's handling of Covid was met with arrests, vaccine activists punished and those brave enough to speak out about human rights in general incarcerated. Sometimes Beijing's response to quite reasonable expressions of disquiet borders on the Orwellian.

In the middle of 2022, people who had taken official advice to buy property off-plan to beat inflation found that the projects had not been completed. From Liaoning Province in the north to Guangdong in the south, where up to 320 projects across a hundred sites had been affected, people took to the streets. But instead of trying to address their concerns, Beijing employed the Covid rules to raise the demonstrators' status to red, which forbade them from congregating or travelling. An even more serious outbreak of opposition to the regime occurred in late 2022, when Covid rules were blamed for the unnecessary deaths which followed a fire in a locked-down block of flats. The tragedy prompted almost unprecedented countrywide protests accompanied by calls for the resignation of Xi and the entire CCP. Inevitably, anyone brave enough to defy the authorities in such a public way risks being set upon by uniformed and plainclothes police officers, who among other ordinances, invoke the arcane charge of 'picking quarrels and provoking people'. This law dating from 1979 was originally aimed at genuine hooligans and anti-social individuals who commit run-of-the-mill public order offences. However, it soon morphed into a catch-all charge for anything and everything which incurred the displeasure of the establishment, breaches of which can lead to prison sentences of between five and ten years.

Failing to secure redress by peaceful means, some people adopt other methods. In faint echoes of the rebellions against the Qings, and for which an equally terrible price is paid, violence is used.

A Century of Humiliation

In February 1997, ethnic Uyghur Moslem separatists seeking independence for Xinjiang Province planted three bombs on buses in the capital Urumqi. They killed nine and injured another seventy-four people, and another bomb in Beijing in March killed two people and injured thirty more. The inevitable police crackdown resulted in peaceful demonstrators being killed and increasingly draconian measures being imposed on the general population. From 2009, Uyghurs have allegedly been subjected to treatment which many human rights groups have claimed to be tantamount to ethnic cleansing or even genocide. They are prevented from practising their religion, performing burial rites, staging traditional marriage ceremonies, and from wearing long beards or head and face coverings. They are also forced to eat pork and drink alcohol whilst being banned from eating halal food. They cannot give their children Muslim names or make the pilgrimage to Mecca and their shrines and temples have been desecrated and built over. They are monitored day and night and have to admit government agents into their homes to ensure they are not breaking the rules.

The families of those who are suspected of transgressing are broken up and their children sent to orphanages, where they are allegedly brainwashed and stripped of their cultural identities. An even worse fate awaits their parents. They are committed to vast re-education camps where they are humiliated and routinely abused on a daily basis, including sleep deprivation, drugs, electric shock treatment and rape. They are used as cheap or unpaid labour in the state-owned Xinjiang Production and Construction Corps or in local factories where they are closely monitored, segregated, abused by the managers and subjected to further re-education. If they resist they face being returned to their camps. All attempts to condemn their treatment by human rights groups and Western governments are dismissed as fabrications. In 2021, British Parliamentarian Sir Iain Duncan Smith MP and five colleagues found themselves placed under sanctions for speaking out, although the rift led in turn to a refusal to permit Chinese officials from attending Queen Elizabeth II's Lying in State in September 2022.

Whilst millions of its own people remain mired in poverty, Beijing is suspected of spending billions to spread soft power around the world. Key to this policy was the much lauded Belt and Road Initiative, launched in 2013 as a strategy to improve regional cooperation along the original Silk Road. Its authors also hope to create new land and maritime Silk Roads between Europe, Asia, Africa and the Middle East. It has seen over US$843 billion committed to over 13,000 infrastructure projects, Beijing selling the entire enterprise as one of mutually beneficial philanthropy. It predicts that the rewards could be considerable, with each of the 138 countries involved so far expected to increase their GDPs by an average of 10 per cent. Taken at face value, the business model appears equitable enough, with investments recouped through income generated by each project. This could include passenger traffic from an airport, ticket sales and tolls collected from railways, roads and bridges, or port dues and taxes from ships.

Problems have arisen when the projected return on investment fails to meet expectations. Finance is primarily through Chinese investment banks and they, acting on behalf of the Chinese government, can call in the loans or impose severe conditions for keeping the scheme afloat. Hambantota Port in Sri Lanka is cited as a case in point, an expensive project which proved to be a white elephant when it failed to attract sufficient business. In 2017, when income fell short of that necessary to service its debts, further financial relief was agreed in return for a ninety-nine-year lease. In another scheme, the China Harbour Engineering Company invested US$1.4bn in the construction of Colombo Port City. It was also granted a ninety-nine year lease plus a forty-three per cent stake. Although some analysts dispute these interpretations of events, blaming instead the government of Sri Lanka for poor choices, others see Beijing pulling the strings. Some have even floated the idea that Colombo is under pressure to support China in the UN when favourable votes are needed. If such assertions seem far-fetched, there is circumstantial evidence to suggest that such tactics may in fact be part of a general trend.

Beijing is also believed to be cultivating greater influence in some of Europe's former African colonies. Kenya owes US$7bn, and other states, also former British colonies, are believed to have fallen under its spell including Nigeria, Zambia, Ghana, South Africa and Tanzania. There are plans for railways in Kenya and a new port in Tanzania, both involving billions in infrastructure investment. Similarly, Algeria and Gabon, onetime French spheres, and Angola and Mozambique, former Portuguese territories, are finding themselves dependent upon Beijing's largesse. As well as infrastructure investments, China has large stakes in various mines in order to guarantee access to vital raw materials. These have come under the spotlight as the result of allegations of abuse of workers by their Chinese managers, echoing the mistreatment once meted out to Chinese labourers. Furthermore, rumours have emerged that Kenya or Tanzania may be coerced into allowing military bases to be built, giving Beijing a stronger foothold on the continent. There are also suspicions of plans to establish a base in the former British colony of the Seychelles in the Indian Ocean, ominously close to the Anglo-US base on Diego Garcia. The former French territory of Djibouti on the Red Sea already hosts a PLA base, ostensibly to protect its interests against the endemic piracy in the area. The Commonwealth Realm of Papua New Guinea in the southwest Pacific, worryingly close to Australia, is believed to have been approached to furnish similar facilities.

Sometimes Beijing is suspected of subversive activity of a different kind to secure influence and advantage. In 2022, lawyer Christine Lee was exposed as an agent operating on behalf of the United Front Work Department, an arm of the CCP created in 1942. Officially its aims are innocuous enough, and include furthering the business interests of expats, offering advice, encouragement and networking. It is believed to insinuate people and organisations in pursuit of information and intelligence gathering and to encourage the spread of Communist ideology. To this end, Lee was found to have donated money to Labour MP Barry Gardiner and LibDem leader Sir Ed Davey, and to have secured access to senior politicians such as Jeremy Corbyn, David Cameron and Theresa May. As well as seeking to garner undue leverage within Parliament, Lee was suspected of exploiting contacts with Ian Duncan Smith MP to obtain details of Uyghur separatists.

In the US, Chinese nationals have been accused of gathering intelligence on government and civilian agencies and politicians, or of masquerading as members of legitimate organisations in order to steal intellectual property and trade secrets. There have emerged reports of 'police stations' in the guise of community centres being established in the cities of other countries which have been used to monitor and intimidate nationals considered to be making a nuisance of themselves. There is also speculation that the equipment and software it installs around the world might contain trojan horses that permit surveillance and intellectual property theft, or allow cyber-attacks to be carried out. Worst-case scenarios include power networks crashing and plunging entire cities into darkness, banking systems being disrupted or state intelligence apparatus being sabotaged. In Britain, these fears were taken seriously enough to prompt the government to stop the involvement of the General Nuclear Power Group in the £20-billion Sizewell C nuclear power station in Suffolk. UK ministers also announced plans to phase out Huawei equipment from all 5G upgrade planning by 2027.

Even the desire of expats to keep in touch, known as *guanxi*, has been suspected of being used to carry out espionage. At one stage President Trump sought to ban the *WeChat* app altogether, whilst Chinese-owned TikTok has aroused fears that the app could be exploited by the Chinese Government to gather the personal data of its 150,000,000 US users. This resulted in Congress banning it from government devices, whilst a number of State Governors had it removed from their computer networks. Whilst it is keen to farm as much data about foreign governments as it can, China is far more reticent when it comes to sharing its own information. SAR-CoV-2, or the Corona virus, is a case in point. Although its source is generally now believed to have been a so-called wet market in the city of Wuhan, other theories include a leak from a laboratory in the city. This possibility mirrors a similar occurrence in 2004 when a pathogen leak caused a minor SARS outbreak. Both theories are vigorously denied by Beijing, which insists that it could just as feasibly have started in the United States, or through imported frozen food. In 2021, a World Health Organisation (WHO) delegation was admitted into the country to uncover the facts, but found their hosts uncooperative, declining to share important data and restricting access to the necessary files.

Yet for all the animus felt towards the political class at home, the vast majority of Chinese around the world are largely welcomed and accepted within their communities. In Peru, the former hell hole where labourers slaved away on guano beds, are refugees who fled from the revolution of 1912, the Communist takeover of 1949 and the violence and upheavals in SE Asia during the 1960s. Its community of 14,000, known as *tusan*, have enjoyed a relatively harmonious existence, and there have been generations of intermarriage with local Peruvian women who consider such unions something of a catch. They have also proven successful in business. Erasmo Wong arrived in the country at the tender age of eleven and founded a supermarket chain in 1942, which became highly successful. His son, Erasmo junior followed in his father's footsteps by becoming a civil engineer, entrepreneur and the owner of television channel Willax. In 2010 he was estimated to be worth US$500,000,000.

Refugees also sought sanctuary in Cuba, more than 130,000 leaving the US from the 1880s onwards. Many went on to become successful businessmen during the island's 1930s and 1940s heyday, but then fell foul of Fidel Castro and his Communist revolution of 1959. Their property and wealth were expropriated and many fled back to the now relatively welcoming US, particularly Florida. Ironically, the man Castro ousted, President Fulgencia Batista, an archetypal tyrant presiding over a corrupt, venal and graft-ridden country, had Chinese heritage. Today, a community of around 114,000 remain on the island, and Cuchillo Street in Havana thrives as the island's Chinatown. Small communities were established in Puerto Rico, Jamaica, Curacao, Belize and French and British Guiana. In the latter particularly, they assimilated almost completely into the culture of the colony and continued to prosper until independence in 1966, when many professionals emigrated. When the country became a republic in 1970 Arthur Chung was elected its first president, and on 27 June 1972 the young nation was among the first South American states to formally recognise the People's Republic of China.

Canada, Australia and the United States have since the Second World War sought to atone for their early mistreatment of Chinese migrants. Having lifted the 1923 restrictions imposed on immigration in 1947, Canada has proven to be an open and welcoming destination for thousands of newcomers, now numbering some 1,700,000, or around five per cent of the population. The push-pull factors are similar to those which drew them to other countries, such as poverty, civil war, the Communist takeover in 1949, and war in Southeast Asia. Their assimilation into Canadian national life is evident by the fact that ethnic Chinese such as Douglas Jung became a Conservative MP in 1957. He had long dedicated himself to the welfare of his fellow Chinese-Canadians, especially those who entered the country without the necessary documentation. Raymond Chan became the first Chinese cabinet minister in 1993 and Philip Lee was appointed Lieutenant-Governor of Manitoba in 2006, one of only three citizens of Chinese descent to have been given such a prominent post. The others were David Lam of British Columbia and Norman Kwong of Alberta. In an effort to draw a line under the racist history of the country, in 2006 Premier David Harper apologised for the imposition of the head tax and offered compensation. Only twenty or so of those affected were still alive at the time.

The 'White Australia' mentality which excluded non-Europeans was applied to the Chinese until the 1960s. The subsequent relaxation of immigration rules allowed thousands of doctors, teachers, academics and business people to flee trouble spots such as Vietnam and Cambodia. Further tranches followed from Hong Kong and Taiwan during the 1980s and 1990s, some made for New Zealand. Here, a quarter of a million reside, mainly in the cities and no longer confined to the periphery of society. Many are well-educated professionals with assets and skillsets that allow them to fit easily into the mainstream of the country.

In the United States, attitudes only began to change in the 1960s. Immigration rules permitted those with special skills to enter the country more easily, and join family already living there, but more recently, issues over trade, Covid and accusations of espionage have again coloured attitudes. Nonetheless, there are no signs of any sudden exodus, quite the contrary, and it remains a key destination for Chinese investment and its millionaire diaspora. Today, there are around 5,400,000 Americans with Chinese roots, the largest Asian ethnic group in the US, and they have contributed hugely to the cultural, economic and political fabric of the country.

Britain's Chinese community could arguably be among its most popular ethnic groups. Though originally small, only 387 Chinese had made Britain their home by 1901, it stands today at around

433,000, around 0.7 per cent of the population. Their experiences have varied greatly over time, and some were shamefully treated in the years immediately following the end of the Second World War. Many of the 20,000 Chinese in the UK by 1945 were seamen who had risked their lives in the Battle of the Atlantic. But with victory won these men were deemed surplus to requirements. The Home Office hatched a secret and illegal plot to have them deported, as outlined in the notorious government paper HO 213/926, or 'Compulsory Repatriation of Undesirable Chinese Seamen'. As a result, around 2,000 men, mainly in Liverpool and many of whom had English wives and children, were arbitrarily rounded up. They were arrested for trivial offences or on trumped-up charges, and then forced to board ships bound for Shanghai, Hong Kong and Singapore. Many were seized with such undue haste that their families thought they had deserted them, unaware they were victims of a scandal predating that of Windrush eighty years later. When in 1946 their wives and girlfriends finally learnt of their fate the *Liverpool Echo* printed the story, but the government denied everything. The scandal remained suppressed along with the infamous file until the story resurfaced in the 1990s. In 2006, the BBC transmitted a documentary on the subject, and the Home Office was examined about the veracity of the claims. In 2010 and 2021 more questions were raised in the House of Commons, but those in authority were reticent to disclose the truth and it remains a little-known and shameful chapter in Sino-British relations.

More recent arrivals have also experienced tragedy. In February 2004 undocumented labourers from Fujian Province were working for a gangmaster picking cockles in Morecambe Bay in Lancashire. They were not only forced to work long hours in horrible conditions for low pay, but were also exposed to the vagaries of unforgiving natural conditions. Twenty or so workers were suddenly overwhelmed by the fast-flowing incoming tide which is a feature of the bay and unable to outrun it, they were nearly all swept away and drowned. Despite the outrage and disgust the tragedy engendered, such conditions prevail today, with tens of thousands hidden in a black economy which exploits and abuses them. Today there are estimated to be some 60,000,000 Chinese living overseas altogether, sending home on average US$67bn in remittances every year. It is calculated that they also account for two-thirds of foreign investment, controlling upwards of US$2 trillion via various organisations such as the Bamboo Network in Southeast Asia. The progress their homeland has made since the end of the Century of Humiliation is astonishing. Like Mao's Great March, and victory in the civil war with Chiang, however, it has not been achieved without tremendous human cost.

The Great Leap Forward Mao initiated in the 1950s created large-scale famines in which millions starved. The numbers simply cannot be established. Some sources give 15 million, some 55 million. As its chief sponsor, he was forced to shoulder most of the responsibility and took a less prominent part until the end of the 1960s, and from 1962 to 1965 a more pragmatic approach was applied to reforming agriculture and industry. Private enterprise and incentives returned to bolster production, and communes were reduced in size. In 1978 further reforms known as the Four Modernisations were put in place, aiming for parity with the West by 2000 in agriculture, industry, science and technology. In 1979 the first four special economic zones were opened, including the city of Zhuhai, which was chosen primarily for its proximity to Hong Kong. It was designed as the trailblazer in attracting direct foreign investment, with more planned for the next decade. The state apparatus itself underwent root and branch reform with younger, brighter, better educated more capable technocrats coming to the fore instead of party placemen.

As a consequence, in 1993 the economy grew by 13 per cent and 9 per cent the following year, and after 1997 the economy continued to grow by 9 per cent annually, lifting it from thirtieth to tenth in international league tables. The US renewed its Most Favoured Nation status in 1996 and in 1999 foreign companies were granted access to Chinese markets in exchange for membership of the World Trade Organisation. In 2000 it surpassed Japan as the country with which the US had the largest trade deficit and membership of the WTO was finalised. In exchange, Beijing agreed to an average cut of eight per cent to its tariffs, and to ending subsidies to farmers and nationalised industry. By 2021 GDP was US$ 17.46 trillion, up 8.1% from 2020, with a trade surplus of US$676.43bn, that with the US alone now at US$153bn. In 1960 its GDP was only

11 per cent of the United States, now it is calculated to be nearer 64 per cent, or US$19.9 trillion, compared to US$25.3 trillion. Per capita disposable income nonetheless remains far lower at US$4,300 compared to the latter's' US$32,000 in 2021, and despite its reputation as the holder of much of the world's debt its own stood in 2021 at US$7 trillion. To the shock of the world's money markets, in April 2023 Russia, Mexico, South Africa and China proposed to use the yuan for their international transactions instead of the US dollar.

As keen to penetrate this huge market as their predecessors had been in the past, today's Western governments face more of a moral dilemma than had been the case in the eighteenth and nineteenth centuries. Then of course they could access opportunities without the need to consider such matters as human rights or Beijing's stance in foreign affairs. But these are hot topics today, and they need to be balanced against the opportunities offered by the world's second largest economy. Post Brexit Britain for example, is keen to secure a free trade agreement. At the same time, ongoing friction regarding Hong Kong ties the British Government's hands somewhat in its efforts to negotiate an equitable arrangement. This dichotomy is magnified when one considers the trade on offer in the old treaty ports and concessions alone. Long since vacated by their European masters, they are now larger and more prosperous than they could ever have imagined.

Guangzhou's population has grown from 2,500,000 in 1950 to nearer 14,000,000 today. The site of the former Thirteen Factories is now a large Cultural Park and Retail Centre, dwarfing the former European concerns, and due to its historic links to the days of humiliation, a popular tourist attraction. It is both an Export Processing Zone and a Free Trade Zone, home to car assembly plants, heavy industry, computer software manufacture and logistics. With a GDP of US$1.92 trillion, it is tenth in the world and the fifth in China. Its stunning architecture reflects this growing wealth and importance, with such avant-garde buildings as the Opera House, known as the 'double pebble', its box-shaped museum and 1,800-foot tall Canton Tower.

Shanghai, today's Shenzhen, accounts for 3.6% of China's total GDP at US$471bn, projected to be US$1.3 trillion by 2035, making it the fifth wealthiest city in the world. It has become a centre for retail, finance, IT, machine and car manufacture and is the world's busiest container port. It also shares with Guangzhou some of the most exciting examples of modern architecture, with the Shanghai Museum, the Grand Theatre, the Oriental Art Centre and the Oriental Pearl Tower alongside the Art Deco style of the world famous bund. Tianjin, with a population of 12,000,000 and GDP of US$247bn was created a Coastal Open City in 1984. In August 2008 it boasted the country's first high speed railway to Beijing, with speeds of 350 kph. In 2008 it co-hosted the Olympic Games and in 2013 the East Asia Games. Its major industries are petrochemicals, textiles, cars, and metalworking, and it is the site of the Airbus 320 assembly plant.

Chefoo, or Yantai, is the second largest city in Shandong Province after Qingdao, famous for its pears and apples, and has the oldest winery. It is also an Economic and Technical Development Area and Export Processing Zone. Bigger brother Qingdao developed rapidly after 2006 at a rate of 18.9 per cent a year, achieving a GDP of US$104bn. It manufactures white goods and electronics, chemicals, rubber, and high tech products. It is also once again the headquarters of the navy's Northern Fleet. The world-famous Tsingtao beer is still brewed here, and much of the old German architecture survives as a popular and quirky tourist attraction, with St Michael's Cathedral still a prominent feature of the skyline.

Dalian now has a population of 7,500,000 and is a financial, machine manufacturing, petrochemical, oil refining, electronics, shipping and logistics centre. It serves over a hundred national and international container shipping routes, and is the eighth busiest port in the world by tonnage. It is also a major tourist magnet for Japan, South Korea and Russia, with its hot springs and ski resorts. Weihaiwei, now Weihai, is another major seaport and fishing centre, with a population of 2,804,000 in 2020. It boasts light industries, grows peanuts and fruit and is an Economic and Technological Development Zone, Export Processing Zone and a Hi-Tech Science Park. It is also another popular tourist spot, drawing many of its visitors from Japan.

The capital Beijing remains at the heart of China's cultural and political life, having become after 3,000 years home to nearly

22,000,000 people. It is eleven times bigger than London, boasts a GDP of US$95bn, an average annual income of US$13,000 and 100 billionaires. Headquarters to 750 financial and other institutions, it is a major centre for electronics, motor car manufacture, machinery, metallurgy, textiles and white goods. Students flock to the Tsinghua and Peking Universities, and thousands of tourists annually gravitate to its numerous historic sites and cultural attractions. These include 197 museums, the Forbidden City and the remains of the Old Summer Palace, wantonly destroyed by Europeans in 1860. Here visitors can contemplate the time when foreigners enjoyed free agency over the country, committing outrages that have never been forgotten. The bitterness this period still engenders among many has prompted speculation as to when or even if, the shadow of the Century of Humiliation will ever be lifted from their shoulders. In 2011, in his speech at the meeting to commemorate the ninetieth anniversary of the founding of the Chinese Communist Party, President Hu Jintao pulled no punches. He blamed successive foreign interventions from 1840 onwards for reducing China to the status of a semi-colonial and semi-feudal society, and committed his country to becoming a modern socialist country by the centenary of the founding of New China. Many point to 2049 as the year by which all outstanding issues such as territorial claims are to be settled. If the prediction made by Sir Robert Hart, former Inspector-General of the Imperial Maritime Custom Service is anything to go by, this date is certainly one to watch. He starkly prophesied that present and future generations of Chinese will not rest until they

> ... take back from foreigners everything foreigners have taken from China, [which] will pay off old grudges with interest; and will carry the Chinese flag and Chinese arms into many a place that even fancy will not suggest today, thus preparing for future upheavals and disasters never even dreamed of.[27]

Notes

1 *I Rule All under the Heavens*

1. George Thin, The Tientsin Massacre, p40
2. B. L. Putnam Weale, The Reshaping of the Far East, Vol1. 1905, pp218-219
3. Ibid, p219
4. John Ross, The Manchus. 1891, page xx
5. Yi Tae-Jin et al, Peace in the East, An Chunggun's Vision for Asia in the Age of Imperialism, p23

2 *Our Celestial Empire Possesses All Things in Prolific Abundance*

1. J.M. Braga, China Landfall 1513, 1955, p5
2. Ibid, p14
3. Ibid, pp14-22
4. Ibid, pp15-21
5. Ibid, p21
6. Rev. W.M. Campbell, Formosa Under The Dutch, 1903, p36
7. Ibid, p35
8. Ibid, p35
9. Chiu Hsin-Hui, The Colonial 'Civilising Process in Dutch Formosa, p37
10. Rev. W.M. Campbell, Formosa Under the Dutch, 1903, p62
11. Ibid, p36
12. Ibid, p497
13. The Jesuits and the Sino-Russian Treaty of Nerchinsk, p58
14. Alexis Krausse, Russia in Asia, A case Study, 1558-1899, p40
15. Ibid, p40
16. Ibid, pp40-41
17. Jan Bremmer, The Rise and Fall of the Afterlife, p28
18. Alexis Krausse, Russia in Asia, A case Study, 1558-1899, p42
19. Source lost
20. Arnold Wright, Twentieth Century Impressions of Hong Kong, Shanghai and Other Treaty Ports, pp18-19
21. James F. Matheson, The Present Position and prospects of the British Trade with China, p84
22. Charles Toogood Downing, 1838, The Fan-Qui in China in 1836-37
23. Aeneas Anderson, A Narrative of the British Embassy to China, pp258
24. Ibid
25. Charles Toogood Downing, The Fan-Qui in China in 1836-37, pp178-197
26. Ibid, pp199-200
27. Hosea Morse, Chronicles of the East India Company, p95
28. Ibid, p111

29. John Barrow, Some Account of the Public Life and a Selection from the Unpublished Writings of Earl of Macartney, 1807, p513
30. John Barrow, Travels in China, 1804, pp610-611
31. Ibid, p613
32. Hosea Morse, Chronicles of the East India Company, 1635-1834, p70
33. Ibid, p71
34. John Barrow, Travels in China, p610
35. Aeneas Anderson, A Narrative of the British Embassy to China, p260
36. E. H. Parker, China, Her History, Diplomacy and Commerce, p263
37. John Barrow, Travels in China, 1804, p592
38. Sir George Thomas Staunton, Misc Notes Relating to China, 1822, p276.
39. Hosea Morse, Chronicles of the East India Company, 1635-1834, p65
40. Ibid, p112
41. John Barrow, Some Account of the Public Life of Earl of Macartney, p420
42. Ibid, p514
43. Ibid, p505
44. Hosea Morse, Chronicles of the East India Company, 1635-1834, p219
45. Ibid, p214
46. Ibid, p217
47. Mark Felton, China Station, p11
48. Hosea Morse, Chronicles of the East India Company, 1635-1834, p219
49. Aeneas Anderson, A Narrative of the British Embassy to China, pviii
50. Ibid, p78
51. Ibid, pp153-154 52
52. Aeneas Anderson, A Narrative of the British Embassy to China, p182
53. Ibid, p176
54. Sir Edmund Backhouse, Annals and Memoirs of the Court of Peking, pp326-331
55. Ibid, p326
56. Ibid, p331
57. Abel Clarke, Narrative of a Journey to the Interior of Chinal pp108-109
58. Sir George Staunton, Misc Notices Relating to China, p270
59. Henry Ellis, Journal of the Proceedings of the Late Embassy to China, p209
60. Ibid, p211

3 The Vile Dirt of Foreign Countries

1. Charles Toogood Downing, The Fan-Qui in China in 1836-37, pp170-171
2. Ibid, pp178-179
3. Ibid, pp179-180
4. Montgomery Martin, Opium in China, p10
5. Ibid, p3
6. Arnold Wright, Twentieth Century Impressions of Hong Kong, Shanghai and other Treaty Ports, p 46
7. Hosea Morse, Chronicles of the East India Company Trading to China, p79
8. Montgomery Martin, Opium in China, p3
9. Ian Hernon, Britain's Forgotten Wars, p300
10. Montgomery Martin, Opium in China, p13
11. Ian Hernon, Britain's Forgotten Wars, p306
12. H. Hamilton Lindsay, Is the War With China a Just One?, p12
13. Ssu-Yu Teng and John Fairbank, China's Response to the West, 1982, p24
14. H. Hamilton Lindsay, Is the War With China a Just One?, p7
15. Matheson, Present Position and prospects of British Trade with China, p1

Notes

16. H. Hamilton Lindsay, Is the War With China a Just One?, p24
17. Ellis, Journal of the Proceedings of the late Embassy to China, p212
18. Zhindong Mao, Macao History and Society, 2011, p29
19. George Thin, The Tientsin Massacre, pp39-40
20. Prosper Giquel, A Journal of the Chinese Civil War, p39
21. Paul H. Clements, The Boxer Rebellion, 1915, p22
22. Robert Swinhoe, Narrative of the North China Campaign, p385
23. Ian Hernon, Britain's Forgotten Wars, p361
24. Ibid, p377
25. Robert Swinhoe, Narrative of the North China Campaign, p323
26. Ibid, p298
27. Ibid, p299
28. Ibid, p306
29. Arnold Wright, Twentieth Century Impressions of Hong Kong, Shanghai and Other Treaty Ports, 1908, p79
30. Robert Swinhoe, Narrative of the North China Campaign, p329
31. Ibid, pp328-329
32. Ibid, p337
33. Ian Hernon, Britain's Forgotten Wars, p395
34. George Thin, The Tientsin Massacre, p44
35. Ssu-Yu Teng and John Fairbank, China's Response to the West, p14
36. George Thin, The Tientsin Massacre, p24
37. A. H. Carvalho, The Tientsin Massacre, px
38. George Thin, The Tientsin Massacre, p48
39. Ibid, p48
40. J. K. Fairbank, Patterns Behind the Tientsin Massacre, p 480
41. A. H. Carvalho, The Tientsin Massacre, p 9
42. George Thin, The Tientsin Massacre, p4
43. Ibid, p5
44. A. H. Carvalho, The Tientsin Massacre, p 8
45. Ibid, p4
46. Ibid, p42
47. Ibid, p9
48. Ibid, p87
49. S. T. Wang, The Marjary Affair and the Chefoo Agreement, p124
50. Robert Douglas, Li Hungchung, p107
51. S. T. Wang, The Marjary Affair and the Chefoo Agreement, 1940, p35
52. Robert Douglas, Li Hungchung, p149
53. S. Paine, Imperial Rivals: China, Russia and the Disputed Frontier, p121
54. Robert Douglas, Li Hungchung, p152
55. R.S Gundray, China and Her Neighbours, p2
56. Robert Douglas, Li Hungchung, p209
57. John Dodd, Journal of a Blockaded Resident in North Formosa During the Franco-Chinese War, 1884-5, pp6-7
58. Zhindong Mao, Macao History and Society, p30

4 Freedom of Trade for All the World Alike

1. Robert Douglas, Li Hungchung, p204
2. Ssu-Yu Teng and J. Fairbank, China's Response to the West, p72
3. Ibid, pp72-73
4. Lord Charles Beresford, The Break Up of China, pp 283-284
5. E. H. Parker, China, Her History, Diplomacy and Commerce, p259
6. Ibid, p252
7. Luke Kwong, A Mosaic of the Hundred Days, p38
8. Richard Storry, A History of Modern Japan, p50
9. Yi Tae-Jin et al, Peace in the East, p25

10. Robert Douglas, Li Hungchung, p120
11. Yi Tae-Jin eta al, Peace in the East, p29
12. Stanley Lane-Poole, The Life of Sir Harry Parkes, p192
13. Ibid, p194
14. Yi Tae-Jin et al, Peace in the East, p28
15. Peter Duus, The Abacus and the Sword, p35
16. David Gilmour, Curzon, p90
17. R. S. Gundray, China and Her Neighbours, p124
18. Peter Duus, The Abacus and the Sword, p41
19. Ibid, p32
20. Robert Douglas, Li Hungchung, p201
21. Ibid, p202
22. Ibid, p198
23. Ibid, p216
24. Ibid, p216
25. Giichi Ono, Expenditures of the Sino-Japanese War, pp20-21
26. Trumbell White, The War in the East, p606
27. Ibid, pp597-604
28. Ibid, p602
29. The Times, 26 December 1894
30. Treaty of Shimonoseki, Article 1
31. Treaty of Shimonoseki, Article 6
32. North China Herald, 18 January 1895
33. Trumbell White, The War in the East, p669
34. Sidney Gulick, The White Peril in the Far East, p54
35. Paul H. Clements, The Boxer Rebellion, 1915, p27
36. Alfred von Tirpitz, My Memoirs, p103
37. George Steinmetz, The Devil's Handwriting, pp15-16
38. H. C. Thompson, China and the Powers, p183
39. Shantung, Treaties and Agreements, Carnegie Endowment for International Peace, p1
40. Ibid, p3
41. Bryna and David Goodman, Twentieth Century Colonialism, p45
42. B. L. Putnam Weale, The Reshaping of the Far East, Vol1. 1905, p357
43. Westel Willoughby, Foreign Rights and Interests in China, 1920, p276
44. Paul H. Clements, The Boxer Rebellion, p30
45. Ibid, p32
46. Westel Willoughby, Foreign Rights and Interests in China, p236
47. Ibid, p224
48. Paul H. Clements, The Boxer Rebellion, p32
49. Westel Willoughby, Foreign Rights and Interests in China, p241
50. Ibid, p241
51. Ibid, p39
52. Ibid, p238
53. Ibid, p238
54. Ibid, p242
55. Ibid, p46
56. William A. Joseph, (ed.) Politics in China, An Introduction, p44
57. J. O. P. Bland, China Under the Empress Dowager, p132
58. Lord Charles Beresford, The Break Up of China, p14
59. Ibid, pp 357-358
60. Luke Kwong, A Mosaic of the Hundred Days, p63
61. J. O. P. Bland, China Under the Empress Dowager, p119
62. Ibid p134
63. Paul H. Clements, The Boxer Rebellion, 1915, p55
64. J. O. P. Bland, China Under the Empress Dowager, p142
65. Ibid, p161

5 A Piece of Stupidity Which Will Be Remembered for All Time

1. Bay of Plenty Times, 1 September 1897
2. Walter H. Mallory, China: Land of Famine, p69

Notes

3. Marvin Perry, Sources of Western Tradition, p262
4. The Boxer Rising: Reprinted from the Shanghai Mercury, p9
5. David Gilmour, Curzon, p67
6. The Monitor, Volume 46, No.24, 12 March 1898, p492
7. Westel Willoughby, Foreign Rights and Interests in China, p198
8. The Monitor, Volume 46, No 24, 12 March 1898, p492
9. Paul H. Clements, The Boxer Rebellion, p24
10. H. C. Thompson, China and the Powers, p22
11. Robert Massie, Dreadnought, p276
12. H. C. Thompson, China and the Powers, p271
13. The Boxer Rising, Reprinted from the Shanghai Mercury, 1901, p17
14. Ibid, p22
15. Liebowitz and Miller, Fortunate Sons, p238
16. Bryna and David Goodman, Twentieth Century Colonialism, p46
17. Paul H. Clements, The Boxer Rebellion, p80
18. Ibid, p83
19. Ibid, p83
20. Lord Charles Beresford, The Break Up of China, p282
21. The Boxer Rising, Reprinted from the Shanghai Mercury, p20
22. Paul H. Clements, The Boxer Rebellion, p116
23. Ibid, p89
24. Ibid, p93
25. Ibid, p94
26. The Boxer Rising, Reprinted from the Shanghai Mercury, 1901, p98
27. Ibid, p20
28. Ibid, p29
29. Ibid, p62
30. Ibid, p62
31. Ibid, p2
32. Ibid, p35
33. Ibid, p98
34. Ibid, p101
35. Robert Massie, Dreadnought, p278
36. Paul H. Clements, The Boxer Rebellion, p112
37. H. C. Thompson, China and the Powers, p29
38. Liebowitz and Miller, Fortunate Sons, pp241-242
39. J. O. P. Bland, China Under the Empress Dowager, pp 200-201
40. The Boxer Rising, Reprinted from the Shanghai Mercury, 1901, p64
41. J. O. P. Bland, China Under the Empress Dowager, p189
42. Ibid, p193
43. Robert Massie, Dreadnought, p280
44. Tyler Whittle, The Last Kaiser, p189
45. Emil Ludwig, Kaiser Wilhelm II, p241
46. Ibid, p242
47. Robert Massie, Dreadnought, p282
48. J. O. P. Bland, China Under the Empress Dowager, p208
49. The Boxer Rising, from the Shanghai Mercury, 1901, p112
50. Ibid, p114
51. Ibid, p112
52. Charles Emmerson, 1913: The World Before the Great War, p388
53. Ibid, p388
54. Emil Ludwig, Kaiser Wilhelm II, pp240-241
55. Robert Massie, Dreadnought, p286
56. Charles Emmerson, 1913: The World Before the Great War, p387
57. H. C. Thompson, China and the Powers, p144
58. Paul H. Clements, The Boxer Rebellion, 1915, p178
59. Ibid, p183
60. H. C. Thompson, China and the Powers, p154
61. The Anglo-Japanese Alliance, Alfred Dennis, pp10-11

62. Emil Ludwig, Kaiser Wilhelm II, p240
63. Paul H. Clements, The Boxer Rebellion, 1915, pp202-203
64. Westel Willoughby, Foreign Rights and Interests in China, pp219
65. B. L. Putnam Weale, The Reshaping of the Far East, p206
66. W. Willoughby, Foreign Rights and Interests in China, 1920, pp221-222
67. Ibid, p222
68. Martin Gilbert, A History of the Twentieth Century, p183
69. Lawrence James, The Rise and Fall of the British Empire, p453
70. Letters of the Chinese and German Emperors in Regard to the Murder of Baron von Ketteler, p208
71. Ibid, p208

6 They Would Never Try to Fight Us

1. H. C. Thompson, China and the Powers, p184
2. Ibid, p141
3. John Birch, Travels in North and Central China, p71
4. Thomas Cowen, The Russo-Japanese War, p3
5. H. C. Thompson, China and the Powers, p144
6. The Anglo-Japanese Alliance, Alfred Dennis, p5
7. Richard Storry, A History of Modern Japan, p136
8. Thomas Cowen, The Russo-Japanese War, p33
9. Sidney Gulick, The White Peril in the Far East, p140
10. Ibid, p140
11. Thomas Cowen, The Russo-Japanese War, p35
12. The Anglo-Japanese Alliance, Alfred Dennis, p6
13. J. M. Roberts, Europe, 1880-1945 p204
14. The Anglo-Japanese Alliance, Alfred Dennis, p8
15. Ibid, p9
16. Westel Willoughby, Foreign Rights and Interests in China, p301
17. Ibid, p302
18. Ibid, p302
19. Thomas Cowen, The Russo-Japanese War, p32
20. Ibid, p1-2
21. Westel Willoughby, Foreign Rights and Interests in China, 1920, p303
22. Sidney Gulick, The White Peril in the Far East, p162
23. Westel Willoughby, Foreign Rights and Interests in China, 1920, p304
24. Sidney Gulick, The White Peril in the Far East, p138
25. Ibid, p152
26. Westel Willoughby, Foreign Rights and Interests in China, p305
27. W. H. Holmes, An Eyewitness in Manchuria, p20
28. Ibid, p21
29. Thomas F. Logan, Manchuria Land of Opportunities, p75
30. The Anglo-Japanese Alliance, Alfred Dennis, p28
31. Ibid, pp29-30
32. The Annexation of Korea, The American Journal of Int Law, p924
33. Ibid, p924
34. Hong Beom Rhee, Asian Millenarianism, p130
35. Young Ick Lew, Brief History of Korea, p19
36. Bryna and David Goodman, Twentieth Century Colonialism, p46
37. Madeleine Ysu, The Good Immigrants, p43
38. Ibid, p42
39. David Arkush and Leo Lee, Land Without Ghosts, p93
40. Charles Emmerson, 1913: The World Before the Great War, p404

41. Victor Purcell, The Boxer Uprising, A Background Study, p31
42. Jedidiah Kroncke, An Early Tragedy of Comparative Constitutionalism, p562

7 A Place of Dingy Dilapidation

1. Aeneas Anderson, A Narrative of the British Embassy to China, p264
2. Ibid, p262-263
3. Ibid, p263
4. Ibid, p263
5. Ibid, p263
6. Robert Burford, Description of a View of Macao, China, pp3-5
7. Ibid, pp 3-5
8. Ibid, pp3-6
9. David Gilmour, Curzon, p68
10. Arnold Wright, Twentieth Century Impressions of Hong Kong, Shanghai and other Treaty Ports, 1908, p802
11. James Dyer, Macao, The Holy City, p2
12. Ibid, p15
13. Ibid, p8
14. Arnold Wright, Twentieth Century Impressions of Hong Kong, Shanghai and other Treaty Ports, 1908, p802
15. Ibid, p802
16. Ibid, p802
17. Report of 1903 on the Trade of Canton, 1903, pp 5-11
18. Ibid, p11
19. Arnold Wright, Twentieth Century Impressions of Hong Kong, Shanghai and other Treaty Ports, 1908, p784
20. C. A. Middleton Smith, The British in China and Far Eastern Trade, 1920, p124
21. Ibid, p124
22. Ibid, p124
23. John M. Carroll, A Concise History of Hong Kong, p16
24. Ibid, p13
25. Arnold Wright, Twentieth Century Impressions of Hong Kong, Shanghai and other Treaty Ports, p56
26. Zhindong Mao, Macao History and Society, p25
27. Arnold Wright, Twentieth Century Impressions of Hong Kong, Shanghai and other Treaty Ports, p58
28. John M. Carroll, A Concise History of Hong Kong, p20
29. Arnold Wright, Twentieth Century Impressions of Hong Kong, Shanghai and other Treaty Ports, p59
30. Ibid, pp59-60
31. Ibid, p196
32. Lord Charles Beresford, The Break Up of China, p191
33. C. A. Middleton Smith, The British in China and Far Eastern Trade, 1920, p127
34. Montgomery Martin, Opium in China, p15
35. Ibid, p16
36. Robert Swinhoe, Narrative of the North China Campaign, p5
37. Ibid, p5
38. Arnold Wright, Twentieth Century Impressions of Hong Kong, Shanghai and other Treaty Ports, p84
39. John M. Carroll, A Concise History of Hong Kong, 2007, p42
40. Ibid, p42
41. Arnold Wright, Twentieth Century Impressions of Hong Kong, Shanghai and other Treaty Ports, p131
42. C. A. Middleton Smith, The British in China and Far Eastern Trade, p117
43. David Gilmour, Curzon, p68
44. C. A. Middleton Smith, The British in China and Far Eastern Trade, 1920, p133
45. Arnold Wright, Twentieth Century Impressions of Hong Kong, Shanghai and other Treaty Ports, p371
46. Lord Charles Beresford, The Break Up of China, p83

47. Charles Emmerson, 1913: The World Before the Great War, p397
48. C. E. Darwent, Shanghai: A Handbook for Travellers and Residents, p160
49. Ibid, p160
50. Charles Emmerson, 1913: The World Before the Great War, p395
51. C. E. Darwent, Shanghai: A Handbook for Travellers and Residents, p6
52. Arnold Wright, Twentieth Century Impressions of Hong Kong, Shanghai and other Treaty Ports, 1908, p93
53. Charles Emmerson, 1913: The World Before the Great War, p398
54. Ibid, p396
55. C. E. Darwent, Shanghai: A Handbook for Travellers and Residents, p156
56. Ibid, p xiv
57. Ibid, p103
58. Charles Emmerson, 1913: The World Before the Great War, p400
59. Ibid, p400
60. B. St. John, The China Times Guide to Tientsin and Neighbourhood, p10
61. Lord Charles Beresford, The Break Up of China, p23-24
62. Arnold Wright, Twentieth Century Impressions of Hong Kong, Shanghai and other Treaty Ports, p728
63. B. St. John, The China Times Guide to Tientsin and Neighbourhood, p8
64. Ibid, p5
65. Ibid, p6
66. Ibid, p7
67. Ibid, p6
68. Ibid, p27
69. Ibid, p28
70. Lord Charles Beresford, The Break Up of China, p73
71. B. L. Putnam Weale, The Reshaping of the Far East, Vol1, p360
72. H. C. Thompson, China and the Powers, p236
73. R. F. Johnston, Lion and Dragon in Northern China, p2
74. Ibid, p5
75. Colonial Reports, Annual No.1408 Shantung, 1929 p20
76. Ibid, p20
77. James Morris, Farewell the Trumpets, p150
78. R. F. Johnston, Lion and Dragon in Northern China, p85
79. Colonial Reports, Annual No.1408 Shantung, 1929 p17
80. R. F. Johnston, Lion and Dragon in Northern China, p83
81. Colonial Reports, Annual No.1408 Shantung, 1929 pp14-15
82. R. F. Johnston, Lion and Dragon in Northern China, p82
83. Colonial Reports, Annual No.1408 Shantung, 1929 p12
84. Ibid, p7
85. Ibid, p8
86. Ibid, p12
87. Ibid, p23
88. Ibid, p6
89. B. L. Putnam Weale, The Reshaping of the Far East, Vol 1, p324
90. Alfred von Tirpitz, My Memoirs, p104
91. Ibid, p104
92. Margaret MacMillan, The Peacemakers, p335
93. B. L. Putnam Weale, The Reshaping of the Far East, Vol1, pp321-322
94. George Steinmetz, The Devil's Handwriting, p18
95. Alfred von Tirpitz, My Memoirs, p104
96. B. L. Putnam Weale, The Reshaping of the Far East, Vol1, p387
97. Alfred von Tirpitz, My Memoirs, p102

Notes

98. B. L. Putnam Weale, The Reshaping of the Far East, Vol1, pp325-326
99. Ibid, pp326-327
100. Ibid, pp346-348
101. Ibid, p349
102. pp317-318
103. George Lynch, Path of Empire, p50
104. Ibid, p53
105. Ibid, p57
106. Ibid, p58
107. S. Paine, Imperial Rivals: China, Russia and the Disputed Frontier, p320
108. Andrew Molozemoff, Russian Far Eastern Policy 1881-1904, p195
109. Nashuah Telegraph, 13 May 1904
110. Thomas F. Logan, Manchuria Land of Opportunities, p50
111. Ibid, p55
112. W. H. Holmes, An Eyewitness in Manchuria, pp14-15
113. Ibid, p15
114. Ibid, p15
115. Ibid, pp15-16
116. Ibid, p36
117. Ibid, p23
118. Ibid, p35
119. Ibid, p35

8 The Very Scum of the Population

1. Robert Swinhoe, Narrative of the North China Campaign. p2
2. Ibid, p3
3. Ibid, p265
4. Trumbell White, The War in the East, pp136-137
5. Ibid, p137
6. Stewart Watt, Chinese Bondage in Peru, p36
7. Ibid, p32
8. Persia Campbell, Chinese Coolie Emigration, p119
9. Stewart Watt, Chinese Bondage in Peru, p175
10. Persia Campbell, Chinese Coolie Emigration, p120
11. Ibid, p16
12. Emma Christopher, Forced Migration and the Making of Many Middle Kingdom Passages, p170-171
13. Stewart Watt, Chinese Bondage in Peru, p36
14. Ibid, p46
15. Ibid, p56
16. Ibid, p31
17. Ibid, p53
18. Persia Campbell, Chinese Coolie Emigration, pxii
19. Ibid, p7
20. Ibid, p8
21. Ibid, p25
22. Lai Ah Eng, Peasants, Proletarians Prostitutes, p17
23. Gerben Bruinsma (ed.) Histories of Transnational Crime, p57
24. Afro Asia, Fred Ho and Bill Mullen Eds., page 36
25. Lisa Yun, The Coolie Speaks, pp16-17
26. Emma Christopher, Forced Migration, p173
27. Lisa Yun, The Coolie Speaks, p18
28. Stewart Watt, Chinese Bondage in Peru, p63
29. Lisa Yun, The Coolie Speaks, p18
30. Papers Relating to Foreign Affairs, 3 April, 1866
31. Stewart Watt, Chinese Bondage in Peru, pp69-71
32. Stewart Watt, Chinese Bondage in Peru, p63
33. Persia Campbell, Chinese Coolie Emigration, pp135-136
34. Ibid, p136
35. Ibid, p136
36. Rev. H. V. P. Bronkhurst, The Colony of British Guyana and its Labouring Population, p111
37. Persia Campbell, Chinese Coolie Emigration, pp136-137
38. Persia Campbell, Chinese Coolie Emigration, p137
39. Evelyn Hu-Dehart, Coolie Labor in the Nineteenth Century, p43

40. Persia Campbell, Chinese Coolie Emigration, p139
41. Fred Ho and Bill Mullen, Afro Asia, p45
42. Persia Campbell, Chinese Coolie Emigration, p135
43. Lisa Yun, The Coolie Speaks, p36
44. Ibid, p79
45. Evelyn Hu-Dehart, Coolie Labor in the Nineteenth Century, p42
46. Rev. H. V. P. Bronkhurst, The Colony of British Guyana and its Labouring Population, p110)
47. Stewart Watt, Chinese Bondage in Peru, p109
48. Ibid, p111
49. Ibid, p220
50. Ibid, p96
51. Ibid, pp97-98
52. Stewart Watt, Chinese Bondage in Peru, p96
53. Ibid, p177
54. Henry Kirke, Twenty Five Years in British Guiana, p207
55. Rev. Bronkhurst, p104
56. Henry Kirke, Twenty Five Years in British Guiana, p208
57. Papers Relating to Foreign Affairs, US Chargé d'affaires in Macao, 3 April, 1866
58. Henry Kirke, Twenty Five Years in British Guiana, p207
59. Rev. Bronkhurst, p104
60. Ibid, p105
61. Ibid, p105
62. Ibid, p110
63. British Guiana, The Commission of Enquiry into Treatment of Immigrants, The Evidence and Proceedings, Vol 1, 1870, p9
64. Ibid, p79
65. Ibid, p119
66. Ibid, p120
67. Rev. Bronkhurst, p110
68. Persia Campbell, Chinese Coolie Emigration, pp33-35
69. George Payne, An Experiment in Alien Labor, p33
70. Ibid, p34
71. Ibid, p33
72. Rev. Bronkhurst, p108
73. Persia Campbell, Chinese Coolie Emigration, p192
74. Edwin Sabin, Building the Pacific Railway, p111
75. Ibid, p111
76. George Payne, An Experiment in Alien Labor, p68
77. Edwin Sabin, Building the Pacific Railway, p271
78. Ibid, p111
79. Ibid, p111
80. Persia Campbell, Chinese Coolie Emigration, p37
81. Ibid, p42
82. Report of the Royal Commission on Chinese and Japanese Immigration, Session 1902, Ottawa, p278
83. Persia Campbell, Chinese Coolie Emigration, p57
84. Ibid, p57
85. Ibid, p59
86. Ibid, pp58-59
87. Ibid, p59
88. Persia Campbell, Chinese Coolie Emigration, p60
89. Ibid, p64
90. Ibid, p79
91. Ibid, pp79-80
92. Ibid, pp80-83
93. George Payne, An Experiment in Alien Labor, p19
94. Ibid, p20
95. Ibid, p19
96. Ibid, p21
97. Ibid, p14
98. Ibid, p38
99. Persia Campbell, Chinese Coolie Emigration, p207
100. Ibid, p192
101. George Payne, An Experiment in Alien Labor, p6
102. Ibid, p40
103. Ibid, p41
104. Ibid, p8
105. Persia Campbell, Chinese Coolie Emigration, p211
106. Ibid, p211
107. George Payne, An Experiment in Alien Labor, pp48-49

108. Robert Blake, The Conservative Party from Peel to Thatcher, p174
109. Hansard, House of Lords, 16 May 1905, Vol. 146, cc407-58
110. Persia Campbell, Chinese Coolie Emigration, p204
111. Robert Blake, The Conservative Party from Peel to Thatcher, p172
112. Hansard, House of Lords, 16 May 1905, Vol. 146, cc407-58
113. George Payne, An Experiment in Alien Labor, p55
114. Ibid, p68
115. Ibid, p5
116. Persia Campbell, Chinese Coolie Emigration, p63
117. Charles Emmerson, 1913: The World Before the Great War, p400
118. David Lloyd George, War Memories of David Lloyd George, p478
119. Lyn Macdonald, Somme, p198
120. David Lloyd George, War Memories, pp478-479
121. Lyn Macdonald, Somme, p197
122. David Lloyd George, War Memories, p479

9 China Belongs to the Chinese

1. Bruce A. Ellman Wilson and China, p18
2. Shandong Treaties and Agreements, p32
3. Alfred von Tirpitz, My Memoirs, p116
4. Ibid, p117
5. Bruce A. Ellman, Wilson and China, p18
6. Margaret MacMillan, The Peacemakers, p337
7. The Anglo-Japanese Alliance, Alfred Dennis, p48
8. W. H. Holmes, An Eyewitness in Manchuria, pp20-21
9. The Anglo-Japanese Alliance, Alfred Dennis, 1923, p48
10. Shantung Treaties and Agreements, p82
11. Ibid, p83
12. Ibid, p83
13. Thomas F. Millard, The Shantung Case at the Conference, p12
14. Ibid, p60
15. W. H. Holmes, An Eyewitness in Manchuria, p21
16. Alfred Dennis, The Anglo-Japanese Alliance, p52
17. Margaret MacMillan, The Peacemakers, p332
18. Harold Nicolson, Peacemaking 1919, p145
19. Thomas F. Millard, The Shantung Case at the Conference, p45
20. Margaret MacMillan, The Peacemakers, p340
21. Ibid, p339
22. Ibid, p339
23. Ibid, p339
24. Naomi Tamura, Facts About the Shandong Question, p4
25. Ibid, p6
26. Margaret MacMillan, The Peacemakers, p332
27. Thomas F. Millard, The Shantung Case at the Conference, p22
28. Ibid, p27
29. Margaret MacMillan, The Peacemakers, p345
30. Bruce A. Ellman, Wilson and China, p7
31. Thomas F. Millard, The Shantung Case at the Conference, p43
32. Ibid, p27
33. Ibid, p27
34. Vera Schwarcz, The Chinese Enlightenment, p15
35. Ibid, p1
36. Margaret MacMillan, The Peacemakers, p349
37. Shantung Treaties and Agreements, p107
38. Ibid, p108
39. Ibid, p108
40. Ibid, p109

41. Bruce Ellman, Wilson and China, p96
42. S. Paine, Imperial Rivals: China, Russia and the Disputed Frontier, p320
43. Ibid, p320
44. Shantung Treaties and Agreements, p111
45. Ibid, p113
46. Ibid, p111
47. Ibid, p114

10 We Do Not Want to Become Like the Koreans

1. Shantung Treaties and Agreements, p110
2. Ibid, p110
3. Ibid, p110
4. Richard Storry, A History of Modern Japan, p164
5. Ibid, p170
6. Christopher Thorne, Allies of a Kind, p25
7. Lytton Report, p5
8. R. Bassett, Democracy and Foreign Policy, A Case History, p75
9. Ibid, p83
10. Ibid, p14
11. Manchukuo, the Founding of the New State, p4
12. Ibid, p6
13. Ibid, p7
14. Ibid, p6
15. W. H. Holmes, An Eyewitness in Manchuria, p 11
16. R. Bassett, Democracy and Foreign Policy, A Case History, p121
17. Ibid, pp248-249
18. Lytton Report, p18
19. Ibid, p20
20. Ibid, p23
21. Ibid, p18
22. Ibid, p17
23. Ibid, p71
24. Ibid, p18
25. Ibid, p97
26. Ibid, p99
27. Ibid, p107
28. Ibid, p110
29. Ibid, p107
30. Ibid, p108
31. Ibid, p39
32. Ibid, p121
33. Foreign Policy Association Inc, Vol VIII, No.18, International Action on the Lytton Report, p212
34. Telegram, Mr Hsieh Chieh-Shih to US Secretary of State, 7 October 1932
35. CP404 (32), The Lytton Report, Japan and the League of Nations, November 1932, CAB/24/235
36. CP404 (32), The Lytton Report, Japan and the League of Nations, November 1932, CAB/24/235
37. R. Bassett, Democracy and Foreign Policy, A Case History, p273
38. Lord Russell of Liverpool, The Knights of Bushido, p44
39. Ibid, p45
40. David Smith, Less Than Human, p18
41. Laurence Rees, Horror in the East, p34
42. Materials on the Trial of Former Service of the Japanese Army, p12
43. Ibid, pp13-14
44. Peter Li (ed.) The Search for Justice: Japanese War Crimes, p296
45. Materials on the Trial of Former Service of the Japanese Army, p20
46. Ibid, p11
47. Peter Li (ed.) The Search for Justice: Japanese War Crimes, p295
48. Materials on the Trial of Former Service of the Japanese Army, p442
49. Takashi Yoshida, The Making of the "Rape of Nanking", p3-4
50. Richard Storry, A History of Modern Japan, p203
51. Japanese Terror in China, H. Timperley, p78
52. Ibid, p112

53. Timothy Brook, Documents on the Rape of Nanking, p15
54. Ibid, p3
55. Lord Russell of Liverpool, The Knights of Bushido, p47
56. H. Timperley, Japanese Terror in China, p220
57. Ibid, pp220-221
58. H. Timperley, Japanese Terror in China, pp73-74
59. Ibid, p67
60. Ibid, p219
61. Takashi Yoshida, The Making of the "Rape of Nanking", p39
62. Peter Li (ed.) The Search for Justice: Japanese War Crimes, pp295-296
63. W. H. Holmes, An Eyewitness in Manchuria, p 11
64. Ibid, p12
65. Christopher Thorne, Allies of a Kind, p192
66. Ibid, p23
67. Ibid, p308
68. Ibid, p421

11 A Mutually Beneficial Relationship

1. Christopher Thorne, Allies of a Kind, p178
2. Ibid, p311
3. Shu Guang Zhang, Economic Cold War, p50
4. Ibid, p28
5. Ibid, p 26
6. Ibid, pp 26-27
7. Truman Doctrine, 12 March 1947
8. Shu Guang Zhang, Economic Cold War, p43
9. Stephen Ambrose, Rise to Globalism, p167
10. Oystein Tunsjo US Taiwan Policy, Constructing the Triangle, p42
11. Stephen Ambrose, Rise to Globalism, p176
12. Max Hastings, The Korean War, p191
13. Michael Maclear, Vietnam, The Ten Thousand Day War, p187
14. Stephen Ambrose, Rise to Globalism, p301
15. Michael Maclear, Vietnam, The Ten Thousand Day War, p232
16. Stephen Ambrose, Rise to Globalism, p400
17. Justin Wintle, The Vietnam Wars, p179
18. Lawrence James, The Rise and Fall of the British Empire, p630
19. Ibid, p634
20. Ibid, p634
21. Ibid, p635
22. brookings.edu
23. Pew Research, 13 September 2016
24. The New York Times, 24 October 1992
25. Pew Research, 13 September 2016
26. Douglas Lovelace, Terrorism Commentary on Security Documents, p280
27. B. L. Putnam Weale, The Reshaping of the Far East, Vol1, pp210-211

Bibliography and Sources

Published Documents and Papers
An Early Tragedy of Comparative Constitutionalism, Frank Goodnow and the Chinese Republic, Jedidiah Kroncke, Washington International Law Journal, Vol,21 No,3, The Future of Nuclear Power in East Asia, 6-1 2012, p562
Annual Series, Diplomatic and Consular Reports, China Report for the Year 1903 of the Trade of Canton, No.3270, HMSO, London, 1904
Bay of Plenty Times, Volume XXIV, Issue 3592, 1 September 1897
British Guiana, The Commission of Enquiry into the Treatment of Immigrants. The Evidence and Proceedings, Volume One, 1870
China: Land of Famine, American Geographical Society Special Publication No. 6, Walyer Mallory, New York, 1926
China, Plague in Hong Kong in 1897 and 1898, Roundseville Wildman, Public Health Reports 1896-1970
China Perspectives 2013-2014. Chinese Visions of Japan. Special Feature – 40 Years in Paradox: Post-Normalisation of Sino-Japanese Relations. Yinan He.
Chinese Coolie Labor in Cuba in the Nineteenth Century: Free Labor of NeoSlavery, Evelyn Hu-Dehart, University of Colorado at Boulder, Contributions in Black Studies, A Journal of African and Afro-American Studies, Vol.12, Article 5, 1994
Colonial Reports – Annual No.1408 Weihaiwei, Report for 1927, London, Printed and Published by HMSO, 1928
Diplomatic Missions to the Court of China: The Kowtow Question. The American Historical Review, Vol. 2 No. 3, (Apr. 1897) pp 427-442, William Woodville Rockhill
Economic History of Manchuria, compiled in Commemoration of the Decennial of the Bank of Chosen, T. Hoshito, Seoul, Chosen, 1921
Embassy From Their Majesties John and Peter Alexievitz, Emperors of Muscovy Etc. Overland into China in the Years 1693, 1694 and 1695, Adam Brand, Translated from the original in High Dutch, 1698.
Facts About The Shantung Question, Naomi Tamura, 1919
Foreign Policy Reports: International Action on the Lytton Report, November 9, 1932, Vol, VIII, No.18, Raymond Leslie Bueil, Foreign Policy Association Inc. New York

Bibliography and Sources

Foreign Relations of the United States Diplomatic Papers, 1932. The Far East Volume IV, 793.94 Commission/430. Telegram. Mr Hsieh Chieh-Shih to the Secretary of State, 7 October, 1932

Formosa, The Shanghai Mercury, 1896, J.D. Clark

Government of Formosa, Report on the Control of the Aborigines in Formosa, Bureau of Aboriginal Affairs, Taihoku, Formosa, 1911

Hansard, House of Lords, 16 May 1905, Volume 146, cc407-58

Japanese Treatment of Prisoners in 1904-1905, Foreign Officers Reports, Military Affairs, Volume 39, No.3, October 1975, pp115-118, Philip A. Towle

League of Nations, Appeal by the Chinese Government, Report of the Commission of Enquiry, Official No. C.663.M.320 1932, VII, Geneva, 1 October 1932 (The Lytton Report)

Left Behind: Japan's Wartime Defeat and the Stranded Women of Manchukuo, Rowena Ward, The Asia Pacific Journal, Volume 5, Issue 3, Article ID 2374, March 1, 2007,

Letters of the Chinese and German Emperors in Regard to the Murder of Baron von Ketterer, The Advocate of Peace, October 1901

Manchukuo, The Founding of the New State in Manchuria, Japanese Chamber of Commerce, New York, 1933

Manchuria, Land of Opportunities, by South Manchuria Railway Company Ltd. Compiled and Published by Thomas F. Logan, Inc, New York, 1922

Materials on the Trial of Former Servicemen of the Japanese Army Charged with Manufacturing and Employing Bacteriological Weapons. Foreign Languages Publishing, Moscow, 1950. Printed in the USSR

Opium in China, Political, Commercial, Social, 1847 Pamphlet, by R. Montgomery Martin

Papers Relating to Foreign Affairs Accompanying the Annual Message of the President to the Second Session of the Thirty-Ninth Congress. Communication from S. Wells Williams, Charge d'Affaires Macao, to US Secretary of State, William H. Seward, 3 April 1866

Patterns Behind the Tientsin Massacre, Harvard Journal of Asiatic Studies, Vol, 20 No. 3/4, December 1957, pp48-511

Peasants, Proletarians, Prostitutes: A Preliminary Investigation Into The Work Of Chinese Women in Colonial Malaya. Research Notes and Discussion Paper No.59, Institute of Southeast Asian Studies, 1986

Report of the Royal Commission on Chinese and Japanese Immigration, Session 1902, Ottawa

Shanghai, A Handbook For Travellers and Residents To The Chief Objects of Interest In And Around The Foreign Settlements And Native City, Rev. D.E. Darwent, MA Minister of Union Church Shanghai, Kelly and Walsh Ltd. Shanghai

Shantung, Treaties and Agreements, Carnegie Endowment for International Peace, Division of International Law. Pamphlet No.42, Washington 1921

The Anglo-Japanese Alliance, by Alfred L.P. Dennis, University of California Publications, Bureau of International Relations, Vol.1, No.1, pp1-111, University of California Press, Berkeley California 1923

The Annexation of Korea to Japan, The American Journal of International Law, Volume 4, pp923-924, 1 October 1910

The Boxer Rising, A History of the Boxer Trouble in China. Reprinted from the *Shanghai Mercury*, Second Edition. Printed at the Shanghai Mercury Ltd. August 1901

The Korea Society, Brief History of Korea – A Birds Eye View, The Korea Society New York, 2000, Young Ick Lew

The Jesuits and the Sino-Russian Treaty of Nerchinsk (1689), Biblioteca Instituti, S.I. Vol. XVIII, The Diary of Thomas Pereira, S.J. Roma, 1961

The Monitor, Vol.46, Number 24, 12 March 1898

The Nashuah Daily Telegraph, 13 May 1904

The repatriation of the Chinese as a counter-insurgency policy during the Malayan Emergency. Journal of Southeast Asian Studies, 45, pp363-392, doi: 10.1017/SS0022463414000332. Loo Choo Chin (2014)

The Report of the Lytton Commission, M. Thomas Tchou, Institute of America, New York, New York, 1932. Text of a radio address given on 21 November 1932

The Tientsin Massacre, Being Documents Published in the Shanghai Evening Courier, from June 16 to September 10, 1870, Shanghai, A.H. Carvalho, 1870

The Travels of Marco Polo, (The Venetian) Revised from Marden's Translation and edited with introduction by Manuel Komroff, (New York, London: Norton and Company, 1926)

The Use of Foreign Soldiers during the Taiping Rebellion, Alex Gouzales

National Archives

CAB/24/235, CP404 (32) November 1932, CABINET, The Lytton Report, Japan and The League of Nations

Websites

Web.stanford.edu/group/chineserailroad/cgi-bin/website/virtual. Accessed 11 April, 2022
carnegieendowment.org Accessed 16 May 202
cnbc.org Accessed 16 May 2022
pewresearch.org Accessed 16 May 2022
worldbank.org Accessed 16 May 2022
la.china-embassy.gov.cn 30 April 2023

Books

Allan, C. Wilfrid, *The Makers of Cathay* (Shanghai: The Presbyterian Mission Press, 1909)

Ambrose, Stephen E., *Rise to Globalism: American Foreign Policy Since 1945* (London: Penguin, 1983)

Anderson, Aeneas, *A Narrative of the British Embassy to China, in the Years 1792, 1793 and 1794* (London: J. Debrett, 1795)

Anderson, M.S., *The Ascendancy of Europe, 1815-1914*, Third ed. (Harlow: Pearson, 2003)

Arkush, David R,. Lee, Leo O, (Eds.) *Land Without Ghosts: Chinese Impressions of America from the Mind Nineteenth Century to the Present* (Berkeley: University of California Press, 1989)

Bibliography and Sources

Backhouse, Sir Edmund, *Annals and Memoirs of the Court of Peking* (Boston & New York: Houghton Mifflin, 1914)

Barrow, Sir John, *Some Account of the Public Life and a Selection from the Unpublished Writings of the Earl of Macartney* (London: T Cadell& W. Davies, 1807)

Barshay, Andrew E., *The Gods Left First, The Captivity and Repatriation of Japanese PoWs in Northeast Asia 1945-1956* (Los Angeles & London: University of California press, 2013)

Bassett, R., *Democracy and Foreign Policy: A Case History, The Sino-Japanese Dispute, 1931-33* (London: Frank Cass, 1968)

Beresford, Lord Charles, *The Breakup of China* (London: Harper & Bros. 1899)

Birch, John, *Travels in North and Central China* (London: Hurst and Blackett, 1902)

Blake, Robert, *The Conservative Party From Peel To Thatcher* (London: Fontana, 1985)

Bland, J.O.P., Backhouse, E., *China Under the Empress Dowager* (Boston & New York: Houghton Mufflin, 1914)

Braga, J.M., *China Landfall, 1513, Jorge Alvares Voyage to China* (Macao: Imprensa Nacionale, 1955)

Bremmer, Jan, N., *The Rise and Fall of the Afterlife* (London: Routledge, 2002)

Bronkhurst, Reverend, H.V.P., *The Colony of British Guyana and its Labouring Population* (London: T. Woolmer, 1883)

Brook, Timothy (ed.) *Documents of the Rape of Nanking* (Ann Arbor: University of Michigan Press, 2003)

Brook, Timothy, *The Confusions of Pleasure, Commerce and Culture in Ming China* (Los Angeles & London: University of California Press, 1998)

Bruinsma, Gerben, (ed.) *Histories of Transnational Crime* (New York: Springer, 2015)

Burford, Robert, *A Description of a View of Macao in China* (London: G. Nichols, 1840)

Campbell, Persia C., *Chinese Coolie Emigration* (London: P.S. King, 1923)

Campbell, Rev. W.M., *Formosa Under the Dutch* (London: Kegan, Paul, Trench Trubner & Co. Ltd,. 1903)

Carroll, John M., *A Concise History of Hong Kong* (Lanham, MD: Rowman and Littlefield, 2007)

Chaudhuri, K.N., *The Trading World of Asia and the English East India Company, 1660-1760* (London: Cambridge University Press, 2006)

Chen, Joseph T., The May Fourth Movement in Shanghai (Leiden: brill, 1971)

Clarke, Abel, *Narrative of a journal in the Interior of China and of a Voyage to and from that Country in the Years 1816-1817* (London: Hurst, Rees, Orme and Brown, 1818)

Clementi, Cecil, *The Chinese in British Guiana* (Georgetown: Argosy, 1915)

Clements, Paul H., *The Boxer Rebellion: A Political and Diplomatic Review* (London: King and Son, 1915)

Cowen, Thomas, *The Russo-Japanese War* (London: Edward Arnold, 1904)

Dodd, John, *Journal of a Blockaded resident in North Formosa During the Franco-Chinese War, 1884-5* (Hongkong: Daily Press, 1888)

Douglas, Robert K., *Li Hungchung* (London: Bliss, Sands & Foster, 1895)

Downing, Charles, Toogood, *The Fan-Qui in China in 1836-7* (London: Henry Colburn, 1838)

Duus, Peter, *The Abacus and the Sword: The Japanese Penetration of Korea, 1895-1910* (Los Angeles: University of California Press, 1998)
Dyer, James, Macao: *The Holy City, The Gem of the Orient Earth* (Canton: China Baptist Publishing Society, 1905)
Eastman, Lloyd E., *Throne and Mandarins, China's Search For A Policy During the Sino-French Controversy, 1880-1885* (Cambridge Mass: Harvard University Press, 1967)
Elleman, Bruce A., *Wilson and China: A Revised History of the Shandong Question* (New York & London: Sharpe Inc., 2002)
Ellis, Henry, *Journal of the Proceedings of the Late Embassy to China, Vol. III* (London: John Murray, 1818)
Emmerson, Charles, *1913, The World Before the Great War* (London: Vintage Books, 2013)
Felton, Mark, *China Station, The British Military in the Middle Kingdom 1839-1997* (Barnsley: Pen & Sword, 2013)
Fogel, Joshua, A. (ed.) *The Nanjing Massacre, In History and Historiography* (Los Angeles: University of California Press, 2000)
Gilbert, Martin, *A History of the Twentieth Century*, vol 1. (London: HarperCollins, 1997)
Gilbert, Martin, *First World War* (London: HarperCollins, 1994)
Gilmour, David, *Curzon* (London: John Murray, 1994)
Giquel, Prosper, *A Journal of the Chinese Civil War* (1864)
Goodman, Bryna and David (eds.) *Twentieth Century Colonialism and China: Localities, the Everyday, and the World* (Abingdon: Routledge, 2002)
Gruzinski, Serge, *The Eagle and the Dragon, Globalisation and European Dreams of Conquest in China and America in the Sixteenth Century* (Cambridge: Polity Press, 2014)
Gulick, Sidney, L., *The White Peril in the Far East* (New York: Fleming H. Revel, 1905)
Gundray, R.S., *China and her Neighbours, France in Indo-China, Russia and China, India and Tibet* (London: Chapman & Hall, 1893)
Hao, Zhindong, *Macao History and Society* (Hong Kong: Hong Kong University Press, 2011)
Hastings, Max, *The Korean War* (London: Pan, 1987)
Hernon, Ian, *Britain's Forgotten Wars, Colonial Campaigns of the Nineteenth Century* (Stroud: Sutton, 2002)
Ho, Fred, and Mullen, Bill V. (Eds.) *Afro Asia, Revolutionary and Cultural Connections Between African Americans and Asian Americans* (Durham & London: Duke University Press, 2008)
Holmes, W.H., *An Eyewitness in Manchuria* (New York: New York International Publisher, 1933)
Hsin-Hui, Chiu, *The Colonial 'Civilising Process' on Dutch Formosa, 1624-1662* (Leiden: Brill, 2008)
Itoh, Mayumi, *Japanese War Orphans in Manchuria, Forgotten Victims of World War II* (New York: Palgrave MacMillan, 2010)
James, Lawrence, *The Rise and Fall of the British Empire* (London: Abacus, 2001)
Johnston, R.F. *Lion and Dragon in Northern China* (London: John Murray, 1910)
Joseph, William A. (ed.) *Politics in China, An Introduction* (Oxford: Oxford University Press, 2010)

Bibliography and Sources

Kirke, Henry, *Twenty Five Years in British Guiana* (London: Sampson Low, Marston and Co., 1898)

Kwong, Luke, S.K., *A Mosaic of the Hundred Days: Personalities, Politics and Ideas of 1898* (Cambridge Mass: Harvard University Press, 1984)

Lach, Donald F., Van Kley, Edwin J., *Asia in the Making of Europe, Volume III, A Century of Advance* (Chicago and London: University of Chicago Press, 1998)

Lane-Poole, Stanley, *The Life of Sir Harry Parkes, KCB, GCMG, Sometime Her Majesty's Minister to China and Japan* (London: Macmillan and Co., 1894)

Lattimore, Owen, *Manchuria, Cradle of Conflict* (London: Macmillian, 1932)

Leibovitz, Liel & Miller, Matthew, *Fortunate Sons: The 120 Chinese Boys Who Came to America, Went to School, and Revolutionized an Ancient Civilization* (New York & London: W.W. Norton, 2011)

Li, Peter (ed.) *The Search for Justice: Japanese War Crimes* (New Brunswick: Transaction Publishers, 2009)

Lindsay, H. Hamilton, *Is The War With China A Just One?* (London: James Ridgway, 1840)

Lloyd George, David, *War Memories of David Lloyd George* (London; Odhams Press, 1938

Lovelace, Douglas C. Jr, (ed.) *Terrorism Commentary on Security Documents, Vol:147, Assessing the 2017 US National Security Strategy* (Oxford: OUP, 2018)

Low, Harriet, *My Mother's Journal, A Young Lady's Diary of Five Years Spent in Manila, Macao and the Cape of Good Hope, From 1829-1834*, edited by Katharine Hillard (Boston: George M. Ellis, 1900)

Ludwig, Emil, *Kaiser Wilhelm II* (London: Putnam, 1926)

Lynch, George, *Path of Empire* (London: Duckworth and Co., 1903)

Maclear, Michael, *Vietnam, The Ten Thousand Day War* (London: Methuen, 1981)

MacMillan, Margaret, *Peacemakers – The Paris Conference of 1919 And its Attempt to End War* (London: John Murray, 2001)

Macdonald, Lyn, *Somme* (London: Penguin, 1998)

Massie, Robert K. *Dreadnought: Britain, Germany and the Coming of the Great War* (London: Pimlico, 2004)

Matheson, James F., *The Present Position and Prospects of the British Trade with China* (London: Smith, Brand, Cornhill, 1836)

McCord, Edward A., *The Power of the Gun, The Emergence of Modern Chinese Warlordism* (LA: University of California Press, 1993)

Middleton Smith, C.A., *The British in China and Far Eastern Trade* (London: Constable and Co., 1920)

Miers, Suzanne, *Slavery in the Twentieth Century, The Evolution of a Global Problem* (New York: Alta Mira, 2003)

Millard, Thomas F. *The Shantung Case at the Conference* (Shanghai: Millards Review of the Far East, 1921)

Molozemoff, Andrew, *Russian Far Eastern Policy 1881-1904, With Special Emphasis On The Cause Of the Russo-Japanese War* (Los Angeles: University of California Press, 1958)

Morris, James, Farewell the Trumpets, An Imperial Retreat (London: Penguin, 1979)

Morris, James, *Pax Britannica: The Climax of an Empire* (London: Penguin, 1979)

Morse, Hosea, Ballou, *The Chronicles of the East India Company Trading to China 1635-1834, Vol:II* (Oxford: The Clarendon Press, 1926)
Nicolson, Harold, *Peacemaking 1919* (London: Methuen, 1964)
Ono, Giichi, *Expenditures of the Sino-Japanese War* (New York: Oxford University Press, 1922)
Paine, S.C.M, *Imperial Rivals: China, Russia and Their Disputed Frontier* (New York & London: Sharpe Inc., 1996)
Parker, E.H., *China, Her History, Diplomacy and Commerce* (London: John Murray, 1901)
Parthesius Robert, *Dutch Ships in Tropical Waters: Development of the Dutch East India Company (VOC) Shipping Network in Asia, 1595-1660* (Amsterdam: Amsterdam University Press, 2010)
Payne, George E., *An Experiment in Alien* Labor (Chicago: University of Chicago Press, 1912)
Perry, Marvin, *Sources of the Western Tradition, From the Renaissance to the Present* (Boston: Wadsworth, 2014)
Purcell, Victor, *The Boxer Uprising, A Background Study* (Cambridge: Cambridge University Press, 1963)
Rees, Laurence, *Horror in the East, The Brutal Struggle in Asia and the Pacific in WWII* (London: Random House, 2001)
Rhee, Hong Beom, *Asian Millenarianism: An Interdisciplinary Study of the Taiping and Tonghak Rebellions in a Global Context* (New York: Cambria Press, 2007)
Roberts, J.M. *Europe, 1880-1945* (Harlow: Pearson, 2001)
Robbins, Helen, *Our First Ambassador to China, An Account of the Life of George, Earl of Macartney* (London: John Murray, 1908)
Ross, John, *The Manchus, or The Reigning Dynasty of China* (London: Elliot Stock, 1891)
Russell, Lord, of Liverpool, *The Knights of Bushido. A Short History of Japanese War Crimes* (London: Gorgi, 1966)
Sabin, Edwin, L., *Building the Pacific Railway* (Philadelphia & London: J.P. Lippincott, 1919)
St. John, Burton, *The China Times Guide to Tientsin and Neighbourhood* (Tientsin: The China Times, 1908)
Schwarcz, Vera, *The Chinese Enlightenment: Intellectuals and the Legacy of the May Fourth Movement of 1919* (Berkeley: University of Califoria Press, 1986)
Scott, James, Gregory, *France and Tongking, A Narrative of the Campaign of 1884, and the Occupation of Further India* (London: T. Fisher Unwin, 1885)
Shepherd, John, *Statecraft and Political Economy on the Taiwan Frontier, 1600-1800* (Stanford: Stanford University Press, 1993)
Smith, David Livingstone, *Less Than Human: Why We Demean, Enslave and Exterminate Others* (New York: St. Martins, 2011)
Staunton, Sir George Thomas, BART, *Miscellaneous Notices Relating To China And Our Commercial Intercourse With That Country* (London: John Murray, 1822)
Steinmetz, George, *The Devil's Handwriting: Precoloniality and the German Colonial State in Qingdao, Samoa, and Southwest Africa* (Chicago: University of Chicago Press, 2007)
Stevenson, David, *1914-1918, The History of the First World War* (London: Penguin, 2004)

Bibliography and Sources

Storry, Richard, *A History of Modern Japan* (London: Penguin, 1984)
Swinhoe, Robert, *Narrative of the North China Campaign of 1860* (London: Smith, Elder & Co. 1861)
Tae-Jin, Yi, Park, Eugene Y., Larsen, Kirk W., *Peace in the East: An Chunggun's Vision for Asia in the Age of Imperialism* (Lanhan, MD: Lexington Books, 2017)
Takekoshi, Yosabura. *Japanese Rule in Formosa* (London: Longmans, 1907)
Teng, Ssu-yu and Fairbank, John K., *China's Response to the West, A Documentary Study, 1839-1923* (Cambridge, Mass: Harvard University Press, 1982)
Thomson, H,C., *China and the Powers, a Narrative of the Outbreak of 1900* (London: Longman, Green & Co., 1902)
Thorne, Christopher, *Allies Of A Kind: The US, Britain and the War Against Japan, 1941-1945* (Oxford: OUP, 1979)
Thin, George, *The Tientsin Massacre, The Causes of the Late Disturbance And How To Secure Permanent Peace* (London: Blackwood, 1870)
Timperley, H.J. (ed.) *Japanese Terror in China* (Calcutta: Thackers Press, 1938)
Tirpitz, Alfred von, *My Memoirs Volume One* (New York: Mead & Co., 1919)
Tunskjo, Oystein, US Taiwan Policy, Constructing the Triangle (London and
Wang, S.T. *The Marjary Affair and the Chefoo Agreement* (London: Oxford University Press, 1940)
Watt, Stewart, *Chinese Bondage in Peru* (Durham, NC: Duke University Press, 1951
Weale, B.L. Putnam, *The Reshaping of the Far East*, Volume One (New York: Macmillan, 1905)
Weissenbacher, Manfred, *Sources of Power, How Energy Forges Human History*, Vol1 & Vol2 (Oxford: Praeger, 2009)
White, Trumbell, *The War in the East, Japan, China and Corea* (Philadelphia: Ziegler, 1895)
Whittle, Tyler, *The Last Kaiser, A Biography of William II, German Emperor and King of Prussia* (London: Heinemann, 1977)
Willoughby, Westel W., *Foreign Rights and Interests in China* (Baltimore: John Hopkins, 1920)
Wintle, Justin, *The Vietnam Wars* (London: Weidenfeld & Nicolson, 1991)
Wright, Arnold, *Twentieth Century Impressions of Hong Kong, Shanghai, and other Treaty Ports of China* (London: Lloyds Greater British Publishing Co., 1908)
Xing, Hang, *Conflict and Commerce in Maritime East Asia, The Zheng Family and the Shaping of the Modern World, c.1620-1720* (Cambridge, Cambridge University Press, 2015)
Yoshida, Takashi, *The Making of the "Rape of Nanking": History and Memory in Japan, China and the United States* (Oxford: OUP, 2006)
Young, Louise, *Japan's Total Empire: Manchuria and the Culture of Wartime Imperialism* (Berkeley: University of California Press, 1998)
Ysu, Madelaine, Y, *The Good Immigrants: How the Yellow Peril Became the Model Minority* (Princeton: Princeton University Press, 2015)
Yun, Lisa, *The Coolie Speaks, Laborers and African Slaves in Cuba* (Philadelphia: Temple University Press, 2008)
Zhang, Shu Guang, *Economic Cold War: America's Embargo Against China and the Sino-Soviet Alliance, 1949-1963* (Washington: Stanford University Press, 2001)
Zhong, Ziaxin, *Japanese War Orphans – Abandoned Twice By The State* (Abingdon: Routledge, 2022)

Index

Agriculture 92, 108, 188, 190, 199, 257
Aigun, Treaty of 1858 with Russia 74
Alexander the Great, and theories regarding earliest Western contacts with China 28
Anglo-Japanese Alliance, 1902 and implications for China 129
Annam, see also Indo-China 83 et seq
Arrow incident, and Second Opium War 70
Astronomy, and importance of in Imperial fortunes 14, see also Mandate of Heaven
Banner Armies and Bannermen, formation of 22, confront Russians 39- 40, neglect of 65, against British 67, effect of reorganisation on 90, and Russian invasion of Manchuria 123
Beijing, see China
Bi Sheng, and the invention of moveable type 18
Biological Warfare, employment of by Japanese against civilians 217-218, see also Japan
Boxers, and Rebellion of 1900 114-121
Boxer Protocol, provisions and consequences for China 124-125, 205
Brown, Colonel Horace, proposed trade route from India through Burma through Yunnan, and Margary incident 80, see also Chefoo Convention

Buddhism 15, 18, 91, 184
Cairo, conference at in 1943 and abolition of extraterritoriality 224
Canton, see Guangzhou
Canton System 45-46, see also Guangzhou
Cassini Convention with Russia 1896, and granting of railway rights 103 et seq
Cavalry, development of and role in warfare 14
Censorate, and importance of in governing China 25
Ceramics, see porcelain and pottery
Chefoo or Yantai Convention of 1876, impact on Chinese sovereignty 80
Cherry Blossom Society, and role in the growth of Japanese fascism in the 1920s and 1930s 209
Chiang Kai-shek, assumes control of Kuomintang 206, and 'White Terror' 206, and Northern Expedition 207, recognised as President of Nationalist China 207, offensive launched against Communists 207, and Manchuria 209, and Japanese invasion 219 et seq, role in war highly criticised 222, admission as one of the 'Big Five' 223, and secures end of extraterritoriality 224, resumes civil war 224, defeated by Communists and exiled to Taiwan 225

Index

China 17, 21-22, 32-34, 38-39, 42, McCartney Mission to 51-59, 68, response to Taiping Rebellion 69, consequence of opium wars for 71-73, Treaty of Tianjin 74, Chefoo Convention 80-81, Treaty of St Petersburg 82, and Indo-China 83-85, Convention of Calcutta 85, Formosa 93-94, Korea 95-101, Ryukyus 102, Boxers 115-128, Treaty of Portsmouth 132, Tibet 135, 197, Twenty One Demands 198, Fourth of May Movement 204, capture of Beijing by Nationalists 207, and Japanese invasion 218, 221, Chinese Civil War 225, Korean War 226-228, and Viet Minh 229, Hong Kong Handover 223, revanchism 235-239, human rights 248-250, Covid 253, today 259-260, see also entries under individual subjects

China White Paper, and 'loss' of China by US State Department 225

Chinese living and working abroad, deceived and abducted as indentured labour in Cuba, Peru, British Guiana, Dutch Guiana and the Straits Settlements, as labour on the railroads in Canada and the United States, as gold prospectors in Canada Australia and New Zealand, as labourers in Witwatersrand in South Africa and the Western Front in the First World War, resentment towards, discriminatory legislation enacted against and abuse of 169 et seq, the Chinese diaspora today 253 et seq

Chinese Communist Party (CCP) establishment of 206

Chongzhen, emperor, and decline and overthrow of Ming Dynasty 22 et seq

Cixi, dowager empress, 'Old Buddha', role as regent 107, sabotages Hundred Days Reforms 109-110, and Boxers 110 et seq, defeat by Europeans and Japan 123, finally accepts need for reform 135, death of 138

Cohongs and role in the Canton System 46 et seq

Comfort Women, and suffering of in the Second World War 241, 244

Confucianism 18, 110, 134

Crossbow, the development of and significance of in warfare 14

Cultural Revolution, and Mao Zedong's role in 229

Dagu Forts, strategic importance of and conflicts with the West 64, 71, 73, 118-119, 124

Dairen, under Russian and Japanese occupation 133, 159, 167-168, 199, see also Russia

Dalny, see Dairen

Dutch, see Netherlands

East India Company, Dutch 34, French 42, English 43, 60, 62

Eunuchs, and participation in the government and administration of Imperial China 26

Ever Victorious Army, and success of against rebels 69

Examination System for Civil Service, significance and limitations of 19, 26, 88, 91, 108, 135

Extraterritoriality 71, 81, as applied in leased territories 104 et seq, ending of 224

Farming, and earliest developments in 14

Feng Shui and application of in architecture 21, 32, 112

First World War, and China's involvement in 165 et seq

Formosa and Taiwan 23, 34, 36-37, 44, 71, 84-85, 93-95, 101, 224-227, 237

Fort Zeelandia, and Dutch settlements in Formosa 35

Four Class System, and application of by Mongols in consolidating its power 20

Forbidden City, construction of by Yongle emperor 21, at heart of government 23, Matteo Ricci first European to enter 75, violated by Europeans in 1900 121, see also Feng Shui

Fourth of May Movement, and Chinese students opposition to settlement of Shandong question 247

Fujian, and Japanese sphere of influence in 106

Ganghwa, Treaty of 1876 between Korea and Japan, and country's opening up to Japanese encroachment 96

Germany 73, 97, and Qingdao 103-104, and spheres of influence 106, Boxer Rebellion 125, Russian threat 127-128, share of trade 157, Shandong 161-162, 165, 197, and loss to Japan 200-204, recognition of Nationalists 207, see also Qingdao

Gold prospecting, see Chinese abroad

Gong, Prince and role in the Self-Strengthening Movement 87

Grand Council, and Grand Secretariat 24-25

Great Leap Forward, and post war modernisation 257

Great Wall of China, and construction of 15, 20

Green Standard Army, effectiveness of 65, effect of reorganisation on 90, disbanded 137

Guangzhou 31-32, 44-45, Canton System 47-52, Opium trade 59-61, and Opium War 63-66, Arrow incident in precipitates second conflict with Britain 70, development of 144, as base for Sun Yat-Sen 206, bombed by Japanese 219, present day 258

Guangxu emperor and Hundred Days Reforms 108 et seq

Gunpowder, development of 16-17, 19

Han dynasty, and decline of 16

Hiroshima, atomic bomb on 222

HO 213/926, Compulsory Repatriation of Undesirable Chinese Seamen, and scandal of 256, see also Liverpool

Hong Kong 52, 63, 66, Britain takes possession of 67, 78, 145-150, and New Territories 149, Britain seeks to reoccupy after 1945 224, return to China 231-233, threats to civil and human rights in since 1997 234

Huaqiao, see Chinese living and working abroad

Hubus, and role in the Canton System 46, et seq

Hue, Treaty of between France and Vietnam and consequences for Chinese influence 83

Hundred Days Reforms, implementation and failure of 108-111

Indemnities, see Boxer Rebellion

Indentures, see Chinese abroad

Indo-China, see Annam

Italy, and failure to secure concession 106

Japan, 19-20, 35, early Chinese influence in 91-92, Sino-Japanese Treaty 93, the Ryukyus 93, Li-Ito Convention 98, Sino-Japanese War 99-101, securing of concessions 106, Boxer Rebellion 115-117, 125, Russo-Japanese War 129-132, rights to South Manchurian Railway 133, annexation of Korea 134-135, in Shanghai 151, in Tianjin 155, occupation of Dairen 167, occupation of Qingdao 197-198, Twenty One Demands 198, in the First World War 199-200, controversy over Shandong at Versailles 200-205, invasion of Manchuria 210-212, creation of Manchukuo 212-213, Lytton Commission 213-216, atrocities in 216-217, invasion of China 218, rape of Nanking 219, Cairo Conference 224, post war relations 237-243

Jiang Zemin, President, and relations with President Vladimir Putin 235, makes conciliatory visit to Japan 241, and Vietnam 243

Kang Youwei, and role in implementing the Hundred Days Reforms 107-110

Kangxi emperor 37, 42-43, opens ports to trade 44, bans Christian missionaries 75, see also Canton System

Karakhan Declaration, Revolutionary Russian government relinquishes privileges and rights in China 205

Kellogg Pact 1928, the outlawing of war and implications for Chinese sovereignty 210

Kempeitai, Japanese military unit and atrocities committed against Chinese nationals throughout Southeast Asia during the Second World War 222

Korea, see Formosa and Japan

Korean War 227-228

Kowloon, see Hong Kong

Kowtow, or koutou and significance of 27

Index

Koxinga, invasion of Formosa and ejection of Dutch 37
Kuomintang, see Chiang Kai-shek
Kwantung Army, stationed in China by Japan 133, atrocities committed by 216 et seq
Labour, Chinese, see Chinese abroad
Laos, loss of to France 85
League of Nations, and role in Shandong settlement, and Japanese annexation of Manchuria, see Japan
Li Hongzhang and Self-Strengthening Movement 87-88, 90, and Japan 94-98, Boxer Rebellion 119-121, 125, and abuses of Chinese labourers in Peru 180
Lin Zexu, Imperial Commissioner attempts to stem opium importation through Guangzhou 61 et seq
Livadia, Treaty of 1879, and Russian occupation of East Turkestan, 81
Lodestone, Ci-Shi, earliest compass 14
London Naval Treaty of 1930, and attempts to limit size of Japanese Navy 210
Long March, the 207
Macao, Luso-Chinese Agreement cedes to Portugal 33, English try to capture 34, life in 140-144, return to China 231-232
Macartney, George Viscount and abortive embassy to Beijing 52-55
Manchukuo see Japan
Manchuria see Japan
Manchus 23, conquest of Mings 22-23, and Boxers 118, overthrow of 138, see also Qing dynasty
Mandate of Heaven, principle of and importance in maintaining dynastic legitimacy 23 et seq
Mao Zedong, implements land reform 207, and Long March 207, and Chiang 224, establishment of Communist republic 225, 'lean to one side speech 226, Korean War 227-228, break with Moscow 228, invasion of Tibet 229, and Vietnam 231, and Taiwan 237, and Japan 239, failure of post war reforms 237
Margary, Augustus, murder of 80 see also Chefoo Convention

Mianzi, and culture of saving face 27
Ming dynasty, and establishment of 21
Missionaries, earliest visitors 2, 43, afforded official protection and privileges 71, hostility towards 74-76 et seq, accused of abuses against children and Tianjin Massacre 77, expulsion from Korea 95, murders of pretext for seizure of Qingdao, blamed for floods and famines by Chinese, and the Boxers 112, in Macao 158
Mongolia and Mongols, invasion by 19-22, and Japan 199
Mukden, and railway 133, 199, and 'Incident' 210-211, and declaration of state of Manchukuo 212
Nanjing, Treaty of 1842 67 et seq, Japanese atrocities in 219-220
Napier, Lord precipitates First Opium War 61
Nerchinsk, settlement by Russian colonists 39, Treaty of 1689 41
Netherlands, entrepreneurs form trading company 33-34, act as pirates 34, in Formosa 35-37, and the Canton System 44-48, and the exploitation of Chinese labourers and women 173-174, 182
New Territories, see Hong Kong
Nine Power Treaty of 1922, and Japanese promises to respect Chinese sovereignty 208
Nurhaci, founds Qing dynasty and takes first steps in conquest of the Mings 22 et seq
Opium, and importation of, see Guangzhou and Canton System
Opium Wars, see Sino-British Wars
Paddle boat, the development of 17
Panmunjom, Korean War ceasefire agreed at 228
Paper, first manufacture of 16-17, use in currency 19-20
Pearl River, Portuguese first explore 31, and Canton System 46, and Opium Wars 64-66
Peking, see China
People's Liberation Army, PLA 207
People's Republic of China, creation of 225

285

Pescadores, used by Portuguese as a base for piracy 34, annexed by Japan 101

Polo, Marco and earliest contacts with China 29

Porcelain, pottery and ceramics 19, 21, 29-30, and Court of Louis XIV 42, 54

Port Arthur. construction of 89, Japanese capture of and atrocities in during Sino-Japanese War 100, ceded to Japan 101, Russia reverses cession 102, Russia occupies 105, and railway to St Petersburg 129, Japanese attack during Russo-Japanese War 130-132, Russia surrenders to Japan 132

Portugal, seeks route to China 31, popularises opium 29, arrives in India 30, and Malacca 30-31, first explorers arrive in Guangzhou 32, attempt to frustrate English traders in 43-44, and role in the opium trade 60, presence in Shanghai 151, see also Macao

Potsdam Declaration 1945, and ending of extraterritoriality 224

Pu Yi, ascends to Chinese throne but deposed by revolution 138, appointed to head Manchukuo regime as Japanese puppet 213

Qianlong, Emperor, restricts European traders to Guangzhou 45, rejects attempts to liberalise Canton System 49, snubs MacCartney Mission 53-56, condemns opium trade 59

Qing dynasty, founding of 22, invades Formosa 38, neglects armed forces 65-69, rebellions against 69, and Russia 73-74, and French 83-84 destruction of navy 84, and Boxers 113-123, abolition of 138, see also Manchus and China

Qingdao promised to Russia 103, leased to Germany 104, life in 161-165, surrendered to Japan 197-198, and controversy over at Versailles 204, present day 259

Ricci, Matteo, one of earliest Jesuit priests to visit China 75

Rome, earliest contacts with and export of silk to 28-29

Roosevelt, President, and misplaced faith in Chiang 222-223, and hopes for return of Hong Kong to China 224

Rudders, development of 16

Russia, early envoys rebuffed 38, trespass into Chinese territory 39-40, forced to climbdown 40-41, permitted to open consulates 68, resumes encroachments and secures Treaty of Aigun 74, in Turkestan 81, Treaty of St Petersburg 1881 81-82, establishes diplomatic relations with Korea 97, builds railway in Manchuria 102, leases Port Arthur 105, and Boxers 120-121, war with Japan 127-132, and develops Dalny 165-167, Communist government renounces unequal treaties 205, Sino-Soviet split 231, rapprochement with China 235, 258

Russo-Japanese War, see Russia

Self-Strengthening Movement, implementation and shortcomings of 87-91, 96, 101, 109, 137

Senkaku Islands, annexation of by Japan 102, present day disputes over 237, 242

Shaanxi Province, and rebellion in 55, and Great March 207

Shandong, birthplace of Confucious 18, 113, rebellion in 55, naval base on 89, and Qingdao 103,164, famine in 111, missionaries in 112, and Weihaiwei 157-158, and dispute over at Versailles 197-203

Shanghai, and opium wars 67, opening to trade 67, and Boxers 117, 122, life in 150-156, anti-Japanese demonstrations in 213, and Japanese invasion, rapes in 241, present day 258-259

Shenyang, see Mukden

Shi Huang, emperor, defeats Warring States and unites China 15

Shimonoseki, Treaty of 1895, ending of first Sino Japanese War and consequences for China 101-102

Shinzo Abe, Japanese Prime Minister visits China to mend fences 242

Siberia 71, 74, frontier agreed with Russia 74, and Trans-Siberian Railway 102, 161

Sichuan Province, and rebellion in 55

Silk Road 28-29, closure of 80

Index

Silk and sericulture 28, 92, use in making paper 15, theft of process by Justinian I 29
Singapore, and role in opium smuggling 59
Single Port Commerce System of 1757, restricts all foreign trade to Guangzhou 45
Sino-Barbarian Order, Yongle emperor declares all world beyond China to be its vassals 27
Sino-British Wars 61-67, and 1842 Treaty of Tianjin 67-68, and treaty of 1858 71 et seq
Sino-French Wars 61-67, in Indo-China 83-85
Sino-Japanese Wars see Japan
Sino-Soviet relations, see Russia
Song dynasty, establishment of and overthrow by Mongols 19-20
Soviet Union, see Russia
Spain 29, 33-34, and on Formosa 35-36
Special Economic Zones, establishment of 257
St. Petersburg, Treaty of 1881, see Russia
Stalin, Joseph support for Communists in Civil War 226
Staunton, Sir George Thomas, and McCartney Mission 50-55
Stimson, Henry, US Secretary of State, and Japan's invasion of Manchuria 211 et seq
Sui dynasty, founding of 17
Summer Palace Beijing, construction 43, destruction of 72, present day symbol of the Century of Humiliation 260
Sun Yat-sen, leads opposition to monarchy 107, founds Kuomintang 138, returns from exile 139, flees to Japan 139, returns but succumbs to cancer 206
Sun Tzu, and The Art of War, earliest known military manual 14
Taft-Katsura Agreement 1905, United States recognises Japan's 'special interests' in China 132
Taiping Rebellion, threat to dynasty and defeat of 69, 75
Taiwan, see Formosa

Tang dynasty establishment of 17, overthrow of 19, and opium 57
Tea, popularised by Portuguese 29
Thirteen Factories in Guangzhou, and the Canton System 45
Tiananmen Square, and Fourth May Movement 204,1989 massacre and international condemnation of 247
Tianjin, and Dagu forts 64, and opium wars 71,73, murder of missionaries in 76 et seq, military academy established in 91, and Boxers 117 et seq, life in 155 et seq, capture by Japan 218, present day 259, for treaties see Sino-British wars
Tibet, invasions of 17, 20, 23, 85, 135, 229, and McMahon Line 197, and present day territorial disputes with India 235-236
Tientsin, see Tianjin and Sino-British wars
Tirpitz, Admiral Afred von, and potential of Qingdao as a German outpost 108 et seq
Tonkin, and conflict with France 83 et seq
Trans-Siberian Railway, see Siberia
Treaty Ports, see Canton System and separate entries
Tsingtao. See Qingdao
Twenty One Demands, see Japan
United Nations, Nationalist China's ejection from and admission of PRC into 230-231
United States, and pursuit of 'Open Door' policy 106 et seq
Units 731 and 100, and involvement in bacteriological warfare against civilians 217 et seq
Uyghurs, revolt of in East Turkestan 81, present day allegations of persecution of 250
Vereenigde Oost-Indische Compagnie, see East India Company Dutch
Versailles, Peace Conference at and controversy over China policy 201-204, see also Shandong
Vietnam, French involvement in and loss of Chinese influence 82 et seq, and America 229-230, friction with

China and territorial disputes 231, 236, improved relations 243
Vladivostok, and Trans-Siberian Railway 102, Russia militarises 127, and Russo-Japanese War 131
Wade, Thomas and negotiation of Chefoo Convention following killing of Augustus Margary 80
War Crimes, Japanese, see Japan
Warring States Period 15
Wei Boyang, and the earlies experiments with the compounds that would produce gunpowder 15, 17
Weihaiwei 101, life in during British occupation 157-160, present day Weihai 259
Wilhelm, Kaiser and Boxer Rebellion 120-125
Wilson, President Woodrow and responsibility for the Shandong controversy at Peace Conference 201-206
Xi Jinping, President and relations with Russia 235, and religious oppression 248, attends G20 summit 245, and relations with South Korea 245
Xia kingdom, believed to be the first Chinese dynasty 13
Yasukuni Shrine, controversy over and consequences for Sino-Japanese relations 241
Yalu River 94, and Sino-Japanese War 100, and Russo-Japanese War 12, 131, and Korean War 229
Yangtse River, and First Opium War 67, and Japanese invasion 219
Ye Mingchen, Commissioner at Guangzhou and role in Arrow incident 70 et seq

Yellow River earliest civilisation develop around 13, and flooding of 111
Yi Xing, and the earliest clock 17
Yongle, emperor, constructs Forbidden City, sends out fleets of exploration 21, and Sino-Barbarian Order 27
Yuan dynasty establishment of 20, and role in the manufacture of porcelain 29
Yunnan, rebellions in 69, opening up to trade 81, and war with France 83, and Second World War 221
Zanryu Fujin, Chinese war wives, controversy over and return to Japan 240
Zanryu Koji, Chinese war orphans, controversy over and return to Japan 240
Zeng Guofan, and Tianjin Massacre 78, and Self-Strengthening Movement 87-88, and role in attempts to modernise army 89
Zhang Heng, and the earliest earthquake detector 16
Zhang Zuolin Manchurian warlord, provokes clash between China and Japan in 1928 209
Zhou dynasties 14-15, 23
Zongli Yamen, Chinese Foreign Ministry creation of 87, ineffectiveness of 91, 107, and Boxers 116-117, 120, intervenes following reports of abuse of Chinese abroad 177
Zuo Zongtang, and role in the Self-Strengthening Movement 87